OXFORD ENGLISH MEMOIRS AND TRAVELS

General Editor: James Kinsley

Memoirs and Anecdotes of
Dr. Johnson

WILLIAM SHAW

Memoirs of the
Life and Writings of the Late
DR. SAMUEL JOHNSON

HESTHER LYNCH PIOZZI

Anecdotes of the Late
SAMUEL JOHNSON, LL.D.
during the Last Twenty Years
of His Life

Edited with an Introduction by
Arthur Sherbo

LONDON
OXFORD UNIVERSITY PRESS
NEW YORK   TORONTO
1974

Oxford University Press, Ely House, London W1

GLASGOW   NEW YORK   TORONTO   MELBOURNE   WELLINGTON
CAPE TOWN   IBADAN   NAIROBI   DAR ES SALAAM   LUSAKA   ADDIS ABABA
DELHI   BOMBAY   CALCUTTA   MADRAS   KARACHI   LAHORE   DACCA
KUALA LUMPUR   SINGAPORE   HONG KONG   TOKYO

ISBN 0 19 255416 6

Printed in Great Britain
by W & J Mackay Limited, Chatham

Contents

Illustrations

The illustrations appear by kind permission of the following: British Museum: facing pp. 74, 90, 91 (right), 107; John Rylands University of Manchester Library: 139; National Portrait Gallery: 91 (left), 122, 123 138 (top), 154 (left); Radio Times Hulton Picture Library: 106, 138 (bottom), 155; Victoria and Albert Museum: 75.

Introduction

I

Memoirs of the Life and Writings of the Late Samuel Johnson was advertised in the *Morning Chronicle* for 9 June 1785, a publishing event that seems to have gone completely unnoticed, at least as far as reviews in the leading periodicals of the day were concerned. There had been and was to be a spate of anecdotal and biographical material about Johnson, and Shaw seems to have been willing to capitalize on his acquaintance with him. He writes that he first became acquainted with Johnson 'about Christmas' in the year 1774. Shaw was then an unknown, of twenty-five years old, who had been eking out a living as a tutor in Ireland. Johnson's first mention of him comes in a letter to Boswell dated 11 March 1777 in which he speaks of Shaw's 'Erse Grammar', published as *An Analysis of the Galic Language* in 1778, as though unknown to Boswell. Boswell, in an answering letter dated 4 April 1777, reminds Johnson that he, Boswell, put Shaw's book into his hands 'last year' and adds: 'I have received Mr. Shaw's Proposals for its publication, which I can perceive are written *by the hand of a* MASTER.' Johnson wrote Shaw's 'Proposals'; encouraged him to compile and publish his *Galic and English Dictionary,* for a copy of which he and Boswell each subscribed and for which he corrected proofs; persuaded him to leave the Church of Scotland for the Church of England and tried to obtain a chaplaincy 'to one of the new-raised regiments' for him; wrote a letter of introduction for him to Charles Allen; and helped him with his reply to John Clark's attack on his *Enquiry into the Authenticity of the Poems ascribed to Ossian.* Shaw, who is accorded the distinction of being Johnson's 'first actual biographer' by Aleyn Lyell Reade, could have known Johnson, at most, for the ten-year period from 1774 to 1784. For almost two of those years Shaw was in Scotland and Ireland, from spring 1778 to February 1779 compiling his Gaelic dictionary and from July 1779 to August 1780 officiating as minister of the parish of Ardclach in the presbytery of Nairn. He must have visited London during this latter period; the dedication of his *Galic and English Dictionary* is dated 'London, May 26, 1780'. Despite the statement in the *D.N.B.* that he was 'one of the literary coterie which met at Bolt Court and Streatham Park', the latter the home of the Thrales, there is no reference to him in Mrs. Piozzi's *Thraliana* or in Professor Clifford's biography of Mrs. Piozzi. What is more, Johnson's health was very bad in the last few years of his life, and while he recorded the names of most of his visitors in a diary, there is only one entry, 20 March 1782, for a visit by Shaw.[1]

One cannot conclude from the available evidence, always excepting the *Memoirs* itself, that there was any great intimacy between Johnson and Shaw. Indeed, some of the evidence of the *Memoirs* even seems against such an intimacy. While it was true that both men were lexicographers, and hence bound by common interests, there is much reason to believe from the *Memoirs* that Shaw rather disliked Johnson and thought poorly of some of the great man's writings. Thus, after quoting the poignant sentence from the Preface to the *Dictionary* where Johnson writes 'much of my life has always been spent, in provision for the day that was passing over me', Shaw can comment, acidly and inaccurately: 'it is well known Johnson received so much money, that at the very time of adopting this whining language he was in a capacity to have lived at the rate of three hundred pounds a year' (p. 33). As part of his concluding 'character' of Johnson, Shaw saw fit to remark that 'the moment he found himself the idol of fashion, his conceit of his own powers was without restraint or decency' (p. 54). Shaw criticized Johnson's *London* and *The Vanity of Human Wishes*, wrote of the two *Idler* essays added to the collected edition that 'the first [on Pope's epitaphs] abounds in false criticism, the second [on the warlike character of English soldiers] is little more than the vulgar rhodomontade of a pot-house politician, who is always ready to match one of his countrymen against three of any other in the universe' (p. 38), and acquiesced in the charge that Johnson's style was often 'over-wrought or blown' (p. 38). The whole tone of the *Memoirs* leads one to conclude that Shaw, who owed much to Johnson, reacted in the not uncommon fashion of repaying kindness with ingratitude—a fault from which Johnson also suffered. Almost equally pervasive is the feeling that Shaw resented Johnson's successes and his own failures. Possibly some clue to Shaw's feeling of literary frustration may be had from his comments upon what he terms gentlemen-authors. David Hume, he writes, 'always kept himself independant of Booksellers', and, unlike the 'author who writes for subsistence,' was one 'who though able to live without writing, yet sells what he writes with as much anxiety, as if he wrote for a livelihood. This, however, they call a gentlemen-author, and, without much regard to the comparative merit of the two, very often, and very

---

[1] Boswell visited Johnson on 9 April 1779; during the course of his visit 'Shaw came in and Nichols the Printer' (*Private Papers*, xiii. 217).

absurdly, give him the preference' (p. 31).[2] And Shaw had grounds for bitterness since it was not until 20 January 1786 that he won a suit against some of the subscribers to his *Galic Dictionary* (1780) who claimed that since the work was defective they were not bound to pay the rest of the subscription price.

One does not, therefore, come away from a close study of the *Memoirs* with the feeling that the author was the sort of person to whom Johnson would confide some of the incidents of his early life, although, of course, Shaw writes in his Preface that Johnson's 'servants, Mrs. Du Maulin [whose very name he could not get right], who knew him from her infancy, and several others of his most intimate acquaintance, whose names the Editor is not allowed to mention, told him all they knew.' And there was James Elphinston, who had corresponded with Johnson 'for above the space of thirty years', to provide Shaw with 'every sort of information'.[3] Further, Johnson's 'most intimate acquaintance' are unnamed, and Shaw, or his bookseller, for reasons best known to themselves, elected that the work should be anonymous. Actually, the amount of space devoted to the Ossian controversy served as a clue to Shaw's identity, if the coyness of the last paragraph of the Preface had not already alerted the reader to the authorship of the work to follow.

The *Memoirs* abound in errors of fact and of knowledge of Johnson's character. For example, contrary to the soon to be published first-hand accounts, Shaw found it 'not a little singular' that, with Johnson's 'bluntness of address, and . . . coarseness of colloquial expression peculiarly characteristic, he was equally without humour and superior to every species of buffoonery' (p. 54). Shaw errs factually in his account of Blackwall (p. 10), in accepting Davies's mistaken date, on the month of publication of Johnson's advertisement (p. 10), on Johnson's share in the first years of the *Gentleman's Magazine* (p. 14), and on a number of other matters.[4] Sometimes the errors can be traced to Shaw's blind following of Cooke or Tyers in their accounts of Johnson. Indeed, Shaw depended quite heavily on previous accounts for his own narrative, and when these failed him he was not above padding and digression. He has his say on gentlemen-authors, on parliamentary reporting, on poetic imitations, on the stage in England, on lexicography, on Shakespeare's lack of genius, and on Ossian (some twenty pages on this last). And he

[2] Further evidence of Shaw's bitterness towards booksellers occurs on pages 10, 12, 24–5, 31, 35, and 39.

[3] Curiously enough, there is no letter to or from Shaw in Elphinston's *Forty Years' Correspondence Between Geniusses of Boath Sexes, and James Elphinston*, four volumes of letters and two of poetry, published in 1791.

[4] See Explanatory Notes for Shaw's other mistakes.

indulges in overly long critiques of Johnson's two major poems.

Despite these shortcomings, two of Johnson's twentieth-century biographers depend in varying degrees on the *Memoirs*, largely for the account of Johnson's early years. Thus Aleyn Lyell Reade writes of Shaw as one 'who derived his knowledge of the Doctor's early life principally from Dr. Swynfen's daughter, Mrs. Desmoulins, and whose matter also stamps him as a witness of considerable value' (*Gleanings*, iii.97).[5] James Clifford, in the preface to his *Young Samuel Johnson*, writes of 'William Shaw, who secured important information from the daughter [Mrs. Desmoulins] of Johnson's godfather' and from whom, as with other early biographies of Johnson, he 'accepted stories when they appeared credible' and 'discarded others'. For Shaw, depending upon the extent of credibility afforded him, has something to contribute to our knowledge of Johnson's early life, of Michael Johnson and his son's attitude towards him, of Dr. Swinfen, and of Tetty and Johnson's life together as husband and wife. And there are the remarks by and anecdotes of Johnson for which there is no other source. On his attention to duty in his father's bookshop: 'to supersede the pleasures of reading, by the attentions of traffic, was a task he never could master.' On Lord Chesterfield: 'All the celebrated qualities of Chesterfield are like certain species of fruit which is pleasant enough to the eye, but there is no tasting it without danger.' On David Hume: 'my countrymen will not always regard the voice of a Blasphemer as an oracle.' On John Wilkes: 'I hope Mr. Wilkes is now become a friend to the constitution, and to the family on the throne, but I know he has much to unwrite, and more to unsay, before he will be forgiven for what he has been writing and saying for many years.' On revising his definition of 'excise' in the *Dictionary*: 'No, it has done all the mischief, and I owe no complaisance to excisemen or their masters.' On Dr. Fordyce: 'no dirty heresies sticking about him.' There is the retort to a 'Bookseller of eminence' (p. 55) and his remark on Goldsmith to Mrs. Thrale (p. 56)—for all these, students of Johnson's life are grateful.

II

As early as 1768 when Johnson advised her to 'get a little Book' in which to write all the anecdotes and observations that might strike her fancy, Mrs. Piozzi (then Mrs. Thrale) began to devote herself to recording her

---

[5] Although he quotes and cites Shaw's work about fifteen times, he can also describe him as 'the Rev. William Shaw, who wrote briefly and without much encumbrance from dates' (iv. 76).

friend's conversation and whatever she could learn about him. In 1776 her husband gave her six quarto blank books with a label stamped 'Thraliana' on each, and into these she copied stories about Johnson accumulated between 1768 and 1776 as well as other '-ana' she had jotted down. Professor Balderston writes in her introduction to *Thraliana* that 'in the *Anecdotes* are to be found 227 separate fragments, taken from the matrix of the *Thraliana*, recombined, altered, and mixed with new matter', and that the passages borrowed from *Thraliana* 'amount in all to five-ninths of the total bulk of the *Anecdotes*' (p. xxiii). Thus, when Johnson died in December 1784, Mrs. Piozzi, then in Milan, had a fund of material ready to hand in *Thraliana* which she could get into shape quickly, and it was no surprise to her intimates when an advertisement appeared in the newspapers in late June 1785 saying that the *Anecdotes* were 'preparing for the press' and would be 'published with all possible Expedition'.

That the *Anecdotes* were not published until 25 March 1786 was due to the time it took for the manuscript to get to England from Italy and to the need for a cancel at signature K for a page in which Mrs. Piozzi lashed out at an anonymous writer (he was George Steevens) in the *St. James's Chronicle* and at Boswell for slurs on herself and on her husband.[6] What is more, in Boswell's *Journal of a Tour to the Hebrides with Samuel Johnson, LL.D*, published in September 1785, Johnson was reported to have admitted that neither he nor Mrs. Thrale had been able to make their way through Mrs. Elizabeth Montagu's *Essay on Shakespeare*, 1769. On the advice of her friends Mrs. Piozzi agreed to the addition of a postscript. After all these delays the *Anecdotes*, upon their appearance on 25 March 1786, enjoyed a tremendous popularity.[7] Despite the commercial success of the work reviewers were generally agreed in condemning the seemingly gratuitous display of Johnson in a less than favourable light; more than one contemporary reader expressed a similar view. Horace Walpole's comments may stand as one example: he labelled the work 'wretched; a high-varnished preface to a heap of rubbish, in a very vulgar style, and too void of method even for such a farrago', adding that Mrs. Piozzi's 'panegyric is loud in praise of her hero; and almost every fact that she relates disgraces him.'[8] The *English Review* put the whole matter more bluntly and coarsely: 'An

[6] The story of the printing of the *Anecdotes* is told in detail by J. L. Clifford in the *John Rylands Library Bulletin*, xx (1936) and, with other information, in chapter XII of his biography of Mrs. Piozzi.

[7] An edition of 1,000 copies sold out on the first day. A second edition of 1,000 copies and a third edition of 500 appeared respectively on 5 and 11 April; but there was still need for a fourth edition, which duly came out on 5 May.

[8] Quoted in Clifford's biography, p. 265, among other comments.

orthodox tartar may possess a sufficient degree of veneration for the *Delai Lama*, without either worshipping or eating his excrements' (April 1786, p. 259).

By modern standards the making of the *Anecdotes* from the materials of *Thraliana* leaves much to be desired in terms of fidelity, Mrs. Piozzi feeling no compunction about adding, omitting, and changing at will. Her accuracy was immediately questioned by reviewers and later by Boswell. Indeed, Boswell quotes part of Mrs. Piozzi's complaint about having to care for the sick Johnson without the help of her husband and then writes, 'I think it necessary to guard my readers against the mistaken notion of Dr. Johnson's character, which the lady's "Anecdotes" of him suggest' (*Life*, iv. 340–1). He then proceeds to give some examples of inaccuracies and inconsistencies in the *Anecdotes*, invoking the aid of Edmond Malone for this purpose and referring to other places in his biography where he has had to note Mrs. Piozzi's mistakes. Some of these seem now to have been the result of carelessness,[9] but some of the reshaping of the material was doubtless dictated by considerations of style and the understandable wish of an author to make the most of his subject. And one may put down to a desire for greater immediacy the practice of introducing an unnamed person as the object or recipient of a remark by Johnson where *Thraliana* gives no authority for the existence of such a person.[10]

Despite the fact that *Anecdotes of the Late Samuel Johnson, LL.D., during the last twenty years of his Life* was published as by Hesther Lynch Piozzi, one remembers her as Mrs. Thrale in her relationship with Johnson. For it was as the wife of Henry Thrale, one of Johnson's dearest friends, that she met Johnson and became herself very dear to him. Streatham Park became Johnson's second home, and even though the house was masterless on the death of Thrale, it was not until Mrs. Thrale announced her intention to marry Gabriel Piozzi on 30 June 1784 in a letter from Bath that the resentment that was smouldering burst out. 'Madam,' the old, sick man wrote on 2 July,

If I interpret your letter right, you are ignominiously married; if it is yet undone, let us once more talk together. If you have abandoned your children and your religion, God forgive your wickedness; if you have forfeited your fame and your country, may your folly do no further mischief. If the last act is yet to do [Mrs. Thrale was *not* yet married], I who have loved you, esteemed you, reverenced you, and served you, I

[9] Mrs. Piozzi sometimes dates events one year later than they occurred (*HLP*, p. 269). For abbreviated references see *infra*, p. 165.

[10] See *Thraliana*, pp. xxi–xxii, for an example of this. In my notes where 'an eminent trader' or 'a lady of fashion' goes unannotated, it means that there is no way known to me of establishing an identity for what may after all be an entirely fictitious person, created for the moment.

who long thought you the first of womankind, entreat that, before your fate is irrevocable, I may once more see you. I was, I once was, Madam, most truly yours, Sam: Johnson. I will come down if you will permit.

After this, and Mrs. Thrale's properly indignant yet dignified reply, despite epistolary gestures of tenderness and reconciliation from both, the long friendship was over. Indeed Johnson knew his beloved Mrs. Thrale as Mrs. Piozzi for less than half a year; he died shortly after the Piozzis left England for a continental honeymoon.

One must remember, therefore, that the exchange of letters between Johnson and Mrs. Thrale in 1784 is between a sick man, full of his symptoms and their treatment, and a woman thirty-five years younger than he, in health and on the verge of a marriage for love. For the *Anecdotes*, published approximately a year and a half after Johnson's bitter and anguished outbreak at the news of the marriage, reflect Mrs. Piozzi's feelings. After commenting on Mr. Thrale's 'very powerful influence over the Doctor', she goes on to write: 'as I never had any ascendancy at all over Mr. Johnson, except just in the things that concerned his health, it grew extremely perplexing and difficult to live in the house with him, when the master of it was no more; the worse, indeed, because his dislikes grew capricious, and he could scarce bear to have any body come to the house whom it was absolutely necessary for me to see' (pp. 106–7). Dr. Burney, who reviewed the *Anecdotes* in the May 1786 *Monthly Review*, was particularly severe on this passage and equally critical, though more restrained in his language, about Mrs. Piozzi's apology for deserting Johnson and retiring to Bath; the reviewer in the *Critical Review* for April 1786 shared his views on this second passage. Mrs. Piozzi had written:

I was forced to take advantage of my lost lawsuit, and plead inability of purse to remain longer in London or its vicinage. I had been crossed in my intentions of going abroad, and found it convenient, for every reason of health, peace, and pecuniary circumstances, to retire to Bath, where I knew Mr. Johnson would not follow me, and where I could for that reason command some little portion of time for my own use; a thing impossible while I remained at Streatham or at London, as my hours, carriage, and servants had long been at his command, who would not rise in the morning till twelve o'clock perhaps, and oblige me to make breakfast for him till the bell rung for dinner, though much displeased if the toilet was neglected,[11] and though much of the time we passed together was spent in blaming or deriding, very justly, my neglect of œconomy, and waste of that money which might make many families happy. The original reason of our connection, his particularly disordered health and spirits, had been long at an end, and he had no other ailments than old age and general infirmity, which every professor of medicine was ardently zealous and generally attentive to palliate, and to contribute all in their power for the prolongation of a life so valuable.

[11] Compare her earlier statement in the *Anecdotes*: 'Dr. Johnson . . . required less attendance, sick or well, than ever I saw any human creature' (*infra*, p. 150).

Veneration for his virtue, reverence for his talents, delight in his conversation, and habitual endurance of a yoke my husband first put upon me, and of which he contentedly bore his share for sixteen or seventeen years, made me go on so long with Mr. Johnson; but the perpetual confinement I will own to have been terrifying in the first years of our friendship, and irksome in the last; nor could I pretend to support it without help, when my coadjutor was no more (p. 156).

She then went on to state that had it not been for her and her husband the world would have been deprived of some of Johnson's later works, particularly the *Lives of the Poets*. All this was too much for reviewers and the public. Today, however, we can take a longer view and rejoice that Arthur Murphy prevailed on Johnson to visit the wealthy brewer and his pretty young wife one day in January 1765.

Notes on the Texts

William Shaw: *Memoirs*

The text is that of the first edition, the *Memoirs* never having been reprinted, wholly or in part. I have silently corrected a few obvious errors.

Mrs. Piozzi: *Anecdotes*

The text is printed from the British Museum copy of the first edition (8º; 1786), collated with the fourth edition, 1786; these, with the second and third editions and a Dublin edition, also of 1786, were all the editions printed in Mrs. Piozzi's lifetime, although a number of the anecdotes were reprinted in the seventh edition of *The Beauties of Johnson* (1787), pp. xlvi–li. Later editions appeared in 1822 (the year after Mrs. Piozzi's death), 1826, 1831 (incorporated in John Wilson Croker's edition of Boswell's *Life*), 1835 (in a separate volume in Croker's edition of the *Life*),[1] in 1856 (in the Traveller's Library), 1862, 1884 (in *Johnsoniana*, the fifth volume of Alexander Napier's edition of Boswell's *Life*), 1887 (no. 105 in Cassell's National Library, with a short introduction by Henry Morley), 1888, 1892, 1897 (in volume I of G. B. Hill's *Johnsonian Miscellanies*), 1925 (edited by S. C. Roberts), and 1932 (S. C. Roberts's 1925 edition with a few textual changes; *Cambridge Miscellany* no. 7). Dr. Burney in his review of the *Anecdotes* in the *Monthly Review* (May 1786) pointed out two errors in grammar which were corrected in the fourth edition, and there is an errata slip, now very rare, which is found in the second or third editions. The Cambridge University Library has the errata slip in its copy of the second edition. The principal textual variants will be found on p. 163 *infra*.

[1] The *Anecdotes* appear in various reissues of Croker's edition of Boswell's *Life of Johnson*.

Select Bibliography

William Shaw: *Memoirs*

    The fullest list of Shaw's works is found in *Notes and Queries*, seventh series, ix (May 1890), p. 392; the fullest biography is that in the *D.N.B.* which depends much on the account in *Notes and Queries* in May 1890 and a further communication in June 1890, p. 498, from the same contributor. There is no modern study of Shaw, unless it lies concealed in some journal of Gaelic studies; and I have reason to believe that this is not so. (Note that the British Museum Catalogue mistakenly lists him as two men, one a Gaelic scholar and the other the Rector of Chelvey, a fate to which he was subjected in the first edition of the *C.B.E.L.*)

Mrs. Piozzi: *Anecdotes*

    The standard biography is *Hesther Lynch Piozzi (Mrs. Thrale)*, by James L. Clifford, 1941; 2nd edn. corrected, 1952; reprinted 1968. Professor Clifford's appendix of Mrs. Piozzi's 'Chief Published Works' is still the fullest bibliography of her primary works and his 'Select Bibliography' of secondary works on or about Mrs. Piozzi is equally definitive. Chief among the works listed in his 'Select Bibliography' are A. Hayward, *Autobiography, Letters and Literary Remains of Mrs. Piozzi (Thrale)*, 2 vols. (1861) with a second edition the same year incorporating much new material. A. M. Broadly's *Doctor Johnson and Mrs. Thrale* (1910) includes Mrs. Piozzi's Welsh Journal. P. Merritt collected and edited *Piozzi Marginalia* in 1925. Excerpts from the collection of Piozzi MSS. in the John Rylands Library have been printed in the *Bulletin* of the Library, vols. xv, xvi, xx, and lii. Professor Clifford's 'The Printing of Mrs. Piozzi's *Anecdotes of Dr. Johnson*' in vol. xx deserves special notice. *The French Journals of Mrs. Thrale and Dr. Johnson* have been edited by M. Tyson and H. Guppy (1932) and *Thraliana: the Diary of Mrs. Hesther Lynch Thrale (later Mrs. Piozzi)* by Katherine C. Balderston (1942; revised, 2nd edn. 1951). Miss Balderston contributes a rather startling essay on 'Johnson's Vile Melancholy', in which she focuses attention on Dr. Johnson's masochistic leanings, to *The Age of Johnson: Essays Presented to Chauncey Brewster Tinker*

(1949). R. W. Chapman edited *The Letters of Samuel Johnson, with Mrs. Thrale's Genuine Letters to him*, 3 vols. (1952). Mention may also be made of Edward G. Fletcher, 'Mrs. Piozzi on Boswell and Johnson's Tour', in *University of Texas Studies in English* (1953), which describes Mrs. Piozzi's annotated copy of Boswell's *Journal* of the Hebrides tour with Johnson. There is an essay on Mrs. Piozzi in Peter Quennell's *The Singular Preference* (1952). Irma S. Lustig's essay 'Boswell at Work: The "Animadversions" on Mrs. Piozzi', *MLR*, 67 (1972), 11–30, uses the manuscript *Life of Johnson* to study Boswell's revisions in his animadversions on Mrs. Piozzi's *Anecdotes*. Part III of Mary Hyde's 'The Impossible Friendship', appearing in the *Harvard Library Bulletin*, xx (July 1972), 270–317 retells, with some additions, the story of the preparation and publication of the *Anecdotes* (see pp. 298–317). *The Impossible Friendship* was published in book form in 1973.

A Chronology of William Shaw

		Age
1749	(3 Feb.) Shaw born on the Isle of Arran	
1766	Matriculates at Glasgow University	17
1774	Becomes acquainted with SJ ('about Christmas')	25
1777	M.A. Glasgow	28
1778	*An Analysis of the Galic Language*	29
1779	(July) Minister of Ardclach, in the presbytery of Nairn	30
1780	*A Galic and English Dictionary* (2 vols.)	31
1780	(1 Aug.) Resigns Ardclach living	31
1781	(17 May) Elected Fellow of Society of Antiquaries	32
1781	*An Enquiry into the Authenticity of the Poems Ascribed to Ossian*	32
1782	Second edition of *An Enquiry* . . . in which Shaw replies to an attack by Dr. John Clark in 1781	33
1784	*A Rejoinder to an Answer from Mr. Clark on the Subject of Ossian's Poems*	35
1785	*Memoirs of the Life and Writings of the Late Samuel Johnson* (anonymous)	36
1795	(1 May) Becomes Rector of Chelvey, Somerset	46
1800	(Easter) B.D., Emmanuel College, Cambridge	51
1801	*Suggestions Respecting a Plan of National Education, with Conjectures on the Probable Consequences of Non-descript Methodism and Sunday Schools,* published at Bath	52
1802	*The Life of H. More, with a Critical Review of her Writings.* By the Rev. Sir Archibald MacSarcasm, Bart.	53
1831	(16 Sept.) Death of Shaw	83

Chronology of Hesther Lynch Piozzi

WILLIAM SHAW

Memoirs of the
Life and Writings of the Late
DR. SAMUEL JOHNSON

Preface

BESIDES the facts already before the public, the Editor of these *Memoirs* has been favoured with the contributions of those who were long the friends of Doctor Samuel Johnson.

His servants, Mrs. Du Maulin,[1] who knew him from her infancy, and several others of his most intimate acquaintance, whose names the Editor is not allowed to mention, told him all they knew.

The late Mr. Thomas Davies,[2] of Covent-Garden, who lived long in habits of friendship with the Doctor, not only assisted the Editor in detecting several errors, in other accounts of his life, but authenticated to him many facts, which seemed otherwise doubtful. This Gentleman had collected many anecdotes of his friend, but would not mention them, he said, to any person whatever, as he might probably have occasion to use them himself.

But the principal, and most valuable communications in this work, are from Mr. Elphinston,[3] who, with singular readiness and affability, gave the Editor every sort of information which he could desire; and the reader may easily conceive how much might be gleaned by a person of his intelligence and discernment, during a correspondence of the greatest intimacy for above the space of thirty years. The letters and anecdotes, here published, will shew how much, how sincerely, and for what a length of time, these congenial characters regarded each other.

The facts relating to the Ossian controversy are anonymous, unless the authenticity of any of them should be challenged; in that case the author will avow them, as the means of defence are fully in his power.

Memoirs of Dr. Samuel Johnson

THE late Dr. Samuel Johnson, whose story I am now to relate, like every one who arrives at extreme age, survived all his earlier and most of his later acquaintance.

This man was grown grey in literature. He lived in the capacity of an author on the town for a period of near fifty years. The vicissitudes and fortunes of such a situation, protracted to such a length of time, it were impossible even for those who knew him best, to trace with accuracy or state with precision.

The anecdotes of his juvenile days have perished with the companions of his youth. Few interest themselves in the history of a man without property, fame or consequence. Johnson was for many years lost in a multitude of authors, who are occupied only in collecting the occurrences of the day, polishing into form the fugitive ideas of booksellers, or in some of the numerous periodical works which engross so much of the trade, furnishing subjects of fresh speculation for the public mind. And it was not till he derived peculiar lustre from a long series of success in his literary pursuits, that he became an object of general attention and enquiry.

It is now thirty years since he lamented on publishing his Dictionary, that *most of those whom he wished to please were sunk into the grave*.[1] Nor is it when thus loaded with the frailties of age, and tottering under the accumulated decays of nature, that any man is much inclined to multiply connections or commence friendships. So great and universal however was the estimation which his virtuous principles and eminent talents at last procured, that of late it has been deemed a sort of literary discredit not to rank in the number of his acquaintance, his admirers, or his imitators.

Men distinguished by industry or genius as Johnson was, in morals, arts, sciences, or letters, serve the purposes of public utility in a double capacity. Their example stimulates those around them to exertion and perseverance in virtue or excellence. Posterity contemplate also with a

5

mixture of reverence and emulation, the copy of an original which their ancestors were thus contented to follow and applaud.

By exhausting a long laborious life in contributing to the improvement and delight of his countrymen, Johnson finally merited and obtained their general and unfeigned approbation. His enlightened mind, which aimed only at the happiness and perfection of the species, was constantly emitting such effusions of virtuous intelligence as tended equally to clear the head and better the heart; and when his death, which had been for some time expected, was announced, most of his contemporaries regarded the melancholy event with a consternation or sensibility similar to that of a family who has lost its head, or an army whose general falls.

This accounts for that extreme avidity with which every vestige of his genius, his taste, or his humour, is still received by a grateful public. And it will be long before any work, in which he had the least concern, can be indifferent to them. His transcendent abilities, and tried virtues, his oddities, which were alike original and abundant; the variety of his friends and the length of his life, give so many shapes to his story, and such different complexions to the prompt and occasional ebullitions of his wit in different situations, that whoever had the honour of his acquaintance must be in possession of materials which, for the sake of literature and posterity, ought to be recorded.

Litchfield in Staffordshire is now very well known to be the place of Johnson's birth; a circumstance which may probably be recollected by posterity, when this ancient city, like others which have been made immortal by giving birth to great men, is forgotten.

It appears from the parish register, that Johnson was born in the month of September, 1709.[1] His father kept a shop near the market-place, and chiefly dealt in books, stationary ware, and book-binding; articles which, especially in a country situation, where literature is but rarely an amusement, and never a business, could not be very profitable. It was from this circumstance, that Johnson was enabled to say, as he often did, that he could bind a book very well.

Old Mr. Johnson,[2] therefore, whose story being thus blended with that of his son, becomes an object of some attention, might be reputable, but could not be rich. He was a man of reserved manners, but of acknowledged shrewdness. From habits of steadiness and punctuality he acquired great personal respectability. The oldest people in the place would often tell the Doctor, who heard them with a sensible satisfaction, that his father continued to the last such a favourite among the boys, that he was perhaps the only one in town who never received any injury from their petulance and mischief. And it was said by himself, whose regards were incapable of betraying him into the flattery even of a parent, that *he was no careless observer of the passages of the times in which he lived*.[1] His intellectual abilities unimproved and called forth by no interest or emergency, were notwithstanding perhaps but moderate, as it does not follow, that because the son made a figure, the father should be a prodigy. But that he preserved himself by his industry and attention in a state of honesty and independence, that he had prudence enough by no schemes or speculations of any kind to injure his credit with his neighbours, and that whatever disappointments and crosses occurred in his intercourse with the world, he discovered the same innate fund of satisfaction and chearfulness[2] which marked the most prosperous circumstances of his life, are particulars well known, and it is all we do know with certainty about him.

Even in the town of Litchfield, however, where so little is to be made by the practice, we find him letting out part of his house in lodgings. These at the time of Johnson's birth were occupied by a Mr. Swynfen,[3] who had a very pretty country-house on an estate of his own a few miles distant from Litchfield, where he practised physic, and where for that reason he provided himself with occasional accommodation. He was a man of considerable reputation in his profession as a physician, but was still more eminent for the liberality of his mind and the goodness of his heart. This gentleman, having stood godfather for the child, interested himself not a little in whatever related to his subsequent tuition. Though perhaps not affluent he was in easy circumstances, and being of a friendly and susceptible nature, took an early liking to young Johnson, the first openings of whose genius he superintended himself with much satisfaction and confidence. These, though neither sparkling nor premature, as Johnson was always rather solid and saturnine, than volatile or forward, were yet so entirely original and spontaneous, as to afford sufficient indications that his talents were not unhappily turned for literature and science.

He imbibed the elements of erudition at the free grammar-school of Litchfield. A Mr. Hunter[4] had then the direction of the school. To this gentleman's elegant and correct method of teaching, the Doctor has often acknowledged the highest obligations. It was a circumstance he always mentioned with pleasure, that the place of his education had produced a Wollaston, a Newton, a Willis, a Garrick, and a Hawkesworth.[5] The two last particularly, whose names are not unknown to fame, though a few years younger, were both his school-fellows, who then contracted that regard for his character, and confidence in his talents and worth, which afterwards disposed them so readily to list among his pupils and friends.[1] For juvenile attachments often continue to operate through life, and are generally the last to which susceptible minds become insensible.

Thus situated, Johnson entered on the initials[2] of learning, with an eagerness equally persevering and unsatiable. His exterior was always sluggish, and he never did any thing which had the least appearance of gracefulness, taste, dexterity, or dispatch. Even in the act of devouring the sublimest passages of ancient literature, one who knew him not, would have thought him asleep with the book in his hand. But though his diligence discovered no ardour, his perseverance was so singular and exemplary, that all attempts to divert him from the task assigned, or which he assigned himself, were uniformly without effect. The rapacity with which he commenced his primary pursuit, and grasped at every object of classical intelligence, is obvious from the stubbornness of a peculiar habit which he then contracted. To his dying day, he never thought, recollected, or studied, whether in his closet, or in the street, alone, or in company, without putting his huge unweildy body, in the same rolling, aukward posture, in which he was in use, while conning his grammar, or construing his lesson, to sit on the form at school.

He is said, when a mere school-boy, to have read indefatigably, and probably picked up no despicable acquaintance with books, by occasionally attending his father's shop. Here he was, not unfrequently, so absorbed by his predilection for the classical lore of antiquity, as entirely to neglect the business he had in trust. Being often chid for disobliging some of the best of his father's customers and friends, in this manner, he replied with great shrewdness, *that to supersede the pleasures of reading, by the attentions of traffic, was a task he never could master.*

It was, undoubtedly, by lounging here, that he heard many of those biographical and literary anecdotes, which he has since detailed, with so much elegance and vivacity, in his *Lives of the Poets.*[3] To such a mind as Johnson's, thus early smitten with the love of science and philosophy, every thing connected with men of genius and letters, we may well believe, would be eagerly devoured, and tenaciously retained. And it is remarkable, in what an exuberant vein of manly sensibility, those particulars, which he says, *were told him* when a boy, occasionally break from him.

We are not informed at whose expence[4] he was sent to college. His godfather, Dr. Swynfen, was likely enough to be consulted on this occasion. And the gentlemen in the neighbourhood, prompted by his example and zeal, and sensible of the father's inability and the son's genius, probably agreed among themselves, on some mode of thus finishing an education, from which they predicted much public utility.

He was entered, however, of Pembroke-college, Oxford, October 31, 1728.[1] Here he studied several terms,[2] and might have continued longer, nor left the university, as he certainly did, without any degree, but that he could not afford either to continue, or to pay for those honours, to which his proficiency as a scholar must have otherwise entitled him.

His conduct, during no long residence in that illustrious seminary, is but little known, or at least has been marked by no celebrity. He is said to have treated some of the tutors with disrespect, their lectures with negligence, and the rules of the college with rudeness and contumely.[3] But this story, besides being supported by no authority, does not suit the tenor of the Doctor's behaviour, who at the same time that he despised the rules or ceremonies of fashion, in his deportment among the idle, the whimsical, the gay, or the affectedly polite, regarded with reverence every form or regulation, which had instruction or utility for its object.

In such a situation Johnson could not be idle. It was here he contemplated the wisdom of antiquity, and stored his capacious memory with whatever is valuable on record. He was formed by nature for a sedentary and recluse life. His strongest habits were those of indolence and austerity. All his subsequent exertions originated, not in his own choice, but in stern necessity. Labour appeared to him impracticable whenever it was possible to be idle. He had not yet commenced author, nor thought of the profession. His performances then could only be such college exercises as he could not avoid. Some of these were much admired and are still remembered. He particularly translated Pope's Messiah into elegant Latin verse, which afterwards appeared in a volume of poems, published by one Husband.[4]

It is supposed that he remained between two and three years at college, which he left for the place of an usher to a free-school at Market Bosworth in Leicestershire.[5] This laborious capacity he sustained much longer than was expected by any who knew him. All his leisure time was employed assiduously in the pursuit of intellectual acquisition and amusement; and who can say what might have been the consequence of his continuing for life in such a situation. Some may suppose his works to have gained in quality what they might have wanted in quantity. It can hardly be conceived, he would not have produced some memorial of his genius. But it would be rash to say, that such a production must have surpassed in excellence, the most finished of those pieces which actually fell from his pen. How very few gentlemen authors have ever arrived at any superlative distinction or eminence. Writing is an art which can only be acquired by practice. Lyttleton, Chesterfield, Hume, Robertson, and Gibbon, though by means of an independent situation, were never in pay to booksellers,[1] accustomed themselves to literary compositions from their infancy. Johnson, therefore, immersed in a school might have published less, but except he had written much, he could not, with all the advantages of leisure, retirement, and plenty, have written so well as he did, amidst the incessant bustle of a town life, exposed to the constant intrusions of the idle and officious, and precipitated by the frequent pressure of impending want.

Here, by the example and advice, probably of his friend and master, Anthony Blackwall,[2] he formed the plan of establishing an academy of his own. 'Previous however to the accomplishment of this project, we find him residing at Birmingham, in the house of one Warren, a printer. His first essays are said to have been written for a news-paper, published by his landlord, and that he wrote while here, *A Voyage to Abyssinia, by Father Jerome Lobo, a Portuguese Jesuit; with a Continuation of the History of Abyssinia down to the Beginning of the eighteenth Century; and Fifteen Dissertations on various Subjects, relating to the History, Antiquities, Government, Religion, Manners, and Natural History of Abyssinia, and other Countries mentioned by Father Jerome Lobo. By Mr. Le Grand.* He wrote at the same time and in the same place, *Verses on a Lady's presenting a Sprig of Myrtle to a Gentleman*, which have been re-printed in several miscellanies, under the name of Mr. Hammond. They were, as the Doctor declared, very late in life, written for a friend, who was desirous of having, at least from his mistress, the reputation of a poet.'

I give this anecdote to the reader as it appeared in one of our monthly publications. It was incorporated with an account of Johnson's life, which, so far as it went, had all the marks of authenticity.[3] Thus connected, the fact bore an aspect so like that of truth, as must have rendered the omissions, in spite of all my suspicions to the contrary, still inexcusable.

The author of the life of Garrick, who has been intimately acquainted with Johnson for many years, from whom Johnson could not conceal a secret of his heart, or an incident in his story, mentions the beginning of the year 1735, as the time when Johnson undertook the instruction of young gentlemen in the Belles Letters at Litchfield.[4] Garrick and Hawkesworth were of the party who became his pupils on this occasion, and who profited during the short time he acted in that station. It is not certain, nor indeed material to know in what this scheme proved defective. But in May, 1736, we find him advertising a boarding-school at Edial, near Litchfield.

This is a critical period in the life of Johnson. His father could afford him no pecuniary assistance, and he had too much sensibility and manliness to continue a burthen on his friends. Such an establishment could not however be accomplished without money; and the gleanings of a very few years in the situation occupied by Johnson, allowing him to be a rigid œconomist, which he never was, must have been trifling. Thus circumstanced, how then could he raise a sum adequate to the demand? The difficulty will be solved by supposing his marriage to have taken place about this time. Mrs. Porter,[1] whom he married, had been left a widow; her husband died insolvent, but her settlement was secured. Though she had three children, she was still young and handsome. The first advances probably proceeded from her, as her attachment to Johnson was in opposition to the advice and desire of all her relations. Her brother in particular offered to settle a very handsome annuity on her for life, provided she would break her engagements. But nothing would dissuade her. She brought her second husband about seven or eight hundred pounds, a great part of which was expended in fitting up a house for a boarding-school, which they had doubtless concerted between them. But this abortive scheme was likewise of short duration. He has left no documents by which to account for the failure. His manners however sufferable among the petty circle to whom his real merits excused every thing, were far from connecting popularity with his personal intercourse. Parents could not be very fond of putting their children under the care of a man whose size was gigantic, whose temper was arrogant and austere, and whose habits were all clumsy and rude. His mind was as destitute of accommodation as his exterior was of politeness or grace; and to those who estimate genius or worth only by a soft tongue, a smooth face, or ceremonious carriage, his wit would appear insolence, his honesty folly, and his learning pedantry. Such a man was more likely to create aversion, than conciliate friendship, and instead of gathering a school, to be considered by the young and ignorant as a scarecrow. He had too much good sense to overlook so material an inconvenience. It might even strike him as an insuperable obstacle to success, and have its effect in determining him to abandon the whole plan, as romantic or impracticable.[2]

He then adopted the sudden resolution of trying his fortune with the Booksellers in town. This adventure was not perhaps so much the consequence of disappointed expectations, as of his strong propensity for literary pursuits. Mr. Garrick, though his pupil, and inferior both in years and education, was no doubt consulted on this event. The letter which introduced Johnson to a clergyman of great reputation at that time as well as Garrick, however frequently quoted by those who have gone before me on the same subject,[3] cannot with propriety be omitted in this place.

To the Rev. Mr. COLSON.[1]

Litchfield, March 2, 1736.

DEAR SIR,

I had the favour of yours, and am extremely obliged to you; but cannot say I have a greater affection for you upon it than I had before, being so long since so much endeared to you, as well by an early friendship as by your many excellent and valuable qualifications. And had I a son of my own, it would be my ambition, instead of sending him to the university, to dispose of him as this young gentleman is. He and another neighbour of mine, one Mr. Samuel Johnson, set out this morning for London together; David Garrick to be with you early next week, and Mr. Johnson to try his fate with a Tragedy,[2] and to see to get himself employed in some translation either from the Latin or from the French. Johnson is a very good scholar, and a poet, and I have great hopes he will turn out a fine tragedy-writer. If it should any ways lie in your way, I doubt not you will be ready to recommend and assist your countryman.

I am, &c.

GILB. WALMSLEY.[3]

London discloses an endless variety of resources for independent merit. Here capacity and industry can never want encouragement. And when every other expedient has failed, there are still hopes of doing something in a market, where all sorts of commodities are sure to bring their price.

Johnson had not lived to the age of six-and-twenty, without occasionally exercising his talents and acquirements in composition. Walmsley mentions him both as a poet and a scholar, without saying how he knew the fact. But few have the art of writing well who are not fond of shewing it, and Johnson does not seem to possess less vanity than other men.

What reception this friendly introduction procured for him with Mr. Colson, or whether this worthy clergyman was of any real service to him, we are not told. Such manuscripts as he brought to town were now by his direction probably offered to sale. But it does not appear that his *London*, with all its merit, was treated with much respect.[4] This literary market was then, as it generally has been, governed only by principles of knavery, envy, or caprice. Most publishers were the tools of some favorite author, in whose opinion they confided, and whom they caressed on purpose that they might at once monopolize his labours and advice. Pride has been always the foible of the profession. What justice could a stranger expect from an order of men who can never be generous, and seldom civil to one another.

The fact is, Johnson's poem was likely to be on his hand, merely because rejected by some capital Booksellers. He had been strongly importuned by his godfather Dr. Swynfen, before he left Litchfield, to publish it in the country, with a dedication to Dr. Chandler, who was then Bishop of Litchfield and Coventry.[1] But he was determined to solicit no connection with the great. The church had been the primary object of his education, but from principles of religious delicacy he had uniformly declined the honour thus intended for him by his friends. And this was one consideration which probably weighed against the advice of his godfather in the present case. But the shyness of the trade to bring forward this favourite production sufficiently punished his obstinacy; and finding he could not live on poetry, which nobody would purchase, he connected himself with the editors of newspapers,[2] and often depended on the lucubrations of the day for the provisions of to-morrow.

It was in this fugitive and dilitory situation that he got acquainted with Cave,[3] the printer, whose numerous literary projects afforded bread to multitudes.

This enterprising printer Johnson compliments in the following copy of beautiful Latin verses, to which an elegant English version is subjoined, which was done for me on purpose by a friend.

Ad URBANUM

URBANE, nullis fesse laboribus,
URBANE, nullis victe calumniis,
   Cui fronte sertum in erudita
      Perpetuo viret et virebit.

Quid moliatur gens imitantium,
Quid et minetur, sollicitus parum,
   Vacare solis perge Musis,
      Juxta animo studiisq; felix.

Linguæ procacis plumbea spicula,
Fidens, suberbo frange silentio;
   Victrix per obstantes catervas
      Sedulitas animosa tendet.

Intende nervos fortis, inanibus
Risurus olim nisibus æmuli;
   Intende jam nervos, habebis
      Participes operæ Camœnas.

Non ulla Musis pagina gratior,
Quam quæ severis ludicra jungere
   Novit, fatigatamq; nugis
      Utilibus recreare mentem.

13

Texente Nymphis serta Lycoride,
Rosæ ruborem sic Viola adjuvat
Immista, sic Iris refulget
Æthereis variata fucis.

To URBAN [1]

URBAN, whom labour cannot bow,
  Nor calumny subdue;
The wreath that decks thy learned brow,
  Shall bloom for ever new.

Whate'er thy mimicks may design,
  Howe'er thy name revile;
Brave man, to court the Muse be thine,
  On thee the Muse shall smile.

By scornful silence break the dart,
  The tongue envenom'd throws;
Thy diligence and dauntless heart
  Shall force thro' all thy foes.

Proceed, and thou shalt live to see
  Thy rival prostrate laid;
Proceed, and all the Nine to thee
  Shall lend their envied aid.

What page to them more pleasure brings?
  What page like thine refin'd?
Where mirth, succeeding serious things,
  Relieves the weary mind.

So violets with roses twine,
  And livelier blushes rise:
So various colours blended shine,
  When Iris paints the skies.

How this connection commenced, the minute transactions it produced, or how long it continued is yet ascertained by no documents before the public.[2]

Johnson seems to have contributed his share from the beginning in the Gentleman's Magazine.[3] But in such enequal and fugitive compilations, no man is fond of writing any thing otherwise than anonymously. In the year 1738 a few petit pieces[4] however appeared with the initials of his name, which perhaps have been excelled by nothing he has since produced. When these are excepted it will not be very easy amidst the huge mass of materials contained in a magazine, to discriminate even the pen of a Johnson. Of this particular he was himself always singularly shy. He declined pointing out any of his earlier performances, when some of his most intimate friends asked it as a favour. To others he acknowledged that he then wrote many things which merited no distinction from the trash with which they were consigned to oblivion. And whatever the Booksellers may alledge, it is a fact very well known, that a perfect catalogue of his works was a task to which he has always said his own recollection was inadequate.

Great merit has been ascribed to Johnson for the speeches he fabricated for the *Senate of Lilliput*. It was by this disrespectful appellation that he marked his contempt for the British House of Commons. This series of chimerical debates commenced in the year 1740, and were continued for several sessions.[1] He received hints from a person who attended the House regularly for that purpose. The public, who were anxious to know what their delegates were doing, gratefully accepted of Johnson's account as there was not another, and allowed that to be genuine which they had not the means of perceiving an imposture.[2]

Men however who know what it is to report the speeches in parliament, will be struck with nothing mighty extraordinary in all this. It is well known Mr. Woodfall, and Mr. Sheridan,[3] who is certainly next in fame as a Reporter, have sometimes exceeded within the four-and-twenty hours, Johnson's labours for a month. There is a prodigious difference between a man's compassing at his leisure in his study, surrounded with every domestic convenience, and feeling no pressure from the urgent demands of the press, and where he is incessantly molested by the bustle of those at work, and by a thousand circumstances which, though not easily described, are yet peculiarly inimical to recollection.

This is their situation to whom the public are indebted for such accounts of the parliamentary proceedings as are daily detailed in Newspapers. These gentlemen, after sitting for twelve, or sometimes eighteen hours on a stretch, crouded as closly as they can be, without victuals, perchance, or drink, hasten as fast to their respective offices as possible, where they often write six, seven, or eight hours, at the rate of a column an hour. This incredible dispatch, to which the period of diurnal publications indispensibly subjects them, absolutely precludes all revisal, either of their own copy, or any proofs from the press. The wonder is not, therefore, that there should be so many improprieties in style and arrangement, but that there are, in fact, so few.

It is habit only which can unite with such facility any degree of correctness whatever. The mechanism of the business is an art, which practice alone can give. It combines accuracy and readiness of recollection, command of language, sound health, and great rapidity in the liberal use of the pen. In the two former Johnson had undoubtedly few equals, in the two latter he seems materially deficient. Seldom, altogether, free from illness, his constitution could not have supported the drudgery of attendance. And the form of his alphabet,[1] which inclines strongly to the left, instead of the right, is a proof that he was not much master of what may be called an expeditious hand.

His predecessor in this Herculean labour was Guthrie,[2] who, long before he died, was reduced to the necessity of using an amanuensis. Johnson was every way superior, and it is asserted by those who ought to know, that the magazine, during his connection with it, rose considerably in the public estimation. Hawkesworth,[3] his friend and imitator, succeeded him likewise in these cursory productions, and brought with him no inconsiderable share of his master's genius.

While thus employed in the composition of speeches, which never were spoken, his admirers imagined they perceived a striking apposition, in his stile and train of thinking, to the various speakers. This characteristic was, however, the more impossible, that Johnson never, in the whole course of his life, attended one debate in either house of parliament. This was a species of ingenuity, which no instruction could supply. And nothing exposes the mean adulation of his eulogists more, than the absurdity of thus praising him for what was, in its own nature, impracticable.

The *Life of Savage*,[4] it is said, was undertaken and executed with peculiar expedition, in order to convince the proprietor of the Gentleman's Magazine, that Johnson was equal to this laborious employ. And he has often enough asserted, with some degree of ostentation, that he completed this long and well-written life, in little more than six-and-thirty hours.

In 1738 he began a translation of the famous Father Paul's history of the Council of Trent. It is not known on what account this work was laid aside.[5] Though no great progress was ever made in it, a few sheets of it were certainly printed. These, it is to be hoped, will be carefully preserved by some friend to letters; and the public will be highly indebted to the editor, who shall be the first to present it with such an acceptable curiosity.

What Johnson says, in his introduction to the Life of Dryden, is so literally true in his own case, that we may as well make him speak for himself. 'In settling the order of his works there is some difficulty; the time of writing and publishing is not always the same; nor can the first editions be easily found, if even from them could be obtained the necessary information.'[6] The truth is, that during his engagement with Cave, he published several lives, and other detached performances, many of which were collected by his friend, Mr. Davies, and given to the world, a few years ago, under the title of Fugitive Pieces.[7]

Among the earliest of these appeared, *London, a Poem, in Imitation of the third Satire of Juvenal*.[1] This elegant and masterly production, in which the enormities of the metropolis, and the infinite perils to which health, reputation, and virtue, are inevitably exposed by a London life, as well without fortune as with it, could, notwithstanding, hardly find a purchaser in the whole trade. The celebrated Mr. Robert Dodsley, however, was an exception. He saw the satire was aimed with the dexterity of no common poet. Johnson asked only ten guineas, and Dodsley gave it, rather as an encouragement to go on, than from any sanguine expectation of success in the sale of an *Imitation*. Johnson is reported to have boasted among his friends, *that Dodsley was the first bookseller who found out that he had any genius*.[2] We are told that Mr. Pope[3] read the poem with pleasure, who, receiving no satisfactory answer to repeated enquiries after the author, said, 'It cannot be long before my curiosity will be gratified, the writer of this poem will soon be *detérré*'.

Such an opinion, from Pope, was one of the highest compliments which could be made to a young author. Whether it produced any personal friendship, acquaintance, or interview, is not certain; but the rigidness which runs through his criticism, on most of Pope's works, gives some ground of suspicion, that a very early dislike had been conceived against the poet, his verses, or his commentator.[4]

What he has written concerning the imitations of this great man, is not inapplicable to his own. 'The imitations of Horace,' says he, 'seem to have been written as relaxations of his genius. This employment became his favourite by its facility: the plan was ready to his hand, and nothing was required but to accommodate as he could, the sentiments of an old author, to recent facts, or familiar images; but what is easy is seldom excellent: such imitations cannot give pleasure to common readers; the man of learning may sometimes be surprized and delighted by an unexpected parallel; but the comparison requires knowledge of the original, which will likewise often detect strained applications. Between Roman images and English manners, there will be an irreconcileable dissimilitude, and the work will be generally uncouth and party-coloured; neither original nor translated, neither ancient nor modern.'[5]

These were his sentiments, when his judgment was matured by experience, and after a long series of studies, in which many opportunities must have occurred, of a cool and critical discussion of the subject. This may probably account for his writing so little in that way afterwards; for, notwithstanding the very high merit of *London*, as a species of imitation, in no part of his works, perhaps, does he appear more susceptible of criticism, as the few following brief strictures, communicated to me by a warm admirer of Pope,[6] will sufficiently evince. He owned, at the same time, that nothing but Johnson's nibbling, with so much indelicacy, at the beautiful versifications of a poet, whom he had always esteemed the most classical and elegant in the language, could have provoked him to read, what he acknowledged an excellent poem, with such fastidious minuteness.

> Let observation, with extensive view,
> Survey the [world] from China to Peru.
>
> *Johnson's Imitation.*[1]

Let observation survey the world, from China to Peru, and we must allow its *view to be extensive*, whether the poet tell us so or not.

> Who now resolves, from vice and London far,
> To breathe in distant fields a purer air.
>
> *Johnson's Imitation.*

If he was *far* from London, certainly the fields which he breathed in must be *distant*.

> *With slavish tenets taint our poison'd youth.*
>
> Johnson's Imitation.

To taint poison'd youth, is to poison them twice.

> Spurn'd as a beggar, dreaded as a spy,
> Live unregarded, unlamented die.
>
> *Johnson's Imitation.*

Johnson censures Pope's epitaph on himself, which begins,

> Under this stone, or under this sill,
> Or under this turf, &c.

'When a man,' says he, 'is buried, the question under what he is buried, is easily decided. He forgot that though he wrote the epitaph in a state of uncertainty, yet it could not be laid over him till his grave was made. Such is the folly of wit, when it is ill employed.'[2]

Johnson did not die till a considerable number of years had elapsed, though he says he was dying at the time he wrote the above line; he died too exceedingly lamented. He made a mistake on a very serious occasion, as well as the poet whom he censures.

> Fate never wounds more deep the gen'rous heart,
> Than when a blockhead's insult points the dart.

Juvenal says no such thing; it is his sense, tortured to little less than nonsense. What! does a blockhead's insult give the deepest wound? Every old woman can tell us that 'a fool's bolt is soon shot.' No one minds it, but those who are themselves not over wise.

Thy satire point, and animate thy page.
Johnson's Imitation.

Here Johnson is again unlucky in the concluding line of a poem. By pointing the satire, he must animate the page of course. Addison fell into this fault of tautology, as often as Johnson, but Addison was not so severe as Johnson, in criticising others.

This poem, very probably, gives an exact picture of *London*, as it appeared to his mind immediately on his leaving the country, while every rural convenience was yet recollected with regret, and those of the town had been enjoyed only to such a degree, in such company, or under such circumstances, as might rather disgust than gratify. The difficulty of securing a prospect of employment, before he could be known, the shyness of the booksellers, to interest themselves in the fortune or business of a stranger, the wants of futurity, which could hope but little assistance from the present, which was unequal to its own supply, ill health, few friends, exquisite sensibility, and a temper of mind, rather melancholy than chearful, obviously account for the indignant spirit, and strong assemblage of melancholy imagery with which that performance abounds.

Under these impressions he undoubtedly meditated a return to a country situation. The bustle of the town seems to have offended his predilection for retirement, and the occupation of an author, his unconquerable love of ease. Perhaps, Mrs. Johnson might also be consulted on the like occasion, and it is likely, would rather wish to enjoy her old friends, than have the trouble, in so precarious a place as London, to cultivate new ones. It is certain he had solicitations to accept of a school in the neighbourhood of Litchfield,[1] with which he had no other objection to comply but a want of the necessary qualifications.

The following letter ought to have been inserted before, but from the observations just made it will not be misplaced here, especially as it requires more labour than I can bestow, as well as materials, which have not yet been found, to settle the chronology of his publications and transactions, with certainty or precision.

Sir,

'Mr. Samuel Johnson (author of London a Satire, and some other poetical pieces) is a native of this country, and much respected by some worthy gentlemen in his neighbourhood, who are trustees of a charity-school now vacant, the certain salary of which is sixty pounds per annum, of which they are desirous to make him master; but unfortunately he is not capable of receiving their bounty, which would make him happy for life, by not being a Master of Arts, which, by the statutes of this school, the master of it must be. Now these gentlemen do me the honour to think, that I have interest enough in you, to prevail upon you to write to Dean Swift,[1] to persuade the University of Dublin to send a diploma to me, constituting this poor man Master of Arts in their University. They highly extol the man's learning and probity; and will not be persuaded that the University will make any difficulty of conferring such a favour upon a stranger, if he is recommended by the Dean. They say he is not afraid of the strictest examination, though he is of so long a journey; and will venture it, if the Dean thinks it necessary, choosing rather to die upon the road, than be starved to death in —— translating for booksellers, which has been his only subsistence for some time past. I fear there is more difficulty in this affair than these good-natured gentlemen apprehend, especially as their election cannot be delayed longer than the 11th of next month. If you see the matter in the same light as it appears to me, I hope you will burn this, and pardon me for giving you so much trouble about an impracticable thing; but if you think there is a probability of obtaining the favour asked, I am sure your humanity and propensity to relieve merit in distress, will incline you to serve the poor man, without my adding any more to the trouble I have already given you, than assuring you that I am, with great truth,

SIR,

Your most humble Servant,

GOWER.'

Trentham, Aug. 1, 1738.[2]

It is rather odd this letter did not procure a more favourable answer, and that Johnson did not succeed to the school. We know not whether Swift, to whose friend it was addressed, knew any thing of the matter, but it is obvious Johnson has written the life of this very extraordinary genius,[3] as if his mind had been somewhat warped, and he owed the Dean no returns of kindness or gratitude. Whatever the impediment might have been, it ultimately proved insuperable. Johnson, whose sanguine imagination was easily influenced, and all whose hopes, by whatever means exerted, still glowed with incessant fervour, felt long and severely the disappointment.

It seems to be about this time that he planned and executed the poem, which he calls the *Vanity of Human Wishes*, another imitation of his favourite Juvenal.* This however was not brought forward till some time in the year 1759.[4] His situation in the Gentleman's Magazine was even then continued, and is the true reason why Cave became the publisher.[5] The train of thinking is in all respects worthy the author. It

* Tenth Satire.

is a poem which every where discovers the same beauties, and not a few of the same faults, which in the former offend every reader of genuine taste and correctness.

The lines with which we venture to compare a few of Johnson's are quoted from a New Translation of the Tenth Satire of Juvenal, by Thomas Morris, Esq.[1] late Captain of his Majesty's seventeenth Regiment of Foot, published as a specimen of a complete version of that masterly writer.* And when the defects of what goes by the name of Dryden,[2] the similarity between Roman and British vices, and the singular gravity, truth and boldness of Juvenal, are duly considered, who would not wish his proposals may succeed. These quotations are chiefly selected for exhibiting to the English reader, the beauty and defects of Johnson's Imitation, as they who comprehend not the meaning of the ancient poet, are not competent to judge with propriety on his application to modern times.

This communication I likewise owe to the same gentleman,[3] whose pertinent strictures on London have already been inserted.

> 'Yet still one gen'ral cry the sky assails,
> 'And gain and grandeur load the tainted gales;
> 'Few know the toiling statesman's fear or care,
> 'Th' insidious rival and the gaping heir.
>
> *Johnson's Imitation.*

> The supplication in each temple heard,
> By ev'ry mortal to the gods preferr'd,
> Is, to be grac'd with pow'r, with riches blest,
> And in the forum keep the largest chest:
> Let us remember, ere we make our pray'r,
> No aconite is serv'd in earthen ware;
> That apprehend, when cups with jewels shine,
> And the broad gold inflames the Setine wine.
>
> *Translation of the Tenth Satire of Juvenal.*

Juvenal speaks out; but Johnson hints *too obliquely* at the practice of poisoning; a person unacquainted with the original, will not understand his meaning.

> *Load the tainted gales,*

is not much better than

> *Load* the *loaden* gales,
> Or, *taint* the *tainted* gales.

Johnson, speaking of Pope's epitaph[4] says,

> *Op'ning virtues blooming round*

* Subscriptions are taken in by Mr. Murray, in Fleet-Street.

is something like tautology. I think *load the tainted gales* is more like it.

'Or seen a new-made mayor's unweildy state.

Surely Johnson might have made something out of the Lord Mayor's shew, answering to Juvenal's description of the prætor's going to proclaim the shews of the circus. In Juvenal's time the prætor of Rome was not a greater personage than our Lord Mayor, and the figure made by the one now, is full as ridiculous as that made by the other long ago.

'For why did Wolsey, near the steeps of fate,
'On weak foundations raise th'enormous weight?
'Why but to sink beneath misfortune's blow,
'With louder ruin to the gulphs below.
Johnson's Imitation.

Sejanus little thought what he desired,
When to the highest rank his soul aspir'd;
The vast increase of riches pomp, and pow'r,
Was only adding stories to his tow'r,
The more astonishing to make it's fall,
That buried riches, honours, lord and all.
Translation, &c.

That the blow of misfortune might throw down Wolsey is plain enough; that it could demolish a building is not so obvious.

Let art and genius weep.
Johnson's Imitation.

Johnson, speaking of Pope's epitaph,[1] says, 'in another couplet art is used for arts, that a rhyme may be had to heart.' Has he not fallen into the like mistake, without having the same excuse for it.

'Enquirer cease; petitions yet remain,
'Which heav'n may hear, nor deem religion vain.
Johnson's Imitation.

The sense here is strangely broken, and rendered obscure.

'Yet when the sense of sacred presence fires,
'And strong devotion to the skies aspires.
Johnson's Imitation.

Is not this anti-climax? Would it not be better thus?

Yet when devotion to the skies aspires,
And the strong sense of sacred presence fires.

'These goods for man the laws of heav'n ordain.
'These goods he grants, who grants the power to gain.'
Johnson's Imitation.

If Johnson thought Pope blameable for not using the singular *art* instead of the plural arts, for the sake of rhyme; how much more to be condemned is the critic himself, who uses the plural *goods*, instead of the singular *good*, without any reason that I can find, and in open defiance of his own decree? I appeal to his dictionary. Under the word *goods* we find, 1. Moveables in a house. 2. Wares, freight, merchandize: Under the word *good*, 4. Moral qualities.

> And makes that happiness she does not find.
>
> *Johnson's Imitation.*

The expletive *does* in the last line of the poem, and in the most important place in that line, makes a most lame and impotent conclusion.

> 'How wouldst thou shake at Britain's modish tribe,
> 'Dart the quick taunt, and edge the piercing gibe?

The latter line is loaden with useless epithets, and the sense weakened by them. How much better thus!

> *How wouldst thou shake at Britain's modish tribe!*
> *How wouldst thou dart the taunt, and edge the gibe!*

> Till conquest unresisted ceas'd to please,
> And rights submitted left him none to seize.

The whole account of Wolsey is in the present tense. Why the author chose so ungracefully to change the tense in this couplet only, which is in the middle of the account too, I cannot guess: it has a slovenly appearance however; and how easily might it have been avoided, thus:

> *Till conquests unresisted cease to please,*
> *And rights submitted leave him none to seize.*

> *Till captive science yields her last retreat.*
>
> Johnson's Imitation.

The epithet *captive* is not only useless, but nonsensical; for, if science was taken captive, what retreat could she be in possession of? We must hope that the author meant to say, that 'when science yields her last retreat, she becomes a captive:' This, however, is a piece of intelligence scarcely worth relating.

> *Should no disease thy torpid veins invade.*
>
> Johnson's Imitation.

That is, in plain English, should no disease invade thy diseased veins. In short it is a pleonasm, to make up the measure; but not quite so bad as the former.

He views and wonders that they please no more.
Johnson's Imitation.

A trifling change would make this line better.

He views and wonders they should please no more,
No sounds, alas! would touch th'impervious ear.
Johnson's Imitation.

If *no* sounds *would* touch it, *it* certainly *must* be impervious.

Johnson fortunately for his reputation was soon satisfied his *forte* did not lie in making verses. His poetry, though not anywhere loaded with epithets, is destitute of animation. The strong sense, the biting sarcasm, the deep solemnity, which mark his genius, no where assume that union, symmetry, or collected energy, which is necessary to produce a general effect. We are now and then struck with a fine thought, a fine line, or a fine passage, but little interested by the whole. His mode of versifying, which is an imitation of Pope, may bear analization, but after reading his best pieces once, few are desirous of reading them again.

The life of Savage, which was his first biographical essay, had such a reception with the public, or answered the bookseller's purpose so well, that Johnson was encouraged to cultivate this species of composition.[1] For a series of years therefore he was constantly enriching the annals of literature, with new articles of English biography. It is impossible to be exact in stating the dates of these public actions, or giving the history of their origin and composition. The particulars they involve are the less interesting, that they seem to have grown into request only since the fame of the author has been established; that they are distinguished by no other species of excellence than fidelity and perspicuity, and they might still have continued unadmired, and even unknown, but for the superior lustre of subsequent performances.

Osborne[2] shared the honour with Cave and Dodsley, of being one of Johnson's first patrons. An affray with that curious bookseller, gave the trade no very advantageous idea of Johnson's temper. It was hushed at the time, in complaisance to the opulence of the one, but gradually became a subject of speculation, as the reputation of the other increased. Johnson was employed in writing an introduction to the Harleian library, which, as it gave an account of various articles, could not be done in haste. Osborne incessantly urged expedition, and had often recourse to contumelious language. Johnson who had much pride, had also much good-nature, made no other reply to this tiresome impertinence, but that he was as busy as possible. The calculations of booksellers are solely confined to the sale, and seldom involve the various avocations and deliberations which protract composition. The delicate embarrassments of genius are consequently not unfrequently treated with rudeness and vulgarity. No body of men are more uniform and eager in taking advantage of their necessities, who, like Johnson, are reduced to a dependance on their favour. Osborne was base enough to make Johnson feel his situation, by a brutal sarcasm, which he blurted in his face, on finding him reading with great coolness, while the quantum of copy promised by this time, was not yet begun. Johnson, surprised into a passion, by the bookseller's rage and ferocity, started from his seat, without uttering a word, and, with the book in his hand, instantly knocked him down.

Hitherto he had tried his genius as a translator, a satyrist, and a biographer; he was now to appear a philologist. The plan of his Diction-ary, which he displays with so much elegance and dignity in an address to the late Earl of Chesterfield, was published so early as the year 1748.[1] This performance promised something so much like what all men of taste had long thought wanting to the purity, stability, and perfection of our language, exhibited an object of such magnitude to the public mind, and was itself so exquisite a specimen of the happiest arrangement and most polished diction, that it brought Johnson forward to general attention with peculiar advantage. The eyes of all the world were turned on what part the nobleman thus distinguished would now act in concert with the first writer, and interested by the sketch of a work the most laborious and useful of any which even then had roused the curiosity and excited the wonder of an enlightened age. From a secretary of state, still more illustrious for his elegant accomplishments than for his high birth or official situation something like substantial encouragement was expected to an undertaking which aimed at no less than a *standard Dictionary of the English tongue*. His lordship was a competent judge of the subject. He acknowledged its importance and necessity. He occupied a sphere in life, an influence among the great, and a character among the learned, which enabled him to do much. His vanity was not inferior to his power; and had the talents of Johnson stooped to the prostituted language of adulation, his toil had probably been considerably alleviated by the taste, the address, the assiduity and the countenance of Chester-field. But nothing can be conceived more diametrically opposite and irreconcileable than the tempers, the prejudices, the habits, the pursuits, and the peculiarities of these contemporary wits. A semblance of intimacy took place, in which it is not likely that either were sincere. The oddities of the author furnished the peer with a fund of ridicule, and the fastidious elegance of the peer excited only the aversion, contempt, and pity of the author. *All the celebrated qualities of Chesterfield,* (said

Johnson to an intimate friend, to whom he was then in the habit of unbosoming himself on occasion) *are like certain species of fruit which is pleasant enough to the eye, but there is no tasting it without danger.*[1]

In this well written pamphlet it was his ambition to rival the preface to Chambers's Dictionary.[2] How far he succeeded is not easily determined. It will not be denied, that he possesses more energy of language, and perhaps a more beautiful arrangement of the multifarious particulars to which he solicits the public attention, but he certainly wants the simplicity, and indeed is proscribed by his subject from displaying the knowledge, of Chambers.

Chesterfield joined in the general applause which followed the exhibition of a design thus replete with utility in the aim, and originality in the execution. He was proud to have attracted the regards of such a man as Johnson, and flattered himself with the hopes of fresh accession of fame, from being the patron of such a work. But the manners of the operator were so disgusting to this Mæcenas of letters, and learned men, that the only concern he took in the matter was saying a few polite things at his table, and congratulating the lovers of grammar on the improvement which that science would derive from the labours of Johnson. It is a disgrace to his memory, and to the age, that the author of an undertaking so arduous and extensive was not placed beyond the recurrence of necessity, and that while his genius was conferring permanency on their language, the exigencies of his situation impelled him to apply to other means for daily subsistence.

The talents requisite for such an undertaking seldom meet in one man. Its magnitude was enough to stagger any resolution less vigorous, to repress any ardour less manly, to derange any intellect less collected than that of Johnson. But his capacity was competent to the object. His reading was chiefly philological, his taste was improved by an intimate acquaintance with all the classical remains of antiquity, his memory retained with exactness whatever his judgment had matured; and he possessed a penetration or discernment characteristically solid, cool, and discriminating. It was not a composition that depended on the paroxysms of genius, a vigorous imagination, fertility of invention, originality of conception, or brilliancy of style. Patient industry, laborious attention, a determination of forgetting the lassitude of fatigue by a renewal of the task; and a mind, which notwithstanding a thousand avocations and obstacles, like the water in a river, still returned to the same channel, and pursued the same course; were some of the qualifications with which Johnson formed the plan, and entered on the compilation of his Dictionary.

A work thus complicated and prodigious admits great variety in collecting the materials, and frequent relaxations from the exertions it demands. Many are the subjects which would present themselves to the author's mind, from such an association of ideas as must have accompanied the progress of his studies. And it may be rationally conjectured, that he often found relief not only in the society of his select friends, but in a great variety of literary pursuits, the more pleasing probably for the time, that they might appear to others of less importance.

His *Irene* however, which was brought upon the stage in 1749, is generally acknowledged to have been written before he came to town.[1] Why it did not make its appearance sooner, and why it was not better received when it did, are questions which now perhaps cannot be answered.

It would be a singular period in the annals of the English Theatre, in which the reception of authors were regulated by their merit. Johnson's temper was ill calculated for supplicating favours from inferiors. It was not in his heart or his nature, to hang about a manager, to associate with the critics in the green-room,[2] to cultivate an intimacy with spouters, or to interest the patronage of loungers in the lobby of the playhouse. He either did not understand that private pliancy and public ostentation which constitute the mystery of the trade, or had the manliness to regard with contempt, every species of obliquity, even when it leads to success. The plot however, the thoughts, and the diction of his tragedy, are allowed to be beautiful and masterly. But he is sparing of that bustle and incident, which atone for the want of every excellence with a London audience. A performance which exemplified the prescriptions of an Aristotle, was not likely to please a nation tutored in this barbarous taste. It does not abound in doggrel madrigals or epigrammatic rodomontade. It degrades, not scenes of dignified distress with the Pantomime of Harlequin, the gossippings or gibberish of gypsies, or the ribaldry and buffoonery of clowns. It is written only to improve the heart, to elucidate and refine the passions, to connect the interests of humanity with the dictates of reason, and to restore the union of taste and virtue.

But though the principal characters were given to those who at that time excelled in the profession,[3] the expectation of Johnson and his friends was disappointed. The first exhibition was coldly received, and the audience it seems were more disposed to admire the author than to be affected by his scenes. A gentleman who sat in the pit, on that occasion, has told me, that on looking round him he saw nobody using their handkerchief; but the whisper was strong and prevalent, that the *poet was a prodigy of learning*.

Much, especially in tragedy, depends on the actors. Johnson's address was disgusting. He had not made any advances to conciliate their fondness, or to prompt their exertions. His manners were gruff and distant, his language was coarse and oraculous;[1] and though Garrick was of the party, posterity who shall mourn *Irene*, will be rather apt to impute her fate to inanimate acting, than unskilful writing.[2]

Johnson was not of a turn of mind to struggle for any thing not immediately within his reach. Under the auspices of a Garrick, whose assistance and advice he could always command, who can doubt but by a sedulous application he might have excelled in the higher species of the drama?[3] But he who had it in his power to lead, was unwilling to continue acting only a secondary part. Other subjects less hazardous in the issue, and more easy in the execution, were incessantly occurring and engaging his cultivation, with which he ran no risk of a rival, and which, though perhaps less profitable, yet yielded his necessities a readier supply.

His disgust and contempt for the public taste suggested to him the first idea of furnishing the town with a periodical paper twice a week. In such a work he enjoyed the prospect of exposing the taste of his countrymen, and often contributing by the happy application of superior talents, to their correction and refinement. And perhaps it may be doing him no injustice to suppose, that wherever the fashionable levities of taste are censured, he glances obliquely at the usage of *Irene*.[4]

By an incident in the history of the *Rambler*, not generally known, that celebrated work was published at Edinburgh, at the same time the publication of it went on in London.

Mr. Elphinston,[5] well known in the learned world for a variety of valuable publications, both in prose and verse, was the intimate friend of Johnson, and then on a visit to his relations in that part of the united kingdom. The first number came to him under cover, and without a name. But the author could not be concealed; and, in Mr. Elphinston's opinion, there was not, in England, another than Johnson, competent to such an undertaking. He consequently conceived the benevolent design of diffusing the work among his countrymen, as promising much instruction to them, and some profit to the author. It was immediately reprinted in Scotland in a minute and elegant manner. Mr. Elphinston not only superintended the press, and took every possible care of the edition, but likewise enriched it by a new and apposite translation of the mottos. Most of these were retained in the next edition which appeared in London, and Johnson, in a note appended to a collection of them,[6] acknowledges the obligation in the handsomest terms. Indeed this was an instance of attention and friendship, with which, as it well became him, he always expressed the most grateful satisfaction.

In the following letter we learn some particulars relating to this business. The original reception of the Rambler in Scotland is not obscurely hinted, and the author's tenderness for his labours, strongly marked by the solicitude with which he cherishes the partiality which his friend had conceived in their favour. The original, in Johnson's own hand-writing, is still in Mr. Elphinston's possession. The writer's regard for true learning and worth, is happily illustrated by his kind attention to the celebrated Ruddiman.[1] The honourable testimony which he bears to the virtue of that venerable man, was a proof that his heart was always in unison with the wise and good, whoever they were, or wherever they lived.

DEAR SIR,

'I cannot but confess the failures of my correspondence, but hope the same regard which you express for me on every other occasion, will incline you to forgive me. I am often, very often ill, and when I am well, am obliged to work: and indeed have never much used myself to punctuality. You are however not to make unkind inferences, when I forbear to reply to your kindness: for be assured, I never receive a letter from you without great pleasure, and a very warm sense of your generosity and friendship, which I heartily blame myself for not cultivating with more care. In this, as in many other cases, I go wrong in opposition to conviction: for I think scarce any temporal good equally to be desired with the regard and familiarity of worthy men. I hope we shall be sometime nearer to each other, and have a more ready way of pouring out our hearts.

I am glad that you still find encouragement to proceed in your publication, and shall beg the favour of six more volumes, to add to my former six, when you can, with any convenience, send them me. Please to present a set in my name to Mr. Ruddiman; of whom I hear, that his learning is not his highest excellence.

'I have transcribed the mottos and returned them, I hope not too late; of which I think many very happily performed. Mr. Cave has put the last in the Magazine,[2] in which I think he did well. I beg of you to write soon, and to write often, and to write long letters; which I hope in time to repay you, but you must be a patient creditor. I have however this of gratitude, that I think of you with regard, when I do not perhaps give the proofs which I ought of being

SIR, your most obliged,
and most humble servant,
SAM. JOHNSON.'

To Mr. Elphinston. [*Without any date*].[3]

From this soothing and friendly letter, Johnson seems to have been much flattered by the success of his Rambler in North-Britain. Indeed he always acknowledged, that it was by far the best edition of the work. It was, in fact, much more correct than the original one in London, though published under his own eye: for his friend spared no attention, which could by any means contribute to the author's reputation.

About this time Mr. Elphinston lost his mother, which affected him so deeply, that Johnson thought it his duty to write to him on the occasion: which, by the way, was a subject on which no writer, ancient or modern, ever excelled him. The letter breathes a spirit of the most elevated piety and of the tenderest consolation; and being handed about while the publication of the Rambler went on in Edinburgh, considerably promoted the circulation of it, especially among religious readers. We may judge of his sincerity in that letter, by a perusal of the papers in the Rambler of nearly the same date. He had heard the news from Mrs. Strahan,[1] sister to Mr. Elphinston; and wrote in all probability his fifty-second and fifty-fourth numbers[2] under that impression.

DEAR SIR,

'You have, as I find by every kind of evidence, lost an excellent mother; and I hope you will not think me incapable of partaking of your grief. I have a mother now eighty-two years of age, whom therefore I must soon lose, unless it please God that she rather should mourn for me. I read the letters in which you relate your mother's death to Mrs. Strahan; and think I do myself honour when I tell you that I read them with tears, but tears are neither to me nor to you of any farther use, when once the tribute of nature has been paid. The business of life summons us away from useless grief, and calls us to the exercise of those virtues of which we are lamenting our deprivation. The greatest benefit which one friend can confer upon another, is to guard, and incite, and elevate his virtues. This your mother will still perform, if you diligently preserve the memory of her life, and of her death: a life, so far as I can learn, useful and wise; innocent; and a death resigned, peaceful, and holy. I cannot forbear to mention, that neither reason nor revelation denies you to hope, that you may encrease her happiness by obeying her precepts; and that she may, in her present state, look with pleasure, upon every act of virtue to which her instructions or example have contributed. Whether this be more than a pleasing dream, or a just opinion of separate spirits, is indeed of no great importance to us, when we consider ourselves as acting under the eye of God: yet surely there is something pleasing in the belief, that our separation from those whom we love is merely corporeal; and it may be a great incitement to virtuous friendship, if it can be made probable, that union which has received the divine approbation, shall continue to eternity.

'There is one expedient, by which you may, in some degree, continue her presence. If you write down minutely what you remember of her from your earliest years, you will read it with great pleasure, and receive from it many hints of soothing recollection, when time shall remove her yet farther from you, and your grief shall be matured to veneration. To this, however painful for the present, I cannot but advise you, as to a source of comfort and satisfaction in the time to come: for all comfort and all satisfaction, is sincerely wished you by, Dear Sir,

Your most obliged,
most obedient,
and most humble servant,
SAM. JOHNSON.'

To Mr. Elphinston.
Sept. 25, 1750.

In the history of literature, the price of copy would be a desirable piece of information; but to keep this as much in the dark as possible, is one of the mysteries of Bookselling; which, being a lottery throughout, is generally carried on under a mask. His emoluments from the *Rambler* are therefore not generally known. Some accounts have rated them at two, and others, probably not less authentic at, five guineas a week.[1] We are only certain, that from the beginning he retained so much of the property in his own hands, till the work was half finished. He then disposed of the copy entirely, but for how much, or under what conditions we are not acquainted. The moment this fact was known in Edinburgh, the translator of the mottos, who had Johnson's interest supremely at heart, and not deeming himself under any obligation to continue the same exertions for the Booksellers, desisted; though he persevered in otherwise perfecting the edition.

The truth is, even this performance, one of the most masterly and elegant in the language, was but coldly received at first. It was during the publication of the Rambler, that the literary character of *David Hume*[2] broke forth in its strongest lustre. He was the fashionable writer of the day. He had always kept himself independant of Booksellers. This was a circumstance which considerably encreased it with some people, as they are pleased to distinguish between an author who writes for subsistence; and one, who though able to live without writing, yet sells what he writes with as much anxiety, as if he wrote for a livelihood. This, however, they call a gentleman-author,[3] and, without much regard to the comparative merit of the two, very often, and very absurdly, give him the preference.

Such was the prejudice to which Hume owed much of his celebrity, though his merits undoubtedly entitled him to a very large share. His peculiar excentricities and paradoxes, chiefly on moral, philosophical, and religious subjects, procured him an incredible number of votaries in both kingdoms. Nothing appeared in the literary world, about which he was not consulted; and it is well known, the critics of the times, regarded his opinion as sacred and decisive. He mentioned the Rambler,[1] however, with respect; and only regretted there should be so much cant and so much pedantry, in a performance replete with taste, erudition and genius.

This stricture very obviously marred, though it did not absolutely prevent the success of the book. Johnson, when told of the fact, only acknowledged himself the less surprized that his papers had not been more universally read. *My countrymen*, said he, *will not always regard the voice of a Blasphemer as an oracle*. He took no farther notice of the circumstance. Perhaps he might not be altogether inattentive to its influence on the minds of men; in what follows, which is quoted from the last number of the Rambler. 'I am far from supposing,' says he, 'that the cessation of my performance will raise any enquiry; for I have never been much the favourite of the public, nor can boast that in the progress of my undertaking, I have been animated by the rewards of the liberal, the caresses of the great, or the praises of the eminent.'

These, however, were not the only compositions, which occupied the attention of Johnson in consort with his Dictionary. During eight years exhausted in this prodigious work, several petty pieces[2] made their appearance on different occasions, and at different times; which severally operated as so many advertisements of that in which he was principally employed, as tending equally to establish his reputation and conciliate the public confidence in his future labours.

This publication, which appeared in 1755, was accompanied with a preface, in which it is not easy to say, whether genius, erudition, industry, or taste is the predominating feature. But on this occasion he takes an opportunity of stating some complaints, which, as they chiefly refer to his circumstances, peculiarly mark the man, in an apology for keeping back his book so long from the public; and to defeat the censures of the captious, he has this curious passage, which gives a summary account of his own conduct. 'Much of my life,' says he, 'has been lost under the pressure of disease. Much has been trifled away, and much has been always spent in provision for the day that was passing over me.'[3] The first of his complaints is true. He had much ill health. His size was large; but he was not more aukward in his gait, than gross and cumber-ous[1] in his make. In the earlier periods of his life, he was grievously afflicted with the king's evil; but this disease was much abated, if not perfectly cured, long before his death. But from his infancy to his grave he laboured under a complication of maladies, which repeatedly baffled all the powers of physic. Had he failed however in his undertaking, this would rather have condemned the attempt, than justified the want of execution.

He acknowledged himself guilty of trifling away much of his time, and yet his habits of temperance and sobriety are well known. No man ever imputed dissipation to Johnson; but his indolence or aversion to activity, was so notorious as to become proverbial. In truth, he never would work, but in order to eat. He has often confessed composition had no charms for him, and that all the fame and reputation which he acquired by his writings, as well as the numerous and sublime virtues ascribed to them, were comprehended in the single monosyllable *bread*.

The other grievance by which he endeavours to interest the feelings of the reader, is, in my opinion, singularly whimsical: *much of my life has always been spent, in provision for the day that was passing over me*. This was literally putting his situation on a level with that of a mere labourer, whose only dependance is on the sweat of his brow. But it is well known Johnson received so much money, that at the very time of adopting this whining language he was in a capacity to have lived at the rate of three hundred pounds a year.[2]

This was at least no despicable competence, for an individual who had no other family to maintain than Mrs. Johnson and himself.

But he adds: '*the English Dictionary was written amidst inconvenience and distraction, in sickness and in sorrow.*' What those inconveniences and sorrows thus solemnly asserted to have interfered with the tranquil pursuits of laborious study were, he does not inform us. It is however known, that though he never had any children, he was not wholly exempted from domestic inquietude. It has been said that Mrs. Johnson, who was much the elder of the two, had, especially in the latter part of her life, addicted herself to drinking, some say, opium. A suspicion of his conjugal infelicity on this account certainly went abroad, and pro-cured him much commiseration among his friends: and to the disgust occasioned by this cruel misfortune, his various sarcasms on matrimony, his affected indifference to the sex, and the contempt which he frequently pours on all expressions of the tender passions, are generally, perhaps improperly, attributed. Mrs. Johnson was otherwise a lady of great sensibility and worth; so shrewd and cultivated, that in the earlier part of their connection, he was fond of consulting her in all his literary pursuits; and so handsome, that his associates in letters and wit were often very pleasant with him on the strange disparity, which, in this respect, subsisted between husband and wife. Probably he grew peevish by study and disease, and he who piqued himself on his bluntness abroad, was not likely to be very complaisant at home. She disliked the profusion, with which he constantly gave away all the money about him; and he found with astonishment and concern, that whatever he provided or laid up for family exigence, was always gone before he expected.

Notwithstanding these petty differences, they regarded each other with true cordiality and affection. Both suffered from oddities, which it was impossible to conquer; but mutually reposed a stedfast confidence, while it was their happiness to live together, Johnson often said he never knew how dear she was to him, till he lost her. Her death affected him so deeply, that he grew almost insensible to the common concerns of life. He then stayed little within, where her image was always recalled by whatever he heard or saw. Study disgusted him, and books of all kinds were equally insipid. He carefully avoided his friends, and associated most with such company as he never saw before. And when he thought himself a burden, and felt the pressure of time becoming insupportable, the only expedient he had was to walk the streets of London. This for many a lonesome night was his constant substitute for sleep. An impression thus forcible and serious, time and vicissitude only could erase. And it was not till he found his mind somewhat composed, and his heart considerably at ease, that he began to relish the blessings of life, to enjoy his friends, and to resume his studies.

The following plain inscription to the memory of Mrs. Johnson, was then among the first productions of his pen. It is simple and concise, but contains much. Genuine sorrow, is not loquacious. There is something in the original which cannot easily be translated, but the reader may not dislike to see it attempted.

Inscribed on a black marble grave-stone in
Bromley Church, Kent.[1]

Hic conduntur reliquiæ
ELIZABETHAE
Antiqua Jarvisiorum gente
Pentlingæ, apud Leicestrienses, ortæ;
Formosæ, cultæ, ingeniosæ, piæ;
Uxoris, primis nuptiis, Henrici Porter,
Secundis, SAMUELIS JOHNSON,
Qui multum amatum, dinque defletam

Hoc lapide contexit.
Obiit Londin. Mense Mart.
A.D.   M,DCC,LIII.

Or, in English thus:

Here are interred the remains
Of ELIZABETH
Descended from the ancient family of JARVIS
Of PENTLING, in the County of Leicester;
Beautiful, polite, ingenious, pious;
Wife, by her first marriage, of HENRY PORTER,
By her second of SAMUEL JOHNSON,
Who over her much loved and long lamented Remains
Placed this Stone.
She died in London, in the Month of March,
A. D.   M,DCC,LIII.

It was doubted whether the artifices of the booksellers by practising on the public curiosity, would not injure the performance, and raise expectation too high to be satisfied. The enquiries after the publication were eager and universal, and yet the disappointment which attended the event was inconsiderable. It was equally ridiculous in individuals and parties, to expect their discriminating prejudices consulted in the explanation of words. But on no other ground has any solid objection been made to the English Dictionary. It is notwithstanding attacked in the twelfth number of the North Briton,[1] with as much virulence as if it had been intended only as a register of political opinion.

When Johnson was first told of Wilkes's going to court, in consequence of his political conversion, he gave a strong proof of the pertinence of his judgment, as well as of the strength of his memory. *I hope* said he, *Mr. Wilkes is now become a friend to the constitution, and to the family on the throne, but I know he has much to unwrite, and more to unsay, before he will be forgiven for what he has been writing and saying for many years.*

In a compilation which involved so much reading, recollection and correction, rash explanations were unavoidable. The word *Furbelow* he derived originally from *Fur* and *below*, and said it was *fur* sewed on the lower part of the garment. But the fact was, a lady of distinction having once appeared at the French court in this dress, which was entirely of her own invention, was asked what she called it, and answered *c'est un falballa.*[2] His definition of the word *oats*,[3] was rigidly just, but the scurrilous alterations of party rendering the Scotch at that time extremely sore, they were much offended, but so may all mankind think it a disgrace to breathe because this is the mode of life in horses as well as men.

He put such a sense on *pension* or *pensioners*,[1] as furnished petty malignity with a fund of ridicule and sarcasm against himself.

His exposition of the excise[2] was likely to be followed by consequences still more serious and vexatious. Some people then at the head of that obnoxious board, avowed their resentment in such a manner as to threaten a prosecution.

How this matter terminated is not now generally known. In a subsequent edition of the Dictionary, Johnson was desired to alter and soften the article. *No*, said he, *it has done all the mischief, and I owe no complaisance to excisemen or their masters.*

Johnson's connection with Chesterfield came to an eclaircissement, the moment this great work made its appearance. *Moore*, author of the World,[3] and the creature of this nobleman, was employed by him to sound Johnson on the subject of a Dedication. Some time before Johnson had been refused admittance to his Lordship. This, it was pretended, happened by the mistake of a porter, though it is pretty well known, few servants take such liberties without the connivance of their masters. Johnson, who saw through all the disguises of Chesterfield's pride, never forgave the indignity, and treated every apology which was afterwards suggested by the friends and admirers of this nobleman, as an insult. *Moore*, without touching on that point in the most distant manner, expressed his hopes that Johnson would dedicate his Dictionary to Chesterfield. He received a very pointed and direct negative.—'I am under obligations,' said he, 'to no great man, and of all others, Chesterfield ought to know better than to think me capable of contracting myself into a dwarf, that he may be thought a giant.' You are certainly obliged to his Lordship, said *Moore*, for two very elegant papers in the World,[4] and all the influence of his good opinion, in favour of your work, 'You seem totally unacquainted with the true state of the fact,' replied Johnson, 'after making a hazardous and fatiguing voyage round the literary world, I had fortunately got sight of the shore, and was coming into port with a pleasant tide and a fair wind, when my Lord Chesterfield sends out two little cock-boats to tow me in. I know my Lord Chesterfield tolerably well, Mr. Moore. He may be a wit among Lords, but I fancy he is no more than a Lord among wits.'[5]

In the year following,[6] he published the *Political State of Great Britain, Observations on the State of Affairs*, and *Proposals for printing the Dramatic Works of William Shakespear*.

His political performances discover all that solid reasoning and sound information without which Johnson never would write on any thing. In these, published in the year fifty-six, he discusses with his usual penetration and address our political situation in the Western world, and enters into the perplexed question, so strenuously agitated by the Courts of Versailles and London, concerning the boundaries of the colonies. Both pamphlets are replete with shrewdness, sarcasm, and profound attention to the restlessness of ambition, the effects of usurpation, the arrogant claims of princes, and the natural rights of mankind.

Johnson, so early as the year forty-five,[1] had conceived the design of publishing a correct edition of Shakespear's works. But Warburton, whose name was then deservedly high in the republic of letters, proposing at the same time a similar work, Johnson prudently suspended his for the present. The pamphlet, however, which he printed on the occasion, received the approbation of his rival, who, of all other men, was the least guilty of adulation. But Warburton saw Johnson's production, and regarded it as the certain presage of his future eminence. And when that great critic, in the decline of life, was treated with indignity by his contemporaries, Johnson had the manliness to retain his veneration, respect and gratitude to him to the last.[2]

Having therefore finished the undertaking, which then attracted and commanded the most general approbation, he renewed his application to the text of Shakespear.[3] The scope of this work he delineates at large in a pamphlet which he then published, and which is composed with the author's usual manliness, decency, and elegance. He enumerates, as might be expected, the defects of former editors. These he promises to supply. He also specifies the general sources of their errors, which he thinks may be rectified.

From the nature of his former labours, and the consequence which he derived from genius, from industry, and from success, he presumes to think himself better qualified to do his author justice than most of those who preceded him. 'With regard to obsolete or peculiar diction,' says he, 'the editor may perhaps claim some degree of confidence, having had more motives to consider the whole extent of our language than any other man from its first formation. He hopes that, by comparing the works of Shakespear with those of writers who lived at the same time, immediately preceded, or immediately followed him, he shall be able to ascertain his ambiguities, disentangle his intricacies, and recover the meaning of words now lost in the darkness of antiquity.'

He adds what must give the reader a very just and distinct idea of the undertaking. 'When, therefore, any obscurity arises from an allusion to some other book, the passage will be quoted. When the diction is entangled it will be cleared by a paraphrase or interpretation. When the sense is broken by the suppression of part of the sentiments in pleasantry or passion, the connexion will be supplied. When any forgotten custom is hinted, care will be taken to retrieve or explain it.

The meaning assigned to doubtful words will be supported by the authorities of other writers, or by parallel passages of Shakespear himself.'

The only publication in which we find him engaged in the subsequent year is the *Idler*,[1] a periodical work, which he owned to a friend, consisted chiefly of some materials he had gleaned for his Rambler, a few pieces occasionally suggested by reading, accident, or conversation, and others rescued from the fate of volumes in which they had been consigned to oblivion. He amused himself by detailing these elegant and instructive papers in the public prints. They were immediately collected and published in two volumes, but on what terms is not known.[2] Two essays which had not appeared were added, one on the epitaphs of Mr. Pope, and one on the warlike character of our English soldiers.[3] The first abounds in false criticism, the second is little more than the vulgar rhodomontade of a pot-house politician, who is always ready to match one of his countrymen against three of any other in the universe.

There is a common prejudice in the world against second parts.[4] But the *Idler* ought not to be considered as a continuation of the Rambler. It seems, from the introductory number to have been contrived on quite a different plan. And the character of an *Idler* is supported throughout with no inconsiderable share of propriety and spirit. Were I disposed to compare the excellence of these two valuable performances, I should not hesitate to prefer the *Idler*. The leading idea is not only more original, but it associates a greater variety of subjects, in the discussion of which the author had an opportunity of indulging his own feelings, apologizing for his own habits, and pouring out his mind in speculations the more mature, that his heart as well as his genius, was interested; and to such as knew him familiarly it is obvious that he often describes the foibles of his imaginary beings in terms applicable only to his own.

It is not improbable that his *translation of Father Lobo's Voyage to Abyssinia*[5] contributed to facilitate his acquaintance with the tropical language of the Orientals. His powers of imagination were vigorous and active, and notwithstanding the truth of his conceptions, he seems from the first to have been not a little dazzled by splendour of expression. The charge of an over-wrought or blown stile, which has been so frequently, and not altogether unjustly made against his writings, might arise from this taste, which all his experience and strength of mind could never finally suppress.

From the Preface of a work so little known, and yet so laborious, I cannot resist the pleasure of presenting the reader with the following short extract. It exhibits, in my opinion, Johnson's manner, and shews that whatever his improvements afterwards were, his plan of composition, his mode of thinking, and his superiority to the prejudices of the vulgar, must have been original and unvaried.

'The following relation,' says he, 'is so curious and entertaining, and the dissertations that accompany it so judicious and instructive, that the translator is confident his attempt stands in need of no apology, whatever censures may fall on the performance.

'The Portuguese traveller, contrary to the general vein of his countrymen, has amused his reader with no romantic absurdity or incredible fictions; whatever he relates, whether true or not, is at least probable; and he who tells nothing exceeding the bounds of probability, has a right to demand that they should believe him, who cannot contradict him.

'He appears by his modest and unaffected narration to have described things as he saw them, to have copied nature from the life, and to have consulted his senses, not his imagination; he meets with no basilisks that destroy with their eyes, his crocodiles devour their prey without tears, and his cataracts fall from the rocks without deafening the neighbouring inhabitants.

'The reader will here find no regions cursed with irremediable barrenness, or blessed with spontaneous fecundity, no perpetual gloom, or unceasing sunshine; nor are the nations here described either devoid of all sense of humanity or consummate in all private or social virtues. Here are no Hottentots without religion, polity, or articulate language; no Chinese perfectly polite, and completely skilled in all sciences; he will discover, what will always be discovered by a diligent and impartial enquirer, that wherever human nature is to be found, there is a mixture of vice and virtue; a contest of passion and reason, and that the Creator doth not appear partial in his distributions, but has balanced in most countries their particular inconveniences by particular favours.'

It is known to many of the Doctor's friends, that his *Rasselas or Prince of Abyssinia*,[1] was an early conception, on which his ideas were matured long before the completion of the work. He shewed the first lines of it to a Bookseller, who gave him no encouragement to proceed; but the confidence of genius was not to be baffled or repressed by the cold suggestions of interested ignorance. The stroke betrayed the hand of a master, but there wanted the taste of Protogenes[2] to discern it. The outlines of this immortal work could not procure the author credit for twenty guineas.[3] His mother was dying of a good old age. He wished to raise this sum that he might be able to see her on her death-bed. He sat down to finish his plan, and notwithstanding his expeditious composition, she died before he could make it convenient to visit her. The forty-first number of his Idler[1] probably relates to the circumstances of her death. The Prince of Abyssinia was sold to another Bookseller,[2] and had a very considerable sale.

We are now come to the æra of his pension. It originated with Lord Bute,[3] though the Doctor since the odium which attended the administration of that nobleman, drove him to the shades, affected always to give the sole merit of it to his Majesty. The manner by which he received it has been detailed especially since his death, probably by Mr. Murphy,[4] or some one desirous of publishing the concern which he had in the transaction. It was owing however entirely to his own merit, without the solicitation of a mistress or a player in his favour.* He was not the man who would have owed an obligation to the creature or courtezan of any minister on earth.

Johnson had conceived a strong prejudice against Lord Bute. He dined at Mr. Elphinston's but a few days before the pension was proposed. He was there asked, why he had shewn such dislike to the minister; because, said he, he gave the king a wrong education. He had only taught him, added Johnson, to *draw a tree.*[6]

It was not above a day or two after this that the fact was mentioned in the newspapers.[7] Mr. Elphinston hastened to congratulate his friend on this unexpected accession of good fortune. Johnson related the matter circumstantially. Nothing he said could have been given more handsomely. When proposed to his Majesty, a certain Lord, whom he would not name, was abundantly sarcastic on his character, and mentioned his political principles as inimical to the House of Hanover. Lord Bute's answer was, that if these were the Doctor's principles, there was merit in his suppressing them; that if he had not made an improper use of them without any acknowledgement from court, it was not very likely he would, when that should take place, and that it was intended to reward his writings which were before the public, without any regard to such principles as he kept to himself.

Johnson was now in a state of independence; but his habit of literary composition was but little enervated, though no longer excited by necessity. The work which engrossed his attention was his long projected and promised edition of Shakespear. This in 1765 was published by subscription, and especially since joined to the critical labours of Mr. Steevens,[8] is become a valuable acquisition to literary criticism.

His notes in various parts of the work, his explanation of difficult passages, his developement of hidden beauties, his interpretations of obscurities, and his candour and ingenuity in reconciling inconsistencies,

* Memoirs of G. Anne Bellamy.[5]

discover no superficial acquaintance with either men or books. Many think the text not deserving the commentary, few who are judges think the commentary at least not equal to the text. This is the favourite bard of Englishmen, and he owes his immortality to their discernment, as in every other nation his absurdities had probably buried him in oblivion. It was said by one of the Popes,[1] with the usual decency of professional impostors, that a book which required so much explanation as the Bible, ought not to have been written. This witticism applied to Shakespear would be deemed blasphemy, and yet apart from a few splendid passages, what do we find in his plays to justify their excessive popularity, or to give the author that super-eminence which he has so long enjoyed on the English stage? Do they serve to correct the taste, improve the heart, enlighten the understanding, or facilitate any one purpose of public utility. His characters are in fact all monsters, his heroes madmen, his wits buffoons, and his women strumpets, viragos, or idiots. He confounds the relations of things by aiming at no moral object, and for pleasantry often substitutes the grossest obscenity. His creations are as preposterous as they are numerous, and whenever he would declaim his thoughts are vulgar, and his expressions quaint or turgid or obscure. He makes Achilles and other illustrious characters of antiquity hector like bullies in a brothel, and puts in the mouths of his heroines the ribaldry of Billingsgate. There is not a rule in dramatic composition which he does not habitually violate. He is called the poet of nature, and he certainly imitates her deformities with exactness, but seldom aims at that preference of art which consists in copying her excellence. The profusion of intemperate praise which accompanies his memory indicates much oftener an abject deference for the opinion of the multitude than any real sense of intrinsic merit. And many a reader fancies himself charm'd with the beauties, who is only a dupe to the name of an author. Johnson was not a critic to be misled by report, while he could have access to the truth. He even says, that there is *not one of Shakespear's plays which were it now to be exhibited as the work of a contemporary writer, would be heard to the conclusion.*[2] And he states the excellencies and defects of his author in terms so equally pointed and strong, that he has run into paradox, where he meant only to be impartial.

From the party altercations which distinguish British politics, no Englishman of a speculative genius can be altogether free. And whatever principles are espoused, one party will always be disgusted in proportion to the merit with which these are asserted, illustrated, or defended. The abuse to which his pamphlets in favour of government exposed him, are to be attributed to this circumstance. He adopted the ministerial side of the question with all that promptitude of invention, that ardour of genius, that brilliancy of imagination, and that energy of expression which characterise his writings. And the *Patriot*, the *False Alarm*, *Falkland Island*, and *Taxation no Tyranny*, which were published at different times from the year 1760 to about 1775,[1] will be read and admired, when the heats which occasioned them are forgotten.

Prior to the unfortunate failure of Fordyce,[2] Johnson in company with his friends Hawksworth and Goldsmith, often visited that gentleman. An acquaintance consequently commenced between Johnson and the Rev. Dr. James Fordyce, so well known for his popular talents in the pulpit, and his Sermons to young women. These were shown to Johnson and published by his advice. He even interested himself so far in the work as to write the title and the advertisement.[3] The author consulted him with a becoming confidence, and politely attributed much of the success attending that elegant work to his good offices. In truth, Johnson conceived a very favourable opinion of this reverend gentleman. He owned himself fond, he said, of a man, who notwithstanding the illiberality which still debased the literature of his country, had *no dirty heresies sticking about him.*

In the summer of 1773, he set out on a tour to the Hebrides of Scotland. His companion was Mr. Boswell, to whose polite attention and facetious temper he attributes much of the entertainment he received. His account of this journey[4] is written with his usual attention to men and things, the ideas he conceived of the country, and his satyrical turn of thinking. It appeared in 1775, and brought upon the author a world of enemies. He was charged with gross misrepresentation, with consulting his prejudices where he ought to have consulted his eyes, and with substituting for the localities, he affects to point out those only which his cynical opinion had disguised.

But the chief controversy which this work produced was concerning the authenticity of Ossian's Poems.[5] This he denies in the most unqualified terms, and dares the translator to shew his originals. He regarded the whole as an impostor, and an insult on the common sense of mankind, and observed, 'that to revenge incredulity by refusing evidence, is a degree of insolence to which the world is not yet acquainted, and stubborn audacity is the last refuge of guilt.'[6] This challenge was conceived as indelicate, and resented, not by an immediate publication of the MSS, but the grossest menaces. The translator's letter to Johnson on this occasion was probably not preserved; it extorted however the following reply:

'Mr. James Macpherson,
    'I received your foolish and impudent letter. Any violence that shall

be attempted upon me I will do my best to repel; and what I cannot do for myself, the law shall do for me; for I will not be hindered from exposing what I think a cheat, by the menaces of a ruffian. What would you have me retract? I thought your work an imposture; I think so still; and for my opinion I have given reasons, which I here dare you to refute. Your abilities since your Homer are not so formidable, and what I hear of your morality, inclines me to credit rather what you shall prove, than what you shall say.

S. JOHNSON.'[1]

This was dictated from memory only, when Johnson had mislaid the copy he preserved of the original, which General Melville[2] has been heard to repeat verbatim, and which is said to be much more pointed. A meeting however was so certainly expected between these two literary heroes, that for some time after Johnson never went abroad without a stout cudgel, and his antagonist it is also alledged, was furnished with a similar weapon. Whether Macpherson was ashamed of his rudeness in addressing a person of Johnson's age and respectability in foul language, or apprehensive of the consequences which might result from an assault, is uncertain, but the matter never went further.

About Christmas, 1774, the Rev. Mr. Shaw[3] was introduced to Johnson, by the kind offices of Mr. Elphinston. Shaw being a Highland man, the Doctor interrogated him much on his knowledge of the Erse, and whether the Poems of Fingal existed in that language. The answer which Shaw made was, that he often had wished, to be clearly ascertained of the fact, whether they did or did not. This candour and frankness strongly recommended him to Johnson's notice and friendship. He was always pleased when he heard him afterwards mentioned with respect, and when Dr. Beattie,[4] in a conversation on the Ossian controversy, ventured to insinuate something derogatory to the veracity of this gentleman, Johnson's answer was, '*I never before heard so much said against Mr. Shaw, and I do not believe it.*'

The present Earl of Eglintoun,[5] who has an attachment to the Highlanders, and their language, requested of Mr. Shaw, a copy of the MS of his Galic[6] Grammatical Rules, which was granted him, and Mr. Boswell having seen it in the hands of his Lordship, begged leave to lay it before Johnson, as a proof that the Erse had not been neglected. It appears that either his Lordship had forgotten to mention how he got it, or at least that Mr. Boswell did not acquaint the Doctor with that circumstance. For on a morning visit, Shaw soon after paid Johnson, he was asked by him if he knew that MS. as it did not appear to be ancient. The Doctor had been perusing it, and it lay on the table before him. Shaw's name, who had written an Erse Grammar, was prefixed to the MS. which he therefore told the Doctor was his composition, and in his own handwriting.

Johnson immediately instigated him to publish it, and assured him the publication would be attended with both profit and reputation. He accordingly introduced him to Mr. Strahan,[1] who printed it, and when he presented him with a copy, he expressed satisfaction at the mention he made of Mr. Elphinston's English Grammar; and when he came, in perusing the preface, to the following sentence, relative to himself, 'To the advice and encouragement of Dr. Johnson, the friend of letters and humanity, the public is indebted for these sheets,' he, after some pause said, 'Sir, you have treated me handsomely, *you are an honour to your country.*'

Besides a natural turn for the study of language, and the advantages and credit he had now acquired among his countrymen, Shaw turned his thoughts towards making a collection of all the vocables in the Galic language that could be collected from the voice or old books and MSS.[2] Having communicated his idea, in 1778, to the Doctor, and pointed out the difficulties and expence necessary to make the tour of Scotland and Ireland, the limited sale of such a work, and the uncertainty of subscriptions, he replied, that the Scotch ought to raise a fund for the undertaking. Application therefore was made to the Highland Club, of which Shaw had been one of the original founders, and which was instituted for the purpose of encouraging Galic enquiries, but he found that by the underhand dealings of Macpherson and his party, and Shaw's connexion with Johnson, nothing would be contributed. His disappointment he soon communicated to the Doctor, and still expressed the most ardent zeal to record the ancient language of his native country: he said he could muster, of his own property, from two to three hundred pounds towards a journey, and other expences, if he could entertain any hopes of being refunded by the publication. By a speech he made that day on the undertaking, the Doctor fully determined him to set off with the spring, the conclusion of which was; '*Sir, if you give the world a Vocabulary of that language, while the island of Great-Britain stands in the Atlantic Ocean, your name will be mentioned*'. By such a speech, and from such a man, the youthful mind of Shaw went with ardour in pursuit of the objects in question. He performed a journey of 3000 miles, persevered and finished his work at his own expence, and has not to this day been paid their subscriptions by his countrymen.

Before he set out, he laid before the Doctor his plan of collecting and arranging his materials, asked his advice, and received his directions. He told him, that though he did not implicitly believe what was said in defence of, and against the Poems of Ossian, he, however, at present, could bring no proofs to substantiate the allegations for or against them; and that as a secondary work, he would do every thing in his power, to collect specimens, if such could be got, at least be in possession in facts, if not to satisfy the public, to remove all doubts from his own mind, of their spuriousness or authenticity; and that he would afterwards talk or write as he could procure evidence. Of this the Doctor highly approved, though it has been since asserted, that it was previously settled between them what proofs he should find. But they know little of the man, who can believe such scandal; and Shaw seems altogether incapable of acting with such disguise.

The sequel hath verified the sincerity of their mutual declarations; for the enquiry of the one has confirmed the incredulity of the other. What the Doctor doubted Shaw has proved, and the virulence shown by the party for Ossian against Shaw, which has since been refuted, is but a fresh proof of the imposture.

So far was the Doctor interested in the success and fortunes of his coadjutor in this business, that he addressed him to take orders in the Church of England, but he lived not to see him provided for. Upon his going to settle in Kent, in 1780, as a curate, the Doctor wrote to Mr. Allen, the Vicar of St. Nicholas, Rochester, in his favour, the following letter.[1]

'SIR,
'Mr. William Shaw, the gentleman from whom you will receive this, is a studious and literary man; he is a stranger, and will be glad to be introduced into proper company; and he is my friend, and any civility you shall shew him, will be an obligation on,

'SIR,

'your most obedient servant,

Signed   SAM. JOHNSON.'

The enquiry into the authenticity of Ossian was published by his approbation; but he expressed his apprehensions of the treatment that succeeded. He read the whole over to Mrs. Williams,[2] as she has been heard to say, and said that he was much pleased with the proofs adduced of the imposture of Ossian, and the manner in which he retorted the abuse and scandal which Macnicol[3] poured out in his book against him. He gave his advice and assistance in conducting the argument, and often told Shaw, '*We shall prevail in this controversy.*'

The following letter, occasioned by Clark's answer[4] to Shaw's enquiry, which appeared in some of the periodical publications, deserves preservation, as it contains such a recapitulation of the subject in debate, as gave the Doctor much satisfaction.

To Doctor SAMUEL JOHNSON.
'SIR,

The controversy concerning the authenticity of Ossian's Poems is at last decided in your favour. But this detection has produced a spirit of revenge as disgraceful to letters as it is shocking to humanity. Thus the vulgar often mistake for a new star, the blaze of a meteor, whose transitory splendour expires in a stench.

It is, however, to you, Sir, the rational admirers of decency and dispassionate criticism now look up, with anxiety and solicitude, for a vindication of the gentleman, whose character, friends, and prospects have been thus generously sacrificed in defence of truth. He is thought to have written at your instigation. It was at least in confidence of your patronage that he thus manfully avowed his convictions. He is of consequence enough to justify even your interference: nor is innocence beneath the protection of any.

To crush the potent combinations raised by this contest, against every thing dear and interesting to Mr. Shaw, requires the most vigorous exertion of no common abilities. The literati of Scotland have, for the most part, been duped by the translator of these chimerical compositions. Their interest in the republic of letters, especially in this country, is at present very powerful. Some of their moral characters are unfortunately involved in the dispute. And to substantiate a proof that the poems in question are only a mere modern fabrication, at once destroys their veracity as men, and, as they imagine, deeply affects the honour of the country.

For these reasons, every possible effort will naturally be made to re-establish the fallen credit of Ossian. The translator, by every honourable means, no doubt, has at last wriggled himself into parliament,[1] and the Highland clergy will be assiduous to serve him, in proportion as they may now suppose it in his power to return the obligation. Your silence, Sir, while all Grub-street is in an uproar, in a matter which originated with you, will consequently be attended with a new eruption of forgeries, from the same lying spirit that has already belched up so many. These, another fresh abettor of Ossian's ghost will readily detail, in all the ribaldry of detraction, and all the malignant acrimony of disappointment. And poor Shaw may adopt for his eternal motto,

> ——A barbarous noise environs me,
> Of owls and cuckows, asses, apes, and dogs![2]

If a blistered tongue be the most infallible symptom of a diseased stomach, the case of his patients surely demand the most immediate prescriptions of a master.

Malice and Scotch cunning are surely united, and exerted against this unfortunate Enquirer, in a most extraordinary degree. The man, like Job in another case, is, in one moment robbed of his all. As a scholar, a gentleman, a poet, or a preacher, he affords his old Scotch acquaintance only a little ridicule or a vulgar sarcasm. His literary talents are denied, and he is considered as a man, equally destitute of letters, decency, and decorum. Yet Clark, who pronounces thus cavalierly on his ignorance, with almost the same breath, acknowledges himself indebted to his criticism. Strange John Clark, to confess yourself corrected in your favourite Celtic study, by one whom you tell us, so often and so roundly, knows nothing about the matter.

It might well be suspected that he who composed both a grammar and a dictionary, under the patronage of the first lexicographer perhaps in Europe, would probably be deemed by the impartial part of mankind, not altogether incompetent to the task. To render the victory decisive, it was therefore necessary, as far as the blackest aspersions and most contemptible insinuations could go, to ruin his moral reputation. They foresaw his knowledge of the subject could have no weight, but in proportion to his credit with the public. This once destroyed, the argument would necessarily be their own.

In short, these Scotch literati seem to hang together in palming these nostrums on the public, like so many jugglers, equally concerned in the success of some common trick, and Mr. Shaw, for having relinquished his share in the plot, is hooted by the whole honourable fraternity as a traitor. To render his criminality for this unpardonable treachery still more enormous, his religious is classed with his literary apostacy,[1] and both stated as irrefragable evidences that he is utterly destitute of principle. And such is the general provocation which his alacrity and adroitness in this business have given, that he would probably run the same risque on appearing once more in the Highlands of Scotland, with the man, who, after turning King's evidence, should have the temerity to re-visit the cells of Newgate.

It seems therefore incumbent on you, Sir, to state the facts at large, which first led you to a discovery of this monstrous imposition, to rescue your Gallic coadjutor from the odium incurred by espousing your cause, to enter your protest against prostituting a polemical discussion to illiberal invective and virulent detraction, and to account to the public for their conduct, who, under pretence of vindicating a very frivolous truth, have essentially injured the most important virtues. Leaving Mr.

Shaw to struggle thus, in a contest commenced by you, will be considered by your joint opponents, as a damning proof of his delinquency; of their surmises, in your suffering yourself to be imposed on by his artifice; and of your yielding to the weight of their accumulated virulence against him, after defying all that sophistry could do against yourself.

ANTI-OSSIAN.'[1]

In consequence of this letter, had Johnson's health permitted him, during the last six months, he intended to have drawn out and published a state of the controversy[2] from the beginning, to balance the arguments and evidence on both sides, and to pronounce judgment on the whole. This is a piece of criticism now lost, and much to be lamented, as the question concerning the poems attributed to Ossian, from the illiberal construction put on his opinion of their authenticity, interested him as materially as any circumstance of his life.

Though the following letter came into the Editor's hands too late to be inserted in the proper place, it must not be suppressed, as it is the first Mr. Elphinston received from the Doctor, and shews how long a correspondence of the most liberal and friendly nature, has subsisted between them.

To Mr. ELPHINSTON.
'SIR,

I have for a long time intended to answer the Letter which you were pleased to send me, and know not why I have delayed it so long; but that I had nothing particular, either of inquiry or information, to send you: and the same reason might still have the same consequence; but that I find in my recluse kind of Life, that I am not likely to have much more to say, at one time than another, and that therefore I may endanger by an appearance of neglect, long continued, the loss of such an Acquaintance as I know not where to supply. I therefore write now to assure you how sensible I am of the kindness you have always expressed to me, and how much I desire the cultivation of that Benevolence, which, perhaps, nothing but the distance between us has hindered from ripening before this time into Friendship. Of myself I have very little to say, and of any body else less: let me, however, be allowed one thing, and that in my own favour; that I am,

Dear Sir,
Your most humble servant,

April 20, 1749,   SAM. JOHNSON.'

In the year 1778, as appears from the date of the following, his friend, Mr. Elphinston became a widower. Johnson, who had long known the exquisite sensibility of his nature, entered into all his sympathies with his usual tenderness. And it is impossible to read his consolatory epistle on that occasion, without sharing that amiable philanthropy which he then felt, and which formed a very distinguishing trait in his character.

To Mr. ELPHINSTON.
'SIR,
    Having myself suffered what you are now suffering, I well know the weight of your distress, how much need you have of comfort, and how little comfort can be given. A loss, such as yours, lacerates the mind, and breaks the whole system of purposes and hopes. It leaves a dismal vacuity in life, which affords nothing on which the affections can fix, or to which endeavour may be directed. All this I have known, and it is now, in the vicissitude of things, your turn to know it.

    But in the condition of mortal beings, one must lose another. What would be the wretchedness of life, if there was not something always in view, some Being, immutable and unfailing, to whose mercy man may have recourse. Τὸν πρῶτον κινοῦντα ἀκίνητον.[1]

    Here we must rest. The greatest Being is the most benevolent. We must not grieve for the dead as men without hope,[2] because we know that they are in his hands. We have, indeed, not leisure to grieve long, because we are hastening to follow them. Your race and mine have been interrupted by many obstacles, but we must humbly hope for an happy end.

I am, Sir,
Your most humble servant,

Signed   SAM. JOHNSON.'
July 27, 1778.

The Lives of the Poets is one of his greatest, and perhaps was the best finished of his works. It was undertaken so late as the year 1778.[3] The design, originally, was only to have given a general character of each author, and to have fixed, as nearly as possible, the period of publication. But the subject was too fertile and pleasing to be thus briefly dismissed. The booksellers agreed to give him two hundred pounds[4] for no more than this, but his genius expanded with the rich fields that opened to his view, and facts accumulated in proportion as he continued the search.

    He was engaged in this performance by a very general concurrence in the trade, to defeat the project which had been conceived of abridging their monopoly. This was the plan of Mr. Bell, who printed the English poets at, what he called, the Apollo press.[5] His edition was cheap and diminutive, but elegant and likely to be popular. The booksellers were in hopes, the high reputation of Johnson, would, by this undertaking, prove a protection to what they deemed their property.

The only thing to be feared was the declension of those abilities,[1] on which they depended, as he was now arrived at a very advanced age. But he soon convinced them and the public, that notwithstanding the disease and infirmities to which he was reduced, his intellects were still unimpaired. His account of the metaphysical poets, his Memoirs of Dryden, and especially his Critique on Paradise Lost, are, in my opinion, among the happiest efforts of his pen, and written with all the beauty and elegance of which our language is susceptible.

Thus, by a most fortunate choice of his subjects, has this great man in giving at once stability to our tongue, and formation to our taste, established a basis for his own fame, which shall last while a vestige of the one or the other remains.

From this period, the cessation of all his labours, the public seemed anxious about his preservation, in proportion as it every day became more and more certain that they must soon lose him. He was consequently, in the evening of his days particularly, an object of universal attention and enquiry. The progress of his declining health has accordingly been traced in every account hitherto presented of his life and literary pursuits, with a minute and tiresome exactness.

In the year 1783 he was attacked by a stroke of the palsey, which deprived him for some time of the power of speech.[2] But by the assiduity of Dr. Hebberden and Dr. Brocklesby,[3] his usual physicians, he was soon recovered to his wonted state of ill health.

In the month of December of the same year, a club was instituted at the Essex-Head,[4] chiefly on his account, and by several individuals who wished to monopolize his company. He composed rules for its regulation, and seemed to enjoy it while he could give his attendance; but his infirmities continued to increase, and the constant evacuations to which he was subjected by an asthmatic habit, terminated in a dropsy, which in the spring of 1784, confined him some months.[5]

It was now his friend, Sir Joshua Reynolds, conceiving that the genial climate of Italy might help to cherish or eke out a life thus dear to him, and to mankind, signified to the Lord Chancellor[6] how seasonable and acceptable, for that purpose, two hundred a year more would prove to the Doctor. His lordship did not hesitate a moment in mentioning the circumstance in its proper place. But Johnson never was a courtier. Other claims and on other accounts were more pressing. Though the greatest princes in the world would have been glad to confer an obligation on such a man, the necessities of his situation were overlooked. The present is neither an age nor a government, in which merit like his can expect more than bare encouragement.

The Chancellor however found means to acquaint him, in the most delicate manner, that five hundred pounds[1] at his banker's was at his service, and he should think it money well laid out, if in any degree it contributed to his convenience. Johnson's letter on this unexpected occasion, though one of his last, is not the least happy of his productions.[2]

The Right Hon. the Lord Chancellor.
MY LORD,

'After a long and not inattentive observation on mankind, the generosity of your lordship's offer raises in me no less wonder than gratitude. Bounty so liberally bestowed I should gladly receive if my condition made it necessary; for to such a mind who would not be proud to own his obligations? But it hath pleased God to restore me to such a measure of health, that if I should now appropriate so much of a fortune destined to do good, I could not escape from myself the charge of advancing a false claim. My journey to the Continent though I once thought it necessary, was never much encouraged by my physicians, and I was very desirous that your lordship should be told of it by Sir Joshua Reynolds, as an event very uncertain; for if I should grow much better I should not be willing, and if much worse I should not be able to migrate.

'Your Lordship was first solicited without my knowledge; but when I was told that you was pleased to honour me with your patronage, I did not expect to hear of a refusal; yet as I have had no long time to brood hope, and have not rioted in imaginary opulence, this cold reception has been scarce a disappointment; and from your lordship's kindness I have received a benefit which men like you are able to bestow. I shall now live *mihi carior*, with a higher opinion of my own merit.

I am, my Lord,
Your Lordship's most obliged,
Most grateful,
And most humble Servant,
S. JOHNSON.'

To the Right Honourable
the Lord Chancellor.
Sept. 1784.

No event since the decease of Mrs. Johnson so deeply affected him as the very unaccountable marriage of Mrs. Thrale.[3] This woman he had frequently mentioned as the ornament and pattern of her sex. There was no virtue which she did not practise, no feminine accomplishment of which she was not a mistress; hardly any language or science, or art

which she did not know. These various endowments he considered as so
many collateral securities of her worth. They conciliated his confidence
at least in what he thought she was. He consequently entertained a
sincere friendship for her and her family. But her apostacy appeared to
him an insult on his discernment, and on all those valuable qualities for
which he had given her so much credit. The uneasiness and regret which
he felt on this occasion was so very pungent, that he could not conceal it
even from his servants. From that time he was seldom observed to be in
his usual easy good humours. His sleep and appetite, and the satisfaction
he took in his study, obviously forsook him. He even avoided that company which had formerly given him the greatest pleasure. He often was
denied to his dearest friends, who declined mentioning her name to him,
and till the hour of his death he could not wholly dismiss her from his
thoughts.

His dying moments were replete with that piety which adorned his
life. The approaches of death shocked him to a certain degree, because
he did not affect to conceal what he felt. Serenity or fortitude in such an
awful situation, is the gift of few minds. He died in the full conviction of
an eternal world, and the important realities of futurity, were consequently regarded by him with proportionable diffidence and solicitude.

A few days before his decease he sent for Sir Joshua Reynolds, and
told him that he had three favours to ask of him. Sir Joshua, confiding
in the Doctor's good sense and discretion, frankly promised an implicit
compliance with his request. The first was, that though he owed Sir
Joshua thirty pounds, he was not to expect to be repaid. This was
readily granted. The second demand was that Sir Joshua should not
paint on Sundays. To this a small degree of hesitation appeared, but
however no positive objection was made. He desired as his third and last
request that he would regularly every day read more or less of the
scriptures; Sir Joshua bogled most at this, but the Doctor assuming
much earnestness, told him how much he had it at heart, and hoped Sir
Joshua's pledging himself to a dying friend might insure the literal and
punctual performance of a duty, which would for certain be attended
with the best effects, promised to comply.

The dispositions he made in his last will[1] have been variously con-
strued. And some have blamed him much for treating his poor relations
so harshly, by leaving his whole property almost to strangers. He consulted however his own feelings, and we know not his principles
sufficiently to judge of his motives.

He was uniformly through life anxious to communicate happiness to
all about him. He had innumerable pensioners. His house, especially in

the latter part of his life, was an asylum for the indigent and well deserving. It was crouded for years with aged invalids of both sexes. Mrs. Williams,[1] the blind woman, lodged with him from Mrs. Johnson's death till within a few years of his own. He has celebrated Mr. Leveret[2] in a beautiful copy of verses to his memory. He had an annual feast for a numerous collection of old ladies whom he knew, and to whom on this occasion, he always gave his company in preference to any other engagement.

About seven o'clock[3] on Monday evening, the 13th of December, 1785, this great and worthy individual expired in the 75th year of his age without a groan. And perhaps he left few behind him either of equal goodness, ability or reputation.

In estimating the real merit of this elegant and masterly writer, it may be necessary to attend not so much to what he knew as to what he communicated. His most intimate friends could obtain but a partial acquaintance with the former, the public are in full possession of the latter. It seems of very little consequence how the fountain is supplied, while the stream preserves its fulness and its purity. The genius of Johnson from whatever source he drew his information, whether his acquaintance with philosophy or philology was solid or superficial, or whether he was a man of science or only a mere lexicographer, abounded with originality on every subject which occupied his attention. His writings are not theoretical, but he often elucidates general knowledge without obscuring his stile by technical phraseology. How then shall the science of an author, who attaches himself to no particular one, be decided. To infer his ignorance of specific qualities, from his acquaintance with that alone which involves them, is like upbraiding the philosopher who studies the principles of mechanics because he is not a wheelwright, or a watchmaker. Examine all his allusions in his *Ramblers*, his *Idlers*, and his *Lives*, and let his science be estimated in the same proportion as these are adopted with propriety. What is it that has thus enriched his stile, and rendered all his details so much more interesting and original than those of most authors. Is it not the solid and profound reflections of a sagacious, discriminating, and well-informed mind? In fact, it was by passing through this intelligent medium, that his various and literal communications accumulated all their value and importance, and what he has said of Dryden,[4] applies with peculiar propriety to himself. *His works abound with knowledge and sparkle with illustrations. There is scarcely any science or faculty that does not supply him with occasional images and lucky similitudes; every page discovers a mind very widely acquainted both with art and nature, and in full possession of great stores of intellectual wealth.*

To a mind thus manured in learning, science, and knowledge of the world, Johnson added such amplitude of wit as answered all the purposes of petulance, malignity, and amusement. It is however not a little singular, that with a bluntness of address, and a coarseness of colloquial expression peculiarly characteristic, he was equally without humour and superior to every species of buffoonery. All his ideas, in whatever terms he chose to exhibit them, were brilliant, original and correct. He was a painter who seldom dealt in sketches. His pictures might be sometimes preposterous or fanciful, and not unfrequently monstrous for deformity, but were generally well finished. He possessed in an eminent degree the talent of elevating the conversation by an exuberance of classical and interesting sentiment, but in the course of a long life, and in the enjoyment of a numerous and polished acquaintance, gave few specimens of those elegant and social pleasantries which are often to be found in the company of the learned and polite. With a large share of good-nature he could occasionally be unpardonably severe, and he never was more entertaining than when he gave a loose to the sarcastic propensity of his nature at the expence of some character absent or present. The moment he found himself the idol of fashion, his conceit of his own powers was without restraint or decency. He arrogated the distinction of Dictator in all companies, delivered his opinions with oracular promptitude and decision, and spurned with impatience and scorn the most delicate contradiction. His respect for no party, sex, or individual, when the fit of talking had once seized him, could either qualify or suppress a favourite paradox, a rude jest, or a bold apothegm. His witticisms were rather strong and pointed, than exquisitely fine and charming, and more calculated to render us dissatisfied with what we cannot help, than by a group of agreeable associations to excite our gratitude for what we may still enjoy. No man ever discovered more humanity or discovered it in a manner less capable of disguise than he did. His heart was in unison with every thing that could suffer. He had no equal in affording consolation to the sorrowful. Pity always made him serious, and he never deemed that an object of mirth which tended by any means whatever to impair the happiness of society. He had no levity of his own, and was so far from relishing it in others, that he never met with a facetious character in his life which he did not either despise or treat with incivility. In short, his genius was fettered by melancholy and caprice, he was fond of appearing sententious and dispassionate and correct, and even his most sprightly ridicule was generally tinged with reflection and solemnity.

The anecdotes which have been told of him are endless. For many he is doubtless obliged to the fabrications of his friends, as well as his enemies. Report, for a series of years, has given him the credit for most of the best things that have attracted public attention. Some of these appear only an improvement of others, the second edition of what did not please him in the first, or an echo to sayings of which no trace probably remained on his memory but the sound. Whoever would make an accurate collection of them must inviolably adhere to arrangement. A great variety were dropt originally in Booksellers shops, where he always lounged away much of his time, with a few literary and scientific men, whose intimacy and conversation it was his ambition to cultivate; and among people of fashion and distinction, of whose attentions, adulation, and friendship he grew immoderately fond in the later periods of his life.

Long before he broached the idea of his Dictionary, or any other work which chiefly contributed to raise and establish his literary reputation, he was much with a Bookseller of eminence,[1] who frequently consulted him about manuscripts offered for sale, or books newly published. But whenever Johnson's opinion happened to differ from his, he would stare Johnson full in the face, and remark with much gravity and arrogance, *I wish you could write as well.* This Johnson thought was literally telling a professional man that he was an impostor, or that he assumed a character to which he was not equal. He therefore heard the gross imputation once or twice with sullen contempt. One day, however, in the presence of several gentlemen, who knew them both, this bookseller very incautiously threw out the same illiberal opinion. Johnson could suppress his indignation no longer. *Sir,* said he, *you are not competent to decide a question which you do not understand. If your allegations be true, you have the brutality to insult me with what is not my fault, but my misfortune. If your allegation be not true, your impudent speech only shews how much more detestable a liar is than a brute.* The strong conclusive aspect and ferocity of manner which accompanied the utterance of these words, from a poor author to a purse-proud Bookseller, made a deep impression in Johnson's favour, and secured him, perhaps, more respect and civility in his subsequent intercourse with the trade than any other transaction of his life.

Goldsmith,[2] who hated the prudery of Johnson's morals, and the foppery of Hawksworth's manners, yet warmly admired the genius of both, was in use to say among his acquaintance, that Johnson would have made a *decent monk,* and Hawksworth *a good dancing master.*

Johnson often took his revenge. He had sarcasms at will for all persons, and all places. One evening these two wits were in company with Mrs. Thrale, and a large assemblage of fine women: Goldsmith, who was the most aukward creature imaginable in such a situation, over-turned the tea-things as the servant presented him with his dish. He was speechless; and the ladies, after staring at each other, burst into a fit of laughter. Johnson only continued grave, and turning to Mrs. Thrale, *Madam*, said he, *can you tell how a man who shocks so much in company, can give so many charms to his writings?*

Johnson is said never to have forgiven a lady, then present, who whispered to Mrs. Thrale in a voice loud enough to be heard through the whole room, *These gentlemen publish so much delicacy, that they reserve none for private use.*

But whatever may be thought of his genius, his science, or his wit, the benevolence, the seriousness and the religious tendency of his moral productions are eminent and incontestible. He never made any attempt in historical composition. In other walks of literature he had few superiors, and he was undoubtedly one of the most popular authors of the present age. His regards for religion were sacred and inviolable. Those virtues and qualities which administer to the decency and felicity of life, derived from his pen peculiar aid and illustration. He was the friend and advocate of whatever enlarges, heightens, refines, or perfects the happiness of humanity. To this great and prevailing object all his labours had an immediate reference, and his whole life in public and private was consecrated to the welfare and the honour of the species.

HESTHER LYNCH PIOZZI

Anecdotes of the Late
SAMUEL JOHNSON, LL.D.
during the last Twenty Years
of His Life

Preface

I HAVE somewhere heard or read,[1] that the Preface before a book, like the portico before a house, should be contrived, so as to catch, but not detain the attention of those who desire admission to the family within, or leave to look over the collection of pictures made by one whose opportunities of obtaining them we know to have been not unfrequent. I wish not to keep my readers long from such intimacy with the manners of Dr. Johnson, or such knowledge of his sentiments as these pages can convey. To urge my distance from England as an excuse for the book's being ill written, would be ridiculous; it might indeed serve as a just reason for my having written it at all; because, though others may print the same aphorisms and stories, I cannot *here* be sure that they have done so. As the Duke says however to the Weaver, in A Midsummer Night's Dream,[2] 'Never excuse; if your play be a bad one, keep at least the excuses to yourself.'

I am aware that many will say, I have not spoken highly enough of Dr. Johnson; but it will be difficult for those who say so, to speak more highly. If I have described his manners as they were, I have been careful to shew his superiority to the common forms of common life. It is surely no dispraise to an oak that it does not bear jessamine; and he who should plant honeysuckle round Trajan's column, would not be thought to adorn, but to disgrace it.

When I have said, that he was more a man of genius than of learning, I mean not to take from the one part of his character that which I willingly give to the other. The erudition of Mr. Johnson proved his genius; for he had not acquired it by long or profound study: nor can I think those characters the greatest which have most learning driven into their heads, any more than I can persuade myself to consider the river Jenisca[3] as superior to the Nile, because the first receives near seventy tributary streams in the course of its unmarked progress to the sea, while the great parent of African plenty, flowing from an almost invisible source, and unenriched by any extraneous waters, except eleven nameless rivers,[1] pours his majestic torrent into the ocean by seven celebrated mouths.

But I must conclude my Preface, and begin my book, the first I ever presented before the Public; from whose awful appearance in some measure to defend and conceal myself, I have thought fit to retire behind the Telamonian shield,[2] and shew as little of myself as possible; well aware of the exceeding difference there is, between fencing in the school and fighting in the field.——Studious however to avoid offending, and careless of that offence which can be taken without a cause, I here not unwillingly submit my slight performance to the decision of that glorious country, which I have the daily delight to hear applauded in others, as eminently just, generous, and humane.

Anecdotes of the Late
Samuel Johnson, LL.D.

T O O much intelligence is often as pernicious to Biography as too little; the mind remains perplexed by contradiction of probabilities, and finds difficulty in separating report from truth. If Johnson then lamented that so little had ever been said about Butler,[1] I might with more reason be led to complain that so much has been said about himself; for numberless informers but distract or cloud information, as glasses which multiply will for the most part be found also to obscure. Of a life, too, which for the last twenty years was passed in the very front of literature, every leader of a literary company, whether officer or subaltern, naturally becomes either author or critic, so that little less than the recollection that it was *once* the request of the deceased,[2] and *twice* the desire of those whose will I ever delighted to comply with, should have engaged me to add my little book to the number of those already written on the subject. I used to urge another reason for forbearance, and say, that all the readers would, on this singular occasion, be the writers of his life: like the first representation of the Masque of Comus, which, by changing their characters from spectators to performers, was *acted* by the lords and ladies[3] it was *written* to entertain. This objection is however now at an end, as I have found friends,[4] far remote indeed from literary questions, who may yet be diverted from melancholy by my description of Johnson's manners, warmed to virtue even by the distant reflexion of his glowing excellence, and encouraged by the relation of his animated zeal to persist in the profession as well as practice of Christianity.

Samuel Johnson was the son of Michael Johnson, a bookseller at Litchfield, in Staffordshire; a very pious and worthy man, but wrongheaded, positive, and afflicted with melancholy, as his son, from whom alone I had the information, once told me: his business, however, leading him to be much on horseback, contributed to the preservation of his bodily health, and mental sanity; which, when he staid long at home, would sometimes be about to give way; and Mr. Johnson said, that when his work-shop, a detached building, had fallen half down for want of money to repair it, his father was not less diligent to lock the door[1] every night, though he saw that any body might walk in at the back part, and knew that there was no security obtained by barring the front door. '*This* (says his son) was madness, you may see, and would have been discoverable in other instances of the prevalence of imagination,[2] but that poverty prevented it from playing such tricks as riches and leisure encourage.' Michael was a man of still larger size and greater strength than his son, who was reckoned very like him, but did not delight in talking much of his family—'one has (says he) *so* little pleasure in reciting the anecdotes of beggary.' One day, however, hearing me praise a favourite friend with partial tenderness as well as true esteem; Why do you like that man's acquaintance so, said he? Because, replied I, he is open and confiding, and tells me stories of his uncles and cousins; I love the light parts of a solid character. 'Nay, if you are for family history, says Mr. Johnson good-humouredly, *I* can fit you: I had an uncle, Cornelius Ford[3], who, upon a journey, stopped and read an inscription written on a stone he saw standing by the way-side, set up, as it proved, in honour of a man who had leaped a certain leap thereabouts, the extent of which was specified upon the stone: Why now, says my uncle, I could leap it in my boots; and he did leap it in his boots. I had likewise another uncle, Andrew, continued he, my father's brother, who kept the ring[4] in Smithfield (where they wrestled and boxed) for a whole year, and never was thrown or conquered. Here now are uncles for you, Mistress, if that's the way to your heart.' Mr. Johnson was very conversant in the art of attack and defence by boxing, which science he had learned from this uncle Andrew, I believe; and I have heard him descant upon the age when people were received, and when rejected, in the schools once held for that brutal amusement, much to the admiration of those who had no expectation of his skill in such matters, from the sight of a figure which precluded all possibility of personal prowess; though, because he saw Mr. Thrale one day leap over a cabriolet stool,[5] to shew that he was not tired after a chace of fifty miles or more, *he* suddenly jumped over it too; but in a way so strange and so unwieldy, that our terror lest he should break his bones, took from us even the power of laughing.

Michael Johnson was past fifty years old when he married his wife, who was upwards of forty;[6] yet I think her son told me she remained three years childless before he was born into the world, who so greatly contributed to improve it. In three years more she brought another son, Nathaniel, who lived to be twenty-seven or twenty-eight years old,[7] and of whose manly spirit I have heard his brother speak with pride and pleasure, mentioning one circumstance, particular enough, that when the company were one day lamenting the badness of the roads, he enquired where they could be, as he travelled the country more than most people, and had never seen a bad road in his life. The two brothers did not, however, much delight in each other's company, being always rivals for the mother's fondness; and many of the severe reflections on domestic life in Rasselas,[1] took their source from its author's keen recollections of the time passed in his early years. Their father Michael died of an inflammatory fever, at the age of seventy-six,[2] as Mr. Johnson told me: their mother at eighty-nine, of a gradual decay. She was slight in her person, he said, and rather below than above the common size. So excellent was her character, and so blameless her life, that when an oppressive neighbour once endeavoured to take from her a little field she possessed, he could persuade no attorney to undertake the cause against a woman so beloved in her narrow circle: and it is this incident he alludes to in the line of his Vanity of Human Wishes, calling her

The general favourite as the general friend.[3]

Nor could any one pay more willing homage to such a character, though she had not been related to him, than did Dr. Johnson on every occasion that offered: his disquisition on Pope's epitaph placed over Mrs. Corbet,[4] is a proof of that preference always given by him to a noiseless life over a bustling one; for however taste begins, we almost always see that it ends in simplicity; the glutton finishes by losing his relish for any thing highly sauced, and calls for his boiled chicken at the close of many years spent in the search of dainties; the connoisseurs are soon weary of Rubens, and the critics of Lucan;[5] and the refinements of every kind heaped upon civil life, always sicken their possessors before the close of it.

At the age of two years Mr. Johnson was brought up to London by his mother, to be touched by Queen Anne for the scrophulous evil,[6] which terribly afflicted his childhood, and left such marks as greatly disfigured a countenance naturally harsh and rugged, beside doing irreparable damage to the auricular organs, which never could perform their functions since I knew him; and it was owing to that horrible disorder, too, that one eye was perfectly useless to him; that defect, however, was not observable, the eyes looked both alike. As Mr. Johnson had an astonishing memory, I asked him, if he could remember Queen Anne at all? 'He had, he said, a confused, but somehow a sort of solemn recollection of a lady in diamonds, and a long black hood.'

The christening of his brother[7] he remembered with all its circumstances, and said, his mother taught him to spell and pronounce the words *little Natty*, syllable by syllable, making him say it over in the evening to her husband and his guests. The trick which most parents play with their children, that of shewing off their newly-acquired accomplishments, disgusted Mr. Johnson beyond expression; he had been treated so himself, he said, till he absolutely loathed his father's caresses, because he knew they were sure to precede some unpleasant display of his early abilities; and he used, when neighbours came o'visiting, to run up a tree that he might not be found and exhibited, such, as no doubt he was, a prodigy of early understanding. His epitaph upon the duck[1] he killed by treading on it at five years old,

> Here lies poor duck
> That Samuel Johnson trod on;
> If it had liv'd it had been good luck,
> For it would have been an odd one;

is a striking example of early expansion of mind, and knowledge of language; yet he always seemed more mortified at the recollection of the bustle his parents made with his wit, than pleased with the thoughts of possessing it. 'That (said he to me one day) is the great misery of late marriages;[2] the unhappy produce of them becomes the plaything of dotage: an old man's child, continued he, leads much such a life, I think, as a little boy's dog, teized with awkward fondness, and forced, perhaps, to sit up and beg, as we call it, to divert a company, who at last go away complaining of their disagreeable entertainment.' In consequence of these maxims, and full of indignation against such parents as delight to produce their young ones early into the talking world, I have known Mr. Johnson give a good deal of pain by refusing to hear the verses the children could recite, or the songs they could sing; particularly one friend who told him that his two sons should repeat Gray's Elegy to him alternately, that he might judge who had the happiest cadence. 'No, pray Sir,' said he, 'let the dears both speak it at once; more noise will by that means be made, and the noise will be sooner over.' He told me the story himself, but I have forgot who the father was.[3]

Mr. Johnson's mother was daughter to a gentleman in the country, such as there were many of in those days, who possessing, perhaps, one or two hundred pounds a year in land, lived on the profits, and sought not to increase their income: she was therefore inclined to think higher of herself[4] than of her husband, whose conduct in money matters being but indifferent, she had a trick of teizing him about it, and was, by her son's account, very importunate with regard to her fears of spending more than they could afford, though she never arrived at knowing how much that was; a fault common, as he said, to most women who pride themselves on their œconomy. They did not however, as I could understand, live ill together on the whole: 'my father (says he) could always take his horse and ride away for orders when things went badly.' The lady's maiden name was Ford; and the parson who sits next to the punch-bowl in Hogarth's Modern Midnight Conversation was her brother's son. This Ford was a man who chose to be eminent only for vice, with talents that might have made him conspicuous in literature, and respectable in any profession he could have chosen: his cousin has mentioned him in the lives of Fenton and of Broome;[1] and when he spoke of him to me it was always with tenderness, praising his acquaintance with life and manners, and recollecting one piece of advice that no man surely ever followed more exactly: 'Obtain (says Ford) some general principles of every science; he who can talk only on one subject, or act in one department, is seldom wanted, and perhaps never wished for; while the man of general knowledge can often benefit, and always please.' He used to relate, however, another story less to the credit of his cousin's penetration, how Ford on some occasion said to him, 'You will make your way the more easily in the world, I see, as you are contented to dispute no man's claim to conversation excellence, they will, therefore, more willingly allow your pretensions as a writer.'[2] Can one, on such an occasion, forbear recollecting the predictions of Boileau's father, when stroaking the head of the young satirist, *Ce petit bon homme* (says he) *n'a point trop d'esprit*, mais il ne *dira jamais mal de personne*.[3] Such are the prognostics formed by men of wit and sense, as these two certainly were, concerning the future character and conduct of those for whose welfare they were honestly and deeply concerned; and so late do those features of peculiarity come to their growth, which mark a character to all succeeding generations.

Dr. Johnson first learned to read of his mother and her old maid Catharine,[4] in whose lap he well remembered sitting while she explained to him the story of St. George and the Dragon. I know not whether this is the proper place to add, that such was his tenderness, and such his gratitude, that he took a journey to Litchfield fifty-seven years afterwards to support and comfort her in her last illness; he had enquired for his nurse and she was dead.[5] The recollection of such reading as had delighted him in his infancy, made him always persist in fancying that it was the only reading which could please an infant; and he used to condemn me for putting Newbery's books[6] into their hands as too trifling to engage their attention. 'Babies do not want (said he) to hear about babies; they like to be told of giants and castles, and of somewhat which can stretch and stimulate their little minds.' When in answer I would urge the numerous editions and quick sale of Tommy Prudent or Goody Two Shoes: 'Remember always (said he) that the parents *buy* the books, and that the children never read them.' Mrs. Barbauld[7] however had his best praise, and deserved it; no man was more struck than Mr. Johnson with voluntary descent from possible splendour to painful duty.

At eight years old[1] he went to school, for his health would not permit him to be sent sooner; and at the age of ten years his mind was disturbed by scruples of infidelity, which preyed upon his spirits, and made him very uneasy; the more so, as he revealed his uneasiness to no one, being naturally (as he said) 'of a sullen temper and reserved disposition.' He searched, however, diligently but fruitlessly, for evidences of the truth of revelation; and at length recollecting a book he had once seen in his father's shop, intitled, *De Veritate Religionis*,[2] &c. he began to think himself highly culpable for neglecting such a means of information, and took himself severely to task for this sin, adding many acts of voluntary, and to others unknown, penance. The first opportunity which offered (of course) he seized the book with avidity; but on examination, not finding himself scholar enough to peruse its contents, set his heart at rest; and, not thinking to enquire whether there were any English books written on the subject, followed his usual amusements, and considered his conscience as lightened of a crime. He redoubled his diligence to learn the language that contained the information he most wished for; but from the pain which guilt had given him, he now began to deduce the soul's immortality, which was the point that belief first stopped at; and from that moment resolving to be a Christian, became one of the most zealous and pious ones our nation ever produced. When he had told me this odd anecdote of his childhood; 'I cannot imagine (said he) what makes me talk of myself to you so, for I really never mentioned this foolish story to any body except Dr. Taylor,[3] not even to my *dear dear* Bathurst, whom I loved better than ever I loved any human creature; but poor Bathurst is dead!!!'[4]—Here a long pause and a few tears ensued. Why Sir, said I, how like is all this to Jean Jaques Rousseau! as like, I mean, as the sensations of frost and fire, when my child complained yesterday that the ice she was eating *burned* her mouth. Mr. Johnson laughed at the incongruous ideas; but the first thing which presented itself to the mind of an ingenious and learned friend[5] whom I had the pleasure to pass some time with here at Florence, was the same resemblance, though I think the two characters had little in common, further than an early attention to things beyond the capacity of other babies, a keen sensibility of right and wrong, and a warmth of imagination little consistent with sound and perfect health. I have heard him relate another odd thing of himself too, but it is one which every body has heard as well as I: how, when he was about nine years old, having got the play of Hamlet in his hand, and reading it quietly in his father's kitchen, he kept on steadily enough, till coming to the Ghost scene,[6] he suddenly hurried up stairs to the street door that he might see people about him:

such an incident, as he was not unwilling to relate it, is probably in every one's possession now; he told it as a testimony to the merits of Shakespeare: but one day when my son was going to school, and dear Dr. Johnson followed as far as the garden gate, praying for his salvation, in a voice which those who listened attentively, could hear plain enough, he said to me suddenly, 'Make your boy tell you his dreams: the first corruption that entered into my heart was communicated in a dream.' What was it, Sir? said I. '*Do* not ask me,' replied he with much violence, and walked away in apparent agitation. I never durst make any further enquiries. He retained a strong aversion for the memory of Hunter,[1] one of his schoolmasters, who, he said, once was a brutal fellow: 'so brutal (added he), that no man who had been educated by him ever sent his son to the same school.' I have however heard him acknowledge his scholarship to be very great. His next master[2] he despised, as knowing less than himself, I found; but the name of that gentleman has slipped my memory. Mr. Johnson was himself exceedingly disposed to the general indulgence of children, and was even scrupulously and ceremoniously attentive not to offend them: he had strongly persuaded himself of the difficulty people always find to erase early impressions either of kindness or resentment, and said, 'he should never have so loved his mother when a man, had she not given him coffee[3] she could ill afford, to gratify his appetite when a boy.' If you had had children Sir, said I, would you have taught them any thing? 'I hope (replied he), that I should have willingly lived on bread and water to obtain instruction for them; but I would not have set their future friendship to hazard for the sake of thrusting into their heads knowledge of things for which they might not perhaps have either taste or necessity. You teach your daughters the diameters of the planets, and wonder when you have done that they do not delight in your company. No science can be communicated by mortal creatures without attention from the scholar; no attention can be obtained from children without the infliction of pain, and pain is never remembered without resentment.' That something should be learned, was, however, so certainly his opinion, that I have heard him say, how education had been often compared to agriculture, yet that it resembled it chiefly in this: 'that if nothing is sown, no crop (says he) can be obtained.' His contempt of the lady who fancied her son could be eminent without study, because Shakespeare was found wanting in scholastic learning, was expressed in terms so gross and so well known, I will not repeat them here.[4]

To recollect, however, and to repeat the sayings of Dr. Johnson, is almost all that can be done by the writers of his life; as his life, at least since my acquaintance with him, consisted in little else than talking, when he was not absolutely employed in some serious piece of work; and whatever work he did, seemed so much below his powers of performance, that he appeared the idlest of all human beings; ever musing till he was called out to converse, and conversing till the fatigue of his friends, or the promptitude of his own temper to take offence, consigned him back again to silent meditation.

The remembrance of what has passed in his own childhood, made Mr. Johnson very solicitous to preserve the felicity of children; and when he had persuaded Dr. Sumner to remit the tasks usually given to fill up boys' time during the holidays, he rejoiced exceedingly in the success of his negociation, and told me that he had never ceased representing to all the eminent schoolmasters in England, the absurd tyranny of poisoning the hour of permitted pleasure, by keeping future misery before the children's eyes, and tempting them by bribery or falsehood to evade it. 'Bob Sumner (said he), however, I have at length prevailed upon: I know not indeed whether his tenderness was persuaded, or his reason convinced, but the effect will always be the same. Poor Dr. Sumner died, however, before the next vacation.'[1]

Mr. Johnson was of opinion, too, that young people should have *positive*, not *general* rules given for their direction. 'My mother (said he) was always telling me that I did not *behave* myself properly; that I should endeavour to learn *behaviour*, and such cant:[2] but when I replied, that she ought to tell me what to do, and what to avoid, her admonitions were commonly, for that time at least, at an end.'

This, I fear, was however at best a momentary refuge, found out by perverseness. No man knew better than Johnson in how many nameless and numberless actions *behaviour* consists: actions which can scarcely be reduced to rule, and which come under no description. Of these he retained so many very strange ones, that I suppose no one who saw his odd manner of gesticulating, much blamed or wondered at the good lady's solicitude concerning her son's *behaviour*.

Though he was attentive to the peace of children in general, no man had a stronger contempt than he for such parents as openly profess that they cannot govern their children. 'How (says he) is an army governed? Such people, for the most part, multiply prohibitions till obedience becomes impossible, and authority appears absurd; and never suspect that they tease their family, their friends, and themselves, only because conversation runs low, and something must be said.'

Of parental authority, indeed, few people thought with a lower degree of estimation. I one day mentioned the resignation of Cyrus to his father's will, as related by Xenophon, when, after all his conquests, he requested the consent of Cambyses to his marriage with a neighbouring princess; and I added Rollin's applause and recommendation of the example. 'Do you not perceive then (says Johnson), that Xenophon on this occasion commends like a pedant, and Pere Rollin[1] applauds like a slave? If Cyrus by his conquests had not purchased emancipation, he had conquered to little purpose indeed. Can you bear to see the folly of a fellow who has in his care the lives of thousands, when he begs his papa permission to be married, and confesses his inability to decide in a matter which concerns no man's happiness but his own?'—Mr. Johnson caught me another time reprimanding the daughter of my housekeeper for having sat down unpermitted in her mother's presence. 'Why, she gets her living, does she not (said he), without her mother's help? Let the wench alone,' continued he. And when we were again out of the women's sight who were concerned in the dispute: 'Poor people's children, dear Lady (said he) never respect them: I did not respect my own mother, though I loved her: and one day, when in anger she called me a puppy, I asked her if she knew what they called a puppy's mother.' We were talking of a young fellow who used to come often to the house; he was about fifteen years old, or less, if I remember right, and had a manner at once sullen and sheepish. 'That lad (says Mr. Johnson) looks like the son of a schoolmaster; which (added he) is one of the very worst conditions of childhood: such a boy has no father, or worse than none; he can never reflect on his parent but the reflection brings to his mind some idea of pain inflicted, or of sorrow suffered.'[2]

I will relate one thing more that Dr. Johnson said about babyhood before I quit the subject; it was this: 'That little people should be encouraged always to tell whatever they hear particularly striking, to some brother, sister, or servant, immediately before the impression is erased by the intervention of newer occurrences. He perfectly remembered the first time he ever heard of Heaven and Hell (he said), because when his mother had made out such a description of both places as she thought likely to seize the attention of her infant auditor, who was then in bed with her, she got up, and dressing him before the usual time, sent him directly to call a favourite workman[3] in the house, to whom she knew he would communicate the conversation while it was yet impressed upon his mind. The event was what she wished, and it was to that method chiefly that he owed his uncommon felicity of remembering distant occurrences, and long past conversations.'

At the age of eighteen Dr. Johnson quitted school,[4] and escaped from the tuition of those he hated or those he despised. I have heard him relate very few college adventures. He used to say that our best accounts of his behaviour there would be gathered from Dr. Adams[5] and Dr. Taylor,[6] and that he was sure they would always tell the truth. He told me however one day, how, when he was first entered at the university, he passed a morning, in compliance with the customs of the place, at his tutor's chambers; but finding him no scholar, went no more. In about ten days after, meeting the same gentleman, Mr. Jordan,[1] in the street, he offered to pass by without saluting him; but the tutor stopped, and enquired, not roughly either, What he had been doing? 'Sliding on the ice,' was the reply; and so turned away with disdain. He laughed very heartily at the recollection of his own insolence, and said they endured it from him with wonderful acquiescence, and a gentleness that, whenever he thought of it, astonished himself. He told me too, that when he made his first declamation, he wrote over but one copy, and that coarsely; and having given it into the hand of the tutor who stood to receive it as he passed, was obliged to begin by chance and continue on how he could, for he had got but little of it by heart; so fairly trusting to his present powers for immediate supply, he finished by adding astonishment to the applause of all who knew how little was owing to study. A prodigious risque, however, said some one: 'Not at all (exclaims Johnson), no man I suppose leaps at once into deep water who does not know how to swim.'

I doubt not but this story will be told by many of his biographers, and said so to him when he told it me on the 18th of July 1773. 'And who will be my biographer[2] (said he), do you think?' Goldsmith, no doubt, replied I, and he will do it best among us. 'The dog would write it best to be sure, replied he; but his particular malice towards me, and general disregard for truth, would make the book useless to all, and injurious to my character.' Oh! as to that, said I, we should all fasten upon him, and force him to do you justice; but the worst is, the Doctor does not *know* your life; nor can I tell indeed who does, except Dr. Taylor of Ashbourne. 'Why Taylor, said he, is better acquainted with my *heart* than any man or woman now alive; and the history of my Oxford exploits lies all between him and Adams;[3] but Dr. James[4] knows my very early days better than he. After my coming to London to drive the world about a little, you must all go to Jack Hawkesworth[5] for anecdotes: I lived in great familiarity with him (though I think there was not much affection) from the year 1753 till the time Mr. Thrale and you took me up.[6] I intend, however, to disappoint the rogues, and either make you write the life, with Taylor's intelligence; or, which is better, do it myself, after out-living you all. I am now (added he), keeping a diary,[7] in hopes of using it for that purpose some time.' Here the conversation stopped, from my accidentally looking in an old magazine of the year 1768,[8] where I saw the following lines with his name to them, and asked if they were his.

VERSES *said to be written by Dr.* SAMUEL JOHNSON, *at the request of a Gentleman to whom a Lady had given a Sprig of Myrtle.*

WHAT hopes, what terrors, does thy gift create,
Ambiguous emblem of uncertain fate;
The Myrtle, ensign of supreme command,
Consign'd by Venus to Melissa's hand;
Not less capricious than a reigning fair,
Now grants, and now rejects a lover's prayer.
In myrtle shades oft sings the happy swain,
In myrtle shades despairing ghosts complain:
The myrtle crowns the happy lover's heads,
Th'unhappy lover's grave the myrtle spreads:
O then the meaning of thy gift impart,
And ease the throbbings of an anxious heart!
Soon must this bough, as you shall fix his doom,
Adorn Philander's head, or grace his tomb.

'Why now, do but see how the world is gaping for a wonder! (cries Mr. Johnson) I think it is now just forty years ago that a young fellow had a sprig of myrtle given him by a girl he courted, and asked me to write him some verses that he might present her in return. I promised, but forgot; and when he called for his lines at the time agreed on—Sit still a moment (says I), dear Mund,[1] and I'll fetch them thee—so stepped aside for five minutes, and wrote the nonsense you now keep such a stir about.'

Upon revising these Anecdotes, it is impossible not to be struck with shame and regret that one treasured no more of them up; but no experience is sufficient to cure the vice of negligence: whatever one sees constantly, or might see constantly, becomes uninteresting; and we suffer every trivial occupation, every slight amusement, to hinder us from writing down, what indeed we cannot chuse but remember; but what we should wish to recollect with pleasure, unpoisoned by remorse for not remembering more. While I write this, I neglect impressing my mind with the wonders of art, and beauties of nature, that now surround me; and shall one day, perhaps, think on the hours I might have profitably passed in the Florentine Gallery, and reflecting on Raphael's St. John at that time, as upon Johnson's conversation in this moment, may justly exclaim of the months spent by me most delightfully in Italy——

That I priz'd every hour that pass'd by,
Beyond all that had pleas'd me before;
But now they are past, and I sigh
And I grieve that I priz'd them no more.

SHENSTONE.[2]

Dr. Johnson delighted in his own partiality for Oxford; and one day, at my house, entertained five members of the other university with various instances of the superiority of Oxford, enumerating the gigantic names of many men whom it had produced, with apparent triumph. At last I said to him, Why there happens to be no less than five Cambridge men in the room now. 'I did not (said he) think of that till you told me; but the wolf don't count the sheep.' When the company were retired, we happened to be talking of Dr. Barnard, the Provost of Eton, who died about that time;[1] and after a long and just eulogium on his wit, his learning, and his goodness of heart: 'He was the only man too (says Mr. Johnson quite seriously) that did justice to my good breeding;[2] and you may observe that I am well-bred to a degree of needless scrupulosity. No man, (continued he, not observing the amazement of his hearers) no man is so cautious not to interrupt another; no man thinks it so necessary to appear attentive when others are speaking; no man so steadily refuses preference to himself, or so willingly bestows it on another, as I do; no body holds so strongly as I do the necessity of ceremony, and the ill effects which follow the breach of it: yet people think me rude; but Barnard did me justice.' 'Tis pity, said I laughing, that he had not heard you compliment the Cambridge men after dinner to-day. 'Why (replied he) I was inclined to *down* them sure enough; but then a fellow *deserves* to be of Oxford that talks so.' I have heard him at other times relate how he used to sit in some coffee-house there, and turn M——'s[3] C-r-ct-u-s into ridicule for the diversion of himself and of chance comers-in. 'The Elf—da (says he) was too exquisitely pretty; I could make no fun out of that.' When upon some occasions he would express his astonishment that he should have an enemy in the world, while he had been doing nothing but good to his neighbours, I used to make him recollect these circumstances: 'Why child (said he), what harm could that do the fellow? I always thought very well of M——n for a *Cambridge* man; he is, I believe, a mighty blameless character.' Such tricks were, however, the more unpardonable in Mr. Johnson, because no one could harangue like him about the difficulty always found in forgiving petty injuries, or in provoking by needless offence. Mr. Jordan,[4] his tutor, had much of his affection, though he despised his want of scholastic learning. 'That creature would (said he) defend his pupils to the last: no young lad under his care should suffer for committing slight improprieties, while he had breath to defend, or power to protect them. If I had had sons to send to college (added he), Jordan should have been their tutor.'

Sir William Browne the physician,[5] who lived to a very extraordinary age, and was in other respects an odd mortal, with more genius than understanding, and more self-sufficiency than wit, was the only person who ventured to oppose Mr. Johnson, when he had a mind to shine by exalting his favourite university, and to express his contempt of the Whiggish notions which prevail at Cambridge. *He* did it once, however, with surprising felicity: his antagonist having repeated with an air of triumph the famous epigram written by Dr. Trapp,[1]

> Our royal master saw, with heedful eyes,
> The wants of his two universities:
> Troops he to Oxford sent, as knowing why
> That learned body wanted loyalty:
> But books to Cambridge gave, as, well discerning,
> That that right loyal body wanted learning.

Which, says Sir William, might well be answered thus:

> The king to Oxford sent his troops of horse,
> For Tories own no argument but force;
> With equal care to Cambridge books he sent,
> For Whigs allow no force but argument.

Mr. Johnson did him the justice to say, it was one of the happiest extemporaneous productions he ever met with; though he once comically confessed, that he hated to repeat the wit of a whig urged in support of whiggism. Says Garrick to him one day, Why did not you make me a tory, when we lived so much together, you love to make people tories? 'Why (says Johnson, pulling a heap of halfpence from his pocket), did not the king make these guineas?'

Of Mr. Johnson's toryism the world has long been witness, and the political pamphlets written by him in defence of his party, are vigorous and elegant. He often delighted his imagination with the thoughts of having destroyed Junius,[2] an anonymous writer who flourished in the years 1769 and 1770, and who kept himself so ingeniously concealed from every endeavour to detect him, that no probable guess was, I believe, ever formed concerning the author's name, though at that time the subject of general conversation. Mr. Johnson made us all laugh one day, because I had received a remarkably fine Stilton cheese as a present from some person who had packed and directed it carefully, but without mentioning whence it came. Mr. Thrale, desirous to know who we were obliged to, asked every friend as they came in, but nobody owned it: 'Depend upon it, Sir (says Johnson), it was sent by *Junius*.'

The False Alarm,[3] his first and favourite pamphlet, was written at our house between eight o'clock on Wednesday night and twelve o'clock on Thursday night; we read it to Mr. Thrale when he came very late home from the House of Commons: the other political tracts followed in their order. I have forgotten which contains the stroke at Junius; but shall for ever remember the pleasure it gave him to have written it. It was however in the year 1775 that Mr. Edmund Burke made the famous speech in parliament, that struck even foes with admiration, and friends with delight. Among the nameless thousands who are contented to echo

73

those praises they have not skill to invent, *I* ventured, before Dr. Johnson himself, to applaud, with rapture, the beautiful passage in it concerning Lord Bathurst[1] and the Angel; which, said our Doctor, had I been in the house, I would have answered *thus*:

'Suppose, Mr. Speaker, that to Wharton, or to Marlborough,[2] or to any of the eminent whigs of the last age, the devil had, not with any great impropriety, consented to appear; he would perhaps in somewhat like these words have commenced the conversation:

'You seem, my Lord, to be concerned at the judicious apprehension, that while you are sapping the foundations of royalty at home, and propagating here the dangerous doctrine of resistance; the distance of America may secure its inhabitants from your arts, though active: but I will unfold to you the gay prospects of futurity. This people, now so innocent and harmless, shall draw the sword against their mother country, and bathe its point in the blood of their benefactors: this people, now contented with a little, shall then refuse to spare, what they themselves confess they could not miss; and these men, now so honest and so grateful, shall, in return for peace and for protection, see[3] their vile agents in the house of parliament, there to sow the seeds of sedition, and propagate confusion, perplexity, and pain. Be not dispirited then at the contemplation of their present happy state: I promise you that anarchy, poverty, and death shall, by my care, be carried even across the spacious Atlantic, and settle in America itself, the sure consequences of our beloved whiggism.'

This I thought a thing so very particular, that I begged his leave to write it down directly, before any thing could intervene that might make me forget the force of the expressions:[4] a trick, which I have however seen played on common occasions, of sitting steadily[5] down at the other end of the room to write at the moment what should be said in company, either *by* Dr. Johnson or *to* him, I never practised myself, nor approved of in another. There is something so ill-bred, and so inclining to treachery in this conduct, that were it commonly adopted, all confidence would soon be exiled from society, and a conversation assembly-room would become tremendous as a court of justice. A set of acquaintance joined in familiar chat may say a thousand things, which (as the phrase is) pass well enough at the time, though they cannot stand the test of critical examination; and as all talk beyond that which is necessary to the purposes of actual business is a kind of game, there will be ever found ways of playing fairly or unfairly at it, which distinguish the gentleman from the juggler. Dr. Johnson, as well as many of my acquaintance, knew that I kept a common-place book;[6] and he one day said to me good-humouredly, that he would give me something to write in my repository.

Part of the city of Lichfield, including (1) the house where Johnson was born, (2) the market cross, (3) St. Mary's church, (4) the town hall

Pembroke College, 1744, from an engraving after George Vertue for the Oxford Almanac

'I warrant (said he) there is a great deal about me in it: you shall have at least one thing worth your pains; so if you will get the pen and ink, I will repeat to you Anacreon's Dove[1] directly; but tell at the same time, that as I never was struck with any thing in the Greek language till I read *that*, so I never read any thing in the same language since, that pleased me as much. I hope my translation (continued he) is not worse than that of Frank Fawkes.'[2] Seeing me disposed to laugh, 'Nay nay (said he), Frank Fawkes has done them very finely.'

> LOVELY courier of the sky,
> Whence and whither dost thou fly?
> Scatt'ring as thy pinions play,
> Liquid fragrance all the way:
> Is it business? is it love?
> Tell me, tell me, gentle Dove.
>   'Soft Anacreon's vows I bear,
>   Vows to Myrtale the fair;
>   Grac'd with all that charms the heart,
>   Blushing nature, smiling art.
>   Venus, courted by an ode,
>   On the bard her Dove bestow'd.
>   Vested with a master's right
>   Now Anacreon rules my flight:
>   His the letters that you see,
>   Weighty charge consign'd to me:
>   Think not yet my service hard,
>   Joyless talk without reward;
>   Smiling at my master's gates,
>   Freedom my return awaits.
>   But the liberal grant in vain
>   Tempts me to be wild again:
>   Can a prudent Dove decline
>   Blissful bondage such as mine?
>   Over hills and fields to roam,
>   Fortune's guest without a home;
>   Under leaves to hide one's head,
>   Slightly shelter'd, coarsely fed;
>   Now my better lot bestows
>   Sweet repast, and soft repose;
>   Now the generous bowl I sip
>   As it leaves Anacreon's lip;
>   Void of care, and free from dread,
>   From his fingers snatch his bread,
>   Then with luscious plenty gay,
>   Round his chamber dance and play;
>   Or from wine, as courage springs,
>   O'er his face extend my wings;
>   And when feast and frolic tire,
>   Drop asleep upon his lyre.

This is all, be quick and go,
More than all thou canst not know;
Let me now my pinions ply,
I have chatter'd like a pye.'

When I had finished, 'But you must remember to add (says Mr. Johnson) that though these verses were planned, and even begun, when I was sixteen years old, I never could find time to make an end of them before I was sixty-eight.'

This facility of writing, and this dilatoriness ever to write, Mr. Johnson always retained, from the days that he lay a bed and dictated his first publication to Mr. Hector,[1] who acted as his amanuensis, to the moment he made me copy out those variations in Pope's Homer which are printed in the Poets Lives:[2] 'And now (said he, when I had finished it for him), I fear not Mr. Nichols[3] of a pin.'—The fine Rambler on the subject of Procrastination was hastily composed, as I have heard, in Sir Joshua Reynolds's parlour,[4] while the boy waited to carry it up to press: and numberless are the instances of his writing under immediate pressure of importunity or distress. He told me that the character of *Sober* in the Idler,[5] was by himself intended as his own portrait; and that he had his own outset into life in his eye when he wrote the eastern story of Gelaleddin.[6] Of the allegorical papers in the Rambler, Labour and Rest was his favourite;[7] but Serotinus, the man who returns late in life to receive honours in his native country, and meets with mortification instead of respect, was by him considered as a masterpiece in the science of life and manners.[8] The character of Prospero in the fourth volume, Garrick[9] took to be his; and I have heard the author say, that he never forgave the offence. Sophron[10] was likewise a picture drawn from reality; and by Gelidus the philosopher, he meant to represent Mr. Coulson,[11] a mathematician, who formerly lived at Rochester. The man immortalized for purring like a cat was, as he told me, one Busby, a proctor in the Commons.[12] He who barked so ingeniously, and then called the drawer to drive away the dog, was father to Dr. Salter[13] of the Charterhouse. He who sung a song, and by correspondent motions of his arm chalked out a giant on the wall, was one Richardson, an attorney.[14] The letter signed Sunday, was written by Miss Talbot;[15] and he fancied the billets in the first volume of the Rambler, were sent him by Miss Mulso, now Mrs. Chapone.[16] The papers contributed by Mrs. Carter,[17] had much of his esteem, though he always blamed me for preferring the letter signed Chariessa to the allegory, where religion and superstition are indeed most masterly delineated.

When Dr. Johnson read his own satire,[18] in which the life of a scholar is painted, with the various obstructions thrown in his way to fortune and to fame, he burst into a passion of tears one day: the family and Mr. Scott only were present, who, in a jocose way, clapped him on the back, and said, What's all this, my dear Sir? Why you, and I, and *Hercules*, you know, were all troubled with *melancholy*. As there are many gentlemen of the same name, I should say, perhaps, that it was a Mr. Scott who married Miss Robinson, and that I think I have heard Mr. Thrale call him George Lewis,[1] or George Augustus, I have forgot which. He was a very large man, however, and made out the triumvirate with Johnson and Hercules comically enough. The Doctor was so delighted at his odd sally, that he suddenly embraced him, and the subject was immediately changed. I never saw Mr. Scott but that once in my life.

Dr. Johnson was liberal enough in granting literary assistance to others, I think; and innumerable are the prefaces, sermons, lectures, and dedications[2] which he used to make for people who begged of him. Mr. Murphy related in his and my hearing one day, and he did not deny it, that when Murphy joked him the week before for having been so diligent of late between Dodd's sermon and Kelly's prologue, that Dr. Johnson replied, 'Why, Sir, when they come to me with a dead stay-maker and a dying parson,[3] what can a man do?' He *said*, however, that 'he hated to give away literary performances, or even to sell them too cheaply: the next generation shall not accuse me (added he) of beating down the price of literature: one hates, besides, ever to give that which one has been accustomed to sell; would not you, Sir (turning to Mr. Thrale), rather give away money than porter?'[4]

Mr. Johnson had never, by his own account, been a close student, and used to advise young people never to be without a book in their pocket, to be read at bye-times when they had nothing else to do. 'It has been by that means (said he to a boy at our house one day) that all my knowledge has been gained, except what I have picked up by running about the world with my wits ready to observe, and my tongue ready to talk. A man is seldom in a humour to unlock his book-case, set his desk in order, and betake himself to serious study; but a retentive memory will do something, and a fellow shall have strange credit given him, if he can but recollect striking passages from different books, keep the authors separate in his head, and bring his stock of knowledge artfully into play: How else (added he) do the gamesters manage when they play for more money than they are worth?' His Dictionary, however, could not, one would think, have been written by running up and down; but he really did not consider it as a great performance; and used to say, 'that he might have done it easily in two years, had not his health[5] received several shocks during the time.'

When Mr. Thrale, in consequence of this declaration, teized him in the year 1768[1] to give a new edition of it, because (said he) there are four or five gross faults: 'Alas, Sir (replied Johnson), there are four or five hundred faults, instead of four or five; but you do not consider that it would take me up three whole months labour, and when the time was expired the work would not be done.' When the booksellers set him about it however some years after, he went cheerfully to the business, said he was well paid, and that they deserved to have it done carefully.[2] His reply to the person who complimented him on its coming out first,[3] mentioning the ill success of the French in a similar attempt, is well known; and I trust, has been often recorded: 'Why, what would you expect, dear Sir (said he), from fellows that eat frogs?' I have however often thought Dr. Johnson more free than prudent in professing so loudly his little skill in the Greek language:[4] for though he considered it as a proof of a narrow mind to be too careful of literary reputation, yet no man could be more enraged than he, if an enemy, taking advantage of this confession, twitted him with his ignorance; and I remember when the king of Denmark was in England, one of his noblemen was brought by Mr. Colman to see Dr. Johnson at our country-house;[5] and having heard, he said, that he was not famous for Greek literature, attacked him on the weak side; politely adding, that he chose that conversation on purpose to favour himself. Our Doctor, however, displayed so copious, so compendious a knowledge of authors, books, and every branch of learning in that language, that the gentleman appeared astonished. When he was gone home (says Johnson), 'Now for all this triumph, I may thank Thrale's Xenophon here, as, I think, excepting that *one*, I have not looked in a Greek book these ten years; but see what haste my dear friends were all in (continued he) to tell this poor innocent foreigner that I knew nothing of Greek! Oh, no, he knows nothing of Greek!' with a loud burst of laughing.

When Davies printed the Fugitive Pieces[6] without his knowledge or consent; How, said I, would Pope have raved, had he been served so? 'We should never (replied he) have heard the last on't, to be sure; but then Pope was a narrow man: I will however (added he) storm and bluster *myself* a little this time;'—so went to London in all the wrath he could muster up. At his return I asked how the affair ended: 'Why (said he), I was a fierce fellow, and pretended to be very angry, and Thomas was a good-natured fellow, and pretended to be very sorry: so *there* the matter ended: I believe the dog loves me dearly. Mr. Thrale (turning to my husband), what shall you and I do that is good for Tom Davies?[7] We will do something for him, to be sure.'

Of Pope as a writer he had the highest opinion, and once when a lady at our house talked of his preface to Shakespeare as superior to Pope's:

'I fear not, Madam (said he), the little fellow has done wonders.'[1] His superior reverence of Dryden[2] notwithstanding still appeared in his talk as in his writings; and when some one mentioned the ridicule thrown on him in the Rehearsal,[3] as having hurt his general character as an author: 'On the contrary (says Mr. Johnson), the greatness of Dryden's reputation is now the only principle of vitality which keeps the duke of Buckingham's play from putrefaction.'[4]

It was not very easy however for people not quite intimate with Dr. Johnson, to get exactly his opinion of a writer's merit, as he would now and then divert himself by confounding those who thought themselves obliged to say to-morrow what he had said yesterday; and even Garrick, who ought to have been better acquainted with his tricks, professed himself mortified, that one time when he was extolling Dryden in a rapture that I suppose disgusted his friend, Mr. Johnson suddenly challenged him to produce twenty lines in a series[5] that would not disgrace the poet and his admirer. Garrick produced a passage that he had once heard the Doctor commend, in which he *now* found, if I remember rightly, sixteen faults, and made Garrick, look silly at his own table. When I told Mr. Johnson the story, 'Why, what a monkey was David now (says he), to tell of his own disgrace!' And in the course of that hour's chat he told me, how he used to teize Garrick by commendations of the tomb scene in Congreve's Mourning Bride,[6] protesting that Shakespeare had in the same line of excellence nothing as good: 'All which is strictly *true* (said he); but that is no reason for supposing Congreve is to stand in competition with Shakespeare: these fellows know not how to blame, nor how to commend.' I forced him one day, in a similar humour, to prefer Young's description of Night to the so much admired ones of Dryden and Shakespeare,[7] as more forcible, and more general. Every reader is not either a lover or a tyrant, but every reader is interested when he hears that

> Creation sleeps; 'tis as the general pulse
> Of life stood still, and nature made a pause;
> An awful pause—prophetic of its end.[8]

'This (said he) is true; but remember that taking the compositions of Young in general, they are but like bright stepping-stones over a miry road: Young froths, and foams, and bubbles sometimes very vigorously; but we must not compare the noise made by your tea-kettle here with the roaring of the ocean.'

Somebody was praising Corneille one day in opposition to Shakespeare: 'Corneille is to Shakespeare (replied Mr. Johnson) as a clipped hedge is to a forest.'[9] When we talked of Steele's Essays,[10] 'They are too

thin (says our Critic) for an Englishman's taste: mere superficial observations on life and manners, without erudition enough to make them
keep, like the light French wines, which turn sour with standing a while
for want of *body*, as we call it.'

Of a much admired poem, when extolled as beautiful (he replied),
'That it had indeed the beauty of a bubble: the colours are gay (said he),
but the substance slight.' Of James Harris's Dedication to his Hermes[1]
I have heard him observe, that, though but fourteen lines long, there
were six grammatical faults in it. A friend was praising the style of Dr.
Swift; Mr. Johnson did not find himself in the humour to agree with him:
the critic was driven from one of his performances to the other. At length
you *must* allow me, said the gentleman, that there are *strong facts* in the
account of the Four last Years of Queen Anne: 'Yes surely Sir (replies
Johnson), and so there are in the Ordinary of Newgate's account.'[2] This
was like the story which Mr. Murphy tells, and Johnson always acknowledged: How Mr. Rose of Chiswick,[3] contending for the preference of
Scotch writers over the English, after having set up his authors like
nine-pins, while the Doctor kept bowling them down again; at last, to
make sure of victory, he named Ferguson upon Civil Society,[4] and
praised the book for being written in a *new* manner. 'I do not (says Johnson) perceive the value of this new manner; it is only like Buckinger,[5]
who had no hands, and so wrote with his feet.' Of a modern Martial,[6]
when it came out: 'There are in these verses (says Dr. Johnson) too much
folly for madness, I think, and too much madness for folly.' If, however,
Mr. Johnson lamented, that the nearer he approached to his own times,
the more enemies he should make, by telling biographical truths in his
Lives of the later Poets, what may I not apprehend, who, if I relate
anecdotes of Mr. Johnson, am obliged to repeat expressions of severity,
and sentences of contempt? Let me at least soften them a little, by saying, that he did not hate the persons he treated with roughness, or
despise them whom he drove from him by apparent scorn. He really
loved and respected many whom he would not suffer to love him. And
when he related to me a short dialogue that passed between himself and
a writer of the first eminence[7] in the world, when he was in Scotland, I
was shocked to think how he must have disgusted him. Dr. ———
asked me (said he), why I did not join in their public worship when
among them? for (said he) I went to your churches often when in
England. 'So (replied Johnson), I have read that the Siamese sent ambassadors to Louis Quatorze, but I never heard that the king of France
thought it worth while to send ambassadors from his court to that of
Siam'. He was no gentler with myself, or those for whom I had the
greatest regard. When I one day lamented the loss of a first cousin[8]

killed in America—— 'Prithee, my dear (said he), have done with canting: how would the world be worse for it, I may ask, if all your relations
were at once spitted like larks, and roasted for Presto's supper?' Presto
was the dog that lay under the table while we talked.——When we went
into Wales together, and spent some time at Sir Robert Cotton's[1] at
Lleweny, one day at dinner I meant to please Mr. Johnson particularly
with a dish of very young peas. Are not they charming? said I to him,
while he was eating them.—'Perhaps (said he) they would be so—to a
pig.'[2] I only instance these replies, to excuse my mentioning those he
made to others.

When a well-known author published his poems in the year 1777:[3]
Such a one's verses are come out, said I: 'Yes (replied Johnson), and this
frost has struck them in again. Here are some lines I have written to
ridicule them: but remember that I love the fellow dearly, now—for all
I laugh at him.

> Wheresoe'er I turn my view,
> All is strange, yet nothing new:
> Endless labour all along,
> Endless labour to be wrong;
> Phrase that Time has flung away;
> Uncouth words in disarray,
> Trick'd in antique ruff and bonnet,
> Ode, and elegy, and sonnet.'

When he parodied the verses of another eminent writer,[4] it was done
with more provocation, I believe, and with some merry malice. A serious
translation of the same lines, which I think are from Euripides, may be
found in Burney's History of Music.[5]—Here are the burlesque ones:

> Err shall they not, who resolute explore
> Times gloomy backward with judicious eyes;
> And scanning right the practices of yore,
> Shall deem our hoar progenitors unwise.
>
> They to the dome where smoke with curling play
> Announc'd the dinner to the regions round,
> Summon'd the singer blythe, and harper gay,
> And aided wine with dulcet-streaming sound.
>
> The better use of notes, or sweet or shrill,
> By quiv'ring string, or modulated wind;
> Trumpet or lyre—to their harsh bosoms chill,
> Admission ne'er had sought, or could not find.
>
> Oh! send them to the sullen mansions dun,
> Her baleful eyes where Sorrow rolls around;
> Where gloom-enamour'd Mischief loves to dwell,
> And Murder, all blood-bolter'd, schemes the wound.

> When cates luxuriant pile the spacious dish,
> And purple nectar glads the festive hour;
> The guest, without a want, without a wish,
> Can yield no room to Music's soothing pow'r.

Some of the old legendary stories put in verse by modern writers provoked him to caricature them thus one day at Streatham; but they are already well-known, I am sure.

> The tender infant, meek and mild,
>   Fell down upon the stone;
> The nurse took up the squealing child,
>   But still the child squeal'd on.[1]

A famous ballad[2] also, beginning *Rio verde, Rio verde,* when I commended the translation of it, he said he could do it better himself—as thus:

> Glassy water, glassy water,
> Down whose current clear and strong,
> Chiefs confus'd in mutual slaughter,
> Moor and Christian roll along.

But Sir, said I, this is not ridiculous at all. 'Why no (replied he), why should I always write ridiculously?—perhaps because I made these verses to imitate such a one, naming him:[3]

> Hermit hoar, in solemn cell
> Wearing out life's evening gray;
> Strike thy bosom sage! and tell,
> What is bliss, and which the way?
>
> Thus I spoke, and speaking sigh'd,
> Scarce repress'd the starting tear,
> When the hoary Sage reply'd,
> Come, my lad, and drink some beer.'

I could give another comical instance of caricatura imitation. Recollecting some day, when praising these verses of Lopez de Vega,[4]

> *Se aquien los leones vence*
> *Vence una muger hermosa*
> *O el de flaco averguençe*
> *O ella di ser mas furiosa,*

more than he thought they deserved, Mr. Johnson instantly observed, 'that they were founded on a trivial conceit; and that conceit ill-explained, and ill-expressed beside.——The lady, we all know, does not conquer in the same manner as the lion does: 'Tis a mere play of words (added he), and you might as well say, that

> If the man who turnips cries,
> Cry not when his father dies,
> 'Tis a proof that he had rather
> Have a turnip than his father.'

And this humour is of the same sort with which he answered the friend[1] who commended the following line:

> Who rules o'er freemen should himself be free.

'To be sure (said **Dr. Johnson**),

> Who drives fat oxen should himself be fat.'

This readiness of finding a parallel, or making one, was shewn by him perpetually in the course of conversation.-- When the French verses of a certain pantomime[2] were quoted thus,

> *Je suis Cassandre descendüe des cieux,*
> *Pour vous faire entendre, mesdames et messieurs,*
> *Que je suis Cassandre descendüe des cieux;*

he cried out gaily and suddenly, almost in a moment,

> I am Cassandra come down from the sky,
> To tell each by-stander what none can deny,
> That I am Cassandra come down from the sky.

The pretty Italian verses too, at the end of Baretti's book, called 'Easy Phraseology,'[3] he did *all' improviso,* in the same manner:

> *Viva! viva la padrona!*
> *Tutta bella, et tutta buona,*
> *La padrona è un angiolella*
> *Tutta buona e tutta bella;*
> *Tutta bella e tutta buona;*
> *Viva! viva la padrona!*

> Long may live my lovely Hetty!
> Always young and always pretty,
> Always pretty, always young,
> Live my lovely Hetty long!
> Always young and always pretty;
> Long may live my lovely Hetty!

The famous distich too, of an Italian *improvisatore,* who, when the duke of Modena ran away from the comet in the year 1742 or 1743,[4]

> *Se al venir vestro i principi sen' vanno*
> *Deh venga ogni di —— durate un anno;*

'which (said he) would do just as well in our language thus:

If at your coming princes disappear,
Comets! come every day—and stay a year.'

When some one in company commended the verses of M. de Benserade[1]
à son Lit;

> *Theatre des ris et des pleurs,*
> *Lit! où je nais, et où je meurs,*
> *Tu nous fais voir comment voisins,*
> *Sont nos plaisirs, et nos chagrins.*

To which he replied without hesitating,

> 'In bed we laugh, in bed we cry,
> And born in bed, in bed we die;
> The near approach a bed may shew
> Of human bliss to human woe.'

The inscription on the collar of Sir Joseph Banks's goat[2] which had been on two of his adventurous expeditions with him, and was then, by the humanity of her amiable master, turned out to graze in Kent, as a recompence for her utility and faithful service, was given me by Johnson in the year 1777 I think, and I have never yet seen it printed.

> *Perpetui,*[3] *ambitâ, bis terrâ, premia lactis,*
> *Hæc habet altrici Capra secunda Jovis.*

The epigram written at Lord Anson's house[4] many years ago, 'where (says Mr. Johnson) I was well received and kindly treated, and with the true gratitude of a wit ridiculed the master of the house before I had left it an hour,' has been falsely printed in many papers since his death. I wrote it down from his own lips one evening in August 1772, not neglecting the little preface, accusing himself of making so graceless a return for the civilities shewn him. He had, among other elegancies about the park and gardens, been made to observe a temple to the winds, when this thought naturally presented itself *to a wit.*

> *Gratum animum laudo; Qui debuit omnia ventis,*
> *Quam bene ventorum, surgere templa jubet!*

A translation of Dryden's epigram[5] too, I used to fancy I had to myself.

> *Quos laudet vates, Graius, Romanus, et Anglus,*
> *Tres tria temporibus secla dedere suis:*
> *Sublime ingenium Graius,—Romanus habebat*
> *Carmen grande sonans, Anglus utrumque tulit.*
> *Nil majus natura capit; clarare priores*
> *Quæ potuere duos, tertius unus habet:*

from the famous lines written under Milton's picture:

Three poets in three distant ages born,
Greece, Italy, and England did adorn:
The first in loftiness of thought surpast,
The next in majesty; in both the last.
The force of Nature could no further go,
To make a third she join'd the former two.

One evening in the oratorio season of the year 1771, Mr. Johnson went
with me to Covent-Garden theatre;[1] and though he was for the most
part an exceedingly bad playhouse companion, as his person drew
people's eyes upon the box, and the loudness of his voice made it difficult
for me to hear any body but himself; he sat surprisingly quiet, and I
flattered myself that he was listening to the music. When we were got
home however he repeated these verses, which he said he had made at
the oratorio, and he bid me translate them.

IN THEATRO

Tertii verso quatre orbe lustri
Quid theatrales tibi crispe pompæ![2]
Quam decet canos male literatos
                              Sera voluptas!

Tene mulceri fidibus canoris?
Tene cantorum modulis stupere?
Tene per pictas oculo elegante
                              Currere formas?

Inter equales sine felle liber,
Codices veri studiosus inter
Rectius vives, sua quisque carpat
                              Gaudia gratus.

Lusibus gaudet puer otiosis
Luxus oblectat juvenem theatri,
At seni fluxo sapienter uti
                              Tempore restat.

I gave him the following lines in imitation, which he liked well enough, I
think:

When threescore years have chill'd thee quite,
Still can theatric scenes delight?
Ill suits this place with learned wight,
                              May Bates or Coulson[3] cry.

The scholar's pride can Brent[4] disarm?
His heart can soft Guadagni[5] warm?
Or scenes with sweet delusion charm
                              The climacteric eye?[6]

The social club, the lonely tower,
Far better suit thy midnight hour;
Let each according to his power
                              In worth or wisdom shine!

And while play pleases idle boys,
And wanton mirth fond youth employs,
To fix the soul, and free from toys,
>> That useful talk be thine.

The copy of verses in Latin hexameters, as well as I remember, which he wrote to Dr. Lawrence,[1] I forgot to keep a copy of; and he obliged me to resign his translation of the song beginning, *Busy, curious, thirsty fly*, for him to give Mr. Langton,[2] with a promise *not* to retain a copy. I concluded he knew why, so never enquired the reason. He had the greatest possible value for Mr. Langton, of whose virtue and learning he delighted to talk in very exalted terms; and poor Dr. Lawrence had long been his friend and confident. The conversation I saw them hold together in Essex-street one day in the year 1781 or 1782,[3] was a melancholy one, and made a singular impression on my mind. He was himself exceedingly ill, and I accompanied him thither for advice. The physician was however, in some respects, more to be pitied than the patient: Johnson was panting under an asthma and dropsy; but Lawrence had been brought home that very morning struck with the palsy, from which he had, two hours before we came, strove to awaken himself by blisters: they were both deaf, and scarce able to speak besides; one from difficulty of breathing, the other from paralytic debility. To give and receive medical counsel therefore, they fairly sate down on each side a table in the Doctor's gloomy apartment, adorned with skeletons, preserved monsters, &c. and agreed to write Latin billets to each other: such a scene did I never see! 'You (said Johnson) are *timidè* and *gelidè*;' finding that his friend had prescribed palliative not drastic remedies. It is not *me*, replies poor Lawrence in an interrupted voice; 'tis nature that is *gelidè* and *timidè*. In fact he lived but few months after[4] I believe, and retained his faculties still a shorter time. He was a man of strict piety and profound learning, but little skilled in the knowledge of life or manners, and died without having ever enjoyed the reputation he so justly deserved.

Mr. Johnson's health had been always extremely bad since I first knew him, and his over-anxious care to retain without blemish the perfect sanity of his mind, contributed much to disturb it. He had studied medicine diligently in all its branches; but had given particular attention to the diseases of the imagination,[5] which he watched in himself with a solicitude destructive of his own peace, and intolerable to those he trusted. Dr. Lawrence told him one day, that if he would come and beat him once a week he would bear it; but to hear his complaints was more than *man* could support. 'Twas therefore that he tried, I suppose, and in eighteen years contrived to weary the patience of a *woman*.[6] When Mr. Johnson felt his fancy, or fancied he felt it, disordered, his constant recurrence was to the study of arithmetic; and one day that he was totally confined to his chamber, and I enquired what he had been doing to divert himself; he shewed me a calculation which I could scarce be made to understand, so vast was the plan of it, and so very intricate were the figures: no other indeed than the national debt, computing it at one hundred and eighty millions sterling, would, if converted into silver, serve to make a meridian of that metal, I forget how broad, for the globe of the whole earth, the real *globe*. On a similar occasion I asked him (knowing what subject he would like best to talk upon), How his opinion stood towards the question between Paschal and Soame Jennings[1] about number and numeration? as the French philosopher observes that infinity, though on all sides astonishing, appears most so when the idea is connected with the idea of number; for the notion of infinite number, and infinite number we know there is, stretches one's capacity still more than the idea of infinite space: 'Such a notion indeed (adds he) can scarcely find room in the human mind.' Our English author on the other hand exclaims, let no man give himself leave to talk about infinite number, for infinite number is a contradiction in terms; whatever is once numbered, we all see cannot be infinite. 'I think (said Mr. Johnson after a pause) we must settle the matter thus: numeration is certainly infinite, for eternity might be employed in adding unit to unit; but every number is in itself finite, as the possibility of doubling it easily proves: besides, stop at what point you will, you find yourself as far from infinitudes as ever.' These passages I wrote down as soon as I had heard them, and repent that I did not take the same method with a dissertation he made one day that he was very ill, concerning the peculiar properties of the number Sixteen, which I afterwards tried, but in vain, to make him repeat.

As ethics or figures, or metaphysical reasoning, was the sort of talk he most delighted in, so no kind of conversation pleased him less I think, than when the subject was historical fact or general polity. 'What shall we learn from *that* stuff (said he)? let us not fancy like Swift[2] that we are exalting a woman's character by telling how she

> Could name the ancient heroes round,
> Explain for what they were renown'd, &c.'

I must not however lead my readers to suppose that he meant to reserve such talk for *men's* company as a proof of pre-eminence. 'He never (as he expressed it) desired to hear of the *Punic war*[3] while he lived: such conversation was lost time (he said), and carried one away from common life, leaving no ideas behind which could serve *living wight*[4] as warning or direction.'

> How I should act is not the case,
> But how would Brutus in my place?

'And now (cries Mr. Johnson, laughing with obstreperous violence), if these two foolish lines can be equalled in folly, except by the two succeeding ones[1]—shew them me.'

I asked him once concerning the conversation powers of a gentleman[2] with whom I was myself unacquainted—'He talked to me at club one day (replies our Doctor) concerning Catiline's conspiracy—so I withdrew my attention, and thought about Tom Thumb.'

Modern politics fared no better. I was one time extolling the character of a statesman, and expatiating on the skill required to direct the different currents, reconcile the jarring interests, &c. 'Thus (replies he) a mill is a complicated piece of mechanism enough, but the water is no part of the workmanship.'——On another occasion, when some one lamented the weakness of a then present minister,[3] and complained that he was dull and tardy, and knew little of affairs,—'You may as well complain, Sir (says Johnson), that the accounts of time are kept by the clock; for he certainly does stand still upon the stair-head—and we all know that he is no great chronologer.'——In the year 1777, or thereabouts, when all the talk was of an invasion,[4] he said most pathetically one afternoon, 'Alas! alas! how this unmeaning stuff spoils all my comfort in my friends conversation! Will the people never have done with it; and shall I never hear a sentence again without the *French* in it? Here is no invasion coming, and you *know* there is none. Let the vexatious and frivolous talk alone, or suffer it at least to teach you *one* truth; and learn by this perpetual echo of even unapprehended distress, how historians magnify events expected, or calamities endured; when you know they are at this very moment collecting all the big words they can find, in which to describe a consternation never felt, for a misfortune which never happened. Among all your lamentations, who eats the less? Who sleeps the worse, for one general's ill success, or another's capitulation? *Oh, pray* let us hear no more of it!'——No man however was more zealously attached to his party; he not only loved a tory himself, but he loved a man the better if he heard he hated a whig. 'Dear Bathurst[5] (said he to me one day) was a man to my very heart's content: he hated a fool, and he hated a rogue, and he hated a *whig*; he was a very good *hater*.'

Some one mentioned a gentleman[6] of that party for having behaved oddly on an occasion where faction was not concerned:—'Is he not a citizen of London, a native of North America, and a whig? (says Johnson)—Let him be absurd, I beg of you: when a monkey is *too* like a man, it shocks one.'

Severity towards the poor was, in Dr. Johnson's opinion (as is visible in his Life of Addison[7] particularly), an undoubted and constant attendant or consequence upon whiggism; and he was not contented with giving them relief, he wished to add also indulgence. He loved the poor as I never yet saw any one else do, with an earnest desire to make them happy.—What signifies, says some one, giving halfpence to common beggars? they only lay it out in gin or tobacco. 'And why should they be denied such sweeteners of their existence (says Johnson)? it is surely very savage to refuse them every possible avenue to pleasure, reckoned too coarse for our own acceptance. Life is a pill which none of us can bear to swallow without gilding; yet for the poor we delight in stripping it still barer, and are not ashamed to shew even visible displeasure, if ever the bitter taste is taken from their mouths.' In consequence of these principles he nursed whole nests of people in his house, where the lame, the blind, the sick, and the sorrowful found a sure retreat from all the evils whence his little income could secure them: and commonly spending the middle of the week at our house, he kept his numerous family in Fleet-street upon a settled allowance; but returned to them every Saturday, to give them three good dinners, and his company, before he came back to us on the Monday night——treating them with the same, or perhaps more ceremonious civility, than he would have done by as many people of fashion——making the holy scriptures thus the rule of his conduct, and only expecting salvation as he was able to obey its precepts.

While Dr. Johnson possessed however the strongest compassion for poverty or illness, he did not even pretend to feel for those who lamented the loss of a child, a parent, or a friend.——'These are the distresses of sentiment (he would reply) which a man who is really to be pitied has no leisure to feel. The sight of people who want food and raiment is so common in great cities, that a surly fellow like me, has no compassion to spare for wounds given only to vanity or softness.' No man, therefore, who smarted from the ingratitude of his friends, found any sympathy from our philosopher: 'Let him do good on higher motives next time,' would be the answer; 'he will then be sure of his reward.'——It is easy to observe, that the justice of such sentences made them offensive; but we must be careful how we condemn a man for saying what we know to be true, only because it *is* so. I hope that the reason our hearts rebelled a little against his severity, was chiefly because it came from a living mouth.—Books were invented to take off the odium of immediate superiority, and soften the rigour of duties prescribed by the teachers and censors of human kind—setting at least those who are acknowledged wiser than ourselves at a distance. When we recollect however, that for this very reason *they* are seldom consulted and little obeyed, how much cause shall his contemporaries have to rejoice that their living Johnson forced them to feel the reproofs due to vice and folly—while Seneca and Tillotson[1] were no longer able to make impression—except on our shelves. Few things indeed which pass well enough with others would do with him: he had been a great reader of Mandeville,[1] and was ever on the watch to spy out those stains of original corruption, so easily discovered by a penetrating observer even in the purest minds. I mentioned an event, which if it had happened would greatly have injured Mr. Thrale and his family——and then dear Sir, said I, how sorry you would have been! 'I *hope* (replied he after a long pause)—I should have been *very* sorry;—— but remember Rochefoucault's maxim.'[2]——I would rather (answered I) remember Prior's verses,[3] and ask,

> What need of books these truths to tell,
> Which folks perceive that cannot spell?
> And must we spectacles apply,
> To see what hurts our naked eye?

Will *any* body's mind bear this eternal microscope that you place upon your own so? 'I never (replied he) saw one that *would*, except that of my dear Miss Reynolds[4]—and her's is very near to purity itself.'——Of slighter evils, and friends less distant than our own household, he spoke less cautiously. An acquaintance[5] lost the almost certain hope of a good estate that had been long expected. Such a one will grieve (said I) at her friend's disappointment. 'She will suffer as much perhaps (said he) as your horse did when your cow miscarried.'——I professed myself sincerely grieved when accumulated distress crushed Sir George Cole-brook's family;[6] and I was so. 'Your own prosperity (said he) may possibly have so far increased the natural tenderness of your heart, for that aught I know you *may* be a *little sorry*; but it is sufficient for a plain man if he does not laugh when he sees a fine new house tumble down all on a sudden, and a snug cottage stand by ready to receive the owner, whose birth entitled him to nothing better, and whose limbs are left him to go to work again with.'

I used to tell him in jest, that his morality was easily contented; and when I have said something as if the wickedness of the world gave me concern, he would cry out aloud against canting, and protest that he thought there was very little gross wickedness in the world, and still less of extraordinary virtue. Nothing indeed more surely disgusted Dr. John-son than hyperbole; he loved not to be told of sallies of excellence, which he said were seldom valuable, and seldom true. 'Heroic virtues (said he) are the *bons mots* of life; they do not appear often, and when they do appear are too much prized I think; like the aloe-tree, which shoots and flowers once in a hundred years. But life is made up of little things; and that character is the best which does little but repeated acts of beneficence; as that conversation is the best which consists in elegant and pleasing thoughts expressed in natural and pleasing terms. With

A page from Shaw's Analysis of the Galic Language, 1778

24   AN ANALYSIS OF

Of the *second Declension Indefinite.*

Masculine Gender.   Singular Number.

N. *Cretoir,* an animal.
G. *Cretoir,* of an animal.
D. *Do chretoir,* to an animal.
A. *Cretoir,* an animal.
V. *O! chretoir,* O animal!
A. *Le cretoir,* with an animal.

Plural.

N. *Cretoira,* or *cretoiran,* animals.
G. *Chretoira,* of animals.
D. *Do chretoira,* to animals.
A. *Cretoira,* animals.
V. *O! chretoira,* O animals!
A. *Le cretoira,* with animals.

Definitely.

Singular.

N. *An cretoir,* the animal.
G. *A' chretoir,* of the animal.
D. *Do'n chretoir,* to the animal.
A. *An cretoir,* the animal.
V. *O! an cretoir,* O the animal!
A. *Leis an chretoir,* with the animal.

8

Plural.

Title page from Shaw's book on Ossian, 1781

AN
ENQUIRY
INTO THE
AUTHENTICITY
OF THE
Poems ascribed to OSSIAN.

BY

W. SHAW, A.M. F.S.A.

Author of the GALIC DICTIONARY and GRAMMAR,

LONDON:

PRINTED FOR J. MURRAY, Nº 32, FLEET-STREET.

M.DCC.LXXXI.

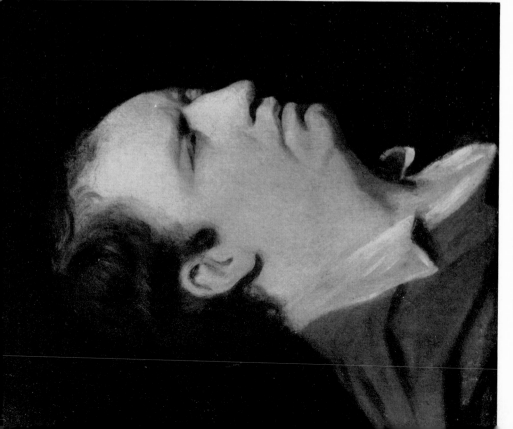

Mrs. Elizabeth Johnson

Samuel Johnson, after Reynolds

regard to my own notions of moral virtue (continued he), I hope I have not lost my sensibility of wrong; but I hope likewise that I have lived long enough in the world, to prevent me from expecting to find any action of which both the original motive and all the parts were good.'

The piety of Dr. Johnson was exemplary and edifying: he was punctiliously exact to perform every public duty enjoined by the church, and his spirit of devotion had an energy that affected all who ever saw him pray in private. The coldest and most languid hearer of the word must have felt themselves animated by his manner of reading the holy scriptures; and to pray by his sick bed, required strength of body as well as of mind, so vehement were his manners, and his tones of voice so pathetic. I have many times made it my request to heaven that I might be spared the sight of his death; and I was spared it![1]

Mr. Johnson, though in general a gross feeder, kept fast in Lent, particularly the holy week, with a rigour very dangerous to his general health; but though he had left off wine[2] (for religious motives as I always believed, though he did not own it), yet he did not hold the commutation of offences by voluntary penance, or encourage others to practice severity upon themselves. He even once said, 'that he thought it an error to endeavour at pleasing God by taking the rod of reproof[3] out of his hands.' And when we talked of convents, and the hardships suffered in them—'Remember always (said he) that a convent is an idle place, and where there is nothing to be *done* something must be *endured*:[4] mustard has a bad taste *per se* you may observe, but very insipid food cannot be eaten without it.'

His respect however for places of religious retirement was carried to the greatest degree of earthly veneration: the Benedictine convent at Paris paid him all possible honours in return, and the Prior and he[5] parted with tears of tenderness. Two of that college[6] being sent to England on the mission some years after, spent much of their time with him at Bolt Court I know, and he was ever earnest to retain their friendship; but though beloved by all his Roman Catholic acquaintance, particularly Dr. Nugent,[7] for whose esteem he had a singular value, yet was Mr. Johnson a most unshaken church of England man; and I think, or at least I once *did* think, that a letter[8] written by him to Mr. Barnard the King's librarian, when he was in Italy collecting books, contained some very particular advice to his friend to be on his guard against the seductions of the church of Rome.

The settled aversion Dr. Johnson felt towards an infidel he expressed to all ranks, and at all times, without the smallest reserve; for though on common occasions he paid great deference to birth or title, yet his regard for truth and virtue never gave way to meaner considerations.

We talked of a dead wit one evening, and somebody praised him—'Let us never praise talents so ill employed, Sir; we foul our mouths by commending such infidels (said he).' Allow him the *lumiéres*[1] at least, intreated one of the company—'I do allow him, Sir (replied Johnson), just enough to light him to hell.'——Of a Jamaica gentleman, then lately dead[2]—'He will not, whither he is now gone (said Johnson), find much difference, I believe, either in the climate or the company.'—— The Abbé Reynal[3] probably remembers that, being at the house of a common friend in London, the master of it approached Johnson with that gentleman so much celebrated in his hand, and this speech in his mouth: Will you permit me, Sir, to present to you the Abbé Reynal? '*No, Sir*,' (replied the Doctor very loud) and suddenly turned away from them both.

Though Mr. Johnson had but little reverence either for talents or fortune, when he found them unsupported by virtue; yet it was sufficient to tell him a man was very pious, or very charitable, and he would at least *begin* with him on good terms, however the conversation might end. He would, sometimes too, good-naturedly enter into a long chat for the instruction or entertainment of people he despised. I perfectly recollect his condescending to delight my daughter's dancing-master with a long argument about *his* art; which the man protested, at the close of the discourse, the Doctor knew more of than himself; who remained astonished, enlightened, and amused by the talk of a person little likely to make a good disquisition upon dancing. I have sometimes indeed been rather pleased than vexed when Mr. Johnson has given a rough answer to a man who perhaps deserved one only half as rough, because I knew he would repent of his hasty reproof, and make us all amends by some conversation at once instructive and entertaining, as in the following cases: A young fellow asked him abruptly one day, Pray, Sir, what and where is Palmira? I heard somebody talk last night of the ruins of Palmira. ' 'Tis a hill in Ireland (replies Johnson), with palms growing on the top, and a bog at the bottom, and so they call it *Palm-mira*.' Seeing however that the lad thought him serious, and thanked him for the information, he undeceived him very gently indeed; told him the history, geography, and chronology of Tadmor in the wilderness,[4] with every incident that literature could furnish I think, or eloquence express, from the building of Solomon's palace to the voyage of Dawkins and Wood.[5]

On another occasion, when he was musing over the fire in our drawing-room at Streatham, a young gentleman[6] called to him suddenly, and I suppose he thought disrespectfully, in these words: Mr. Johnson, Would you advise me to marry? 'I would advise no man to marry, Sir (returns for answer in a very angry tone Dr. Johnson), who is not likely to propagate understanding;' and so left the room. Our companion looked confounded, and I believe had scarce recovered the consciousness of his own existence, when Johnson came back, and drawing his chair among us, with altered looks and a softened voice, joined in the general chat, insensibly led the conversation to the subject of marriage,[1] where he laid himself out in a dissertation so useful, so elegant, so founded on the true knowledge of human life, and so adorned with beauty of sentiment, that no one ever recollected the offence, except to rejoice in its consequences. He repented just as certainly however, if he had been led to praise any person or thing by accident more than he thought it deserved; and was on such occasions comically earnest to destroy the praise or pleasure he had unintentionally given.

Sir Joshua Reynolds mentioned some picture as excellent. 'It has often grieved me, Sir (said Mr. Johnson), to see so much mind as the science of painting requires, laid out upon such perishable materials: why do not you oftener make use of copper? I could wish your superiority in the art you profess, to be preserved in stuff more durable than canvas.' Sir Joshua urged the difficulty of procuring a plate large enough for historical subjects, and was going to raise further objections: 'What foppish[2] obstacles are these! (exclaims on a sudden Dr. Johnson:) Here is Thrale has a thousand tun of copper; you may paint it all round if you will, I suppose; it will serve him to brew in afterwards: Will it not, Sir?' (to my husband who sat by.) Indeed Dr. Johnson's utter scorn of painting was such, that I have heard him say, that he should sit very quietly in a room hung round with the works of the greatest masters, and never feel the slightest disposition to turn them if their backs were outermost, unless it might be for the sake of telling Sir Joshua that he *had* turned them. Such speeches may appear offensive to many, but those who knew he was too blind to discern the perfections of an art which applies itself immediately to our eye-sight, must acknowledge he was not in the wrong.

He delighted no more in music than painting; he was almost as deaf as he was blind: travelling with Dr. Johnson was for these reasons tiresome enough. Mr. Thrale loved prospects, and was mortified that his friend could not enjoy the sight of those different dispositions of wood and water, hill and valley, that travelling through England and France affords a man. But when he wished to point them out to his companion: 'Never heed such nonsense,' would be the reply: 'a blade of grass is always a blade of grass,[3] whether in one country or another: let us if we *do* talk, talk about something; men and women are my subjects of enquiry; let us see how these differ from those we have left behind.'

When we were at Rouen together,[4] he took a great fancy to the Abbé

Roffette, with whom he conversed about the destruction of the order of Jesuits, and condemned it loudly, as a blow to the general power of the church, and likely to be followed with many and dangerous innovations, which might at length become fatal to religion itself, and shake even the foundation of Christianity. The gentleman seemed to wonder and delight in his conversation: the talk was all in Latin, which both spoke fluently, and Mr. Johnson pronounced a long eulogium upon Milton with so much ardour, eloquence, and ingenuity, that the Abbé rose from his seat and embraced him. My husband seeing them apparently so charmed with the company of each other, politely invited the Abbé to England, intending to oblige his friend; who, instead of thanking, reprimanded him severely before the man, for such a sudden burst of tenderness towards a person he could know nothing at all of; and thus put a sudden finish to all his own and Mr. Thrale's entertainment, from the company of the Abbé Roffette.

When at Versailles the people shewed us the theatre. As we stood on the stage looking at some machinery for playhouse purposes: Now we are here, what shall we act, Mr. Johnson,—The Englishman at Paris? 'No, no (replied he), we will try to act Harry the Fifth.'[1] His dislike of the French was well known to both nations, I believe; but he applauded the number of their books and the graces of their style. 'They have few sentiments (said he), but they express them neatly; they have little meat too, but they dress it well.' Johnson's own notions about eating however were nothing less than delicate; a leg of pork boiled till it dropped from the bone, a veal-pye with plums and sugar, or the outside cut of a salt buttock of beef, were his favourite dainties: with regard to drink, his liking was for the strongest, as it was not the flavour, but the effect he sought for, and professed to desire; and when I first knew him, he used to pour capillaire[2] into his Port wine. For the last twelve years however, he left off all fermented liquors. To make himself some amends indeed, he took his chocolate liberally, pouring in large quantities of cream, or even melted butter; and was so fond of fruit, that though he usually eat seven or eight large peaches of a morning before breakfast began, and treated them with proportionate attention after dinner again, yet I have heard him protest that he never had quite as much as he wished of wall-fruit, except once in his life, and that was when we were all together at Ombersley, the seat of my Lord Sandys.[3] I was saying to a friend one day, that I did not like goose; one smells it so while it is roasting, said I: 'But you, Madam (replies the Doctor), have been at all times a fortunate woman, having always had your hunger so forestalled by indulgence, that you never experienced the delight of smelling your dinner before-hand.' Which pleasure, answered I pertly, is to be enjoyed in perfection by such as have the happiness to pass through Porridge-Island* of a morning. 'Come, come (says he gravely), let's have no sneering at what is serious to so many: hundreds of your fellow-creatures, dear Lady, turn another way, that they may not be tempted by the luxuries of Porridge-Island to wish for gratifications they are not able to obtain: you are certainly not better than all of *them*; give God thanks that you are happier.'

I received on another occasion as just a rebuke from Mr. Johnson, for an offence of the same nature, and hope I took care never to provoke a third; for after a very long summer particularly hot and dry, I was wishing naturally but thoughtlessly for some rain to lay the dust as we drove along the Surry roads. 'I cannot bear (replied he, with much asperity and an altered look), when I know how many poor families will perish next winter for want of that bread which the present drought will deny them, to hear ladies sighing for rain, only that their complexions may not suffer from the heat, or their clothes be incommoded by the dust;— for shame! leave off such foppish¹ lamentations, and study to relieve those whose distresses are real.'

With advising others to be charitable however, Dr. Johnson did not content himself. He gave away all he had, and all he ever had gotten, except the two thousand pounds he left behind; and the very small portion of his income which he spent on himself, with all our calculation, we never could make more than seventy, or at most fourscore pounds a year, and he pretended to allow himself a hundred. He had numberless dependents out of doors as well as in, 'who, as he expressed it, did not like to see him latterly unless he brought 'em money.' For those people he used frequently to raise contributions on his richer friends; 'and this (says he) is one of the thousand reasons which ought to restrain a man from drony² solitude and useless retirement. Solitude (added he one day) is dangerous to reason, without being favourable to virtue: pleasures of some sort are necessary to the intellectual as to the corporeal health; and those who resist gaiety, will be likely for the most part to fall a sacrifice to appetite; for the solicitations of sense are always at hand, and a dram to a vacant and solitary person is a speedy and seducing relief. Remember (continued he) that the solitary mortal is certainly luxurious,³ probably superstitious, and possibly mad:⁴ the mind stagnates for want of employment, grows morbid, and is extinguished like a candle in foul air.' It was on this principle that Johnson encouraged parents to carry their daughters early and much into company: 'for what harm can be

* Porridge-Island is a mean street in London, filled with cook-shops for the convenience of the poorer inhabitants; the real name of it I know not, but suspect that it is generally known by, to have been originally a term of derision.

done before so many witnesses? Solitude is the surest nurse of all prurient passions, and a girl in the hurry of preparation, or tumult of gaiety, has neither inclination nor leisure to let tender expressions soften or sink into her heart. The ball, the show, are not the dangerous places: no, 'tis the private friend, the kind consoler, the companion of the easy vacant hour, whose compliance with her opinions can flatter her vanity, and whose conversation can just sooth, without ever stretching her mind, that is the lover to be feared: he who buzzes in her ear at court, or at the opera, must be contented to buzz in vain.' These notions Dr. Johnson carried so very far, that I have heard him say, 'if you would shut up any man with any woman, so as to make them derive their whole pleasure from each other, they would inevitably fall in love, as it is called, with each other; but at six months end if you would throw them both into public life where they might change partners at pleasure, each would soon forget that fondness which mutual dependance, and the paucity of general amusement alone, had caused, and each would separately feel delighted by their release.'

In these opinions Rousseau[1] apparently concurs with him exactly; and Mr. Whitehead's poem called *Variety*,[2] is written solely to elucidate this simple proposition. Prior[3] likewise advises the husband to send his wife abroad, and let her see the world as it really stands——

> Powder, and pocket-glass, and beau.

Mr. Johnson was indeed unjustly supposed to be a lover of singularity. Few people had a more settled reverence for the world than he, or was less captivated by new modes of behaviour introduced, or innovations on the long-received customs of common life. He hated the way of leaving a company without taking notice to the lady of the house that he was going; and did not much like any contrivances by which ease has been lately introduced into society[4] instead of ceremony, which had more of his approbation. Cards,[5] dress, and dancing however, all found their advocates in Dr. Johnson, who inculcated, upon principle, the cultivation of those arts, which many a moralist thinks himself bound to reject, and many a Christian holds unfit to be practised. 'No person (said he one day) goes under-dressed till he thinks himself of consequence enough to forbear carrying the badge of his rank upon his back.' And in answer to the arguments urged by Puritans, Quakers, &c. against showy decorations of the human figure, I once heard him exclaim, 'Oh, let us not be found when our Master calls us, ripping the lace off our waistcoats, but the spirit of contention from our souls and tongues! Let us all conform in outward customs, which are of no consequence, to the manners of those whom we live among, and despise such paltry distinctions.

Alas, Sir (continued he), a man who cannot get to heaven in a green coat, will not find his way thither the sooner in a grey one.'[1] On an occasion of less consequence, when he turned his back on Lord Bolingbroke[2] in the rooms at Brighthelmstone, he made this excuse: 'I am not obliged, Sir (said he to Mr. Thrale, who stood fretting), to find reasons for respecting the rank of him who will not condescend to declare it by his dress or some other visible mark: what are stars and other signs of superiority made for?'

The next evening however he made us comical amends, by sitting by the same nobleman, and haranguing very loudly about the nature and use and abuse of divorces.[3] Many people gathered round them to hear what was said, and when my husband called him away, and told him to whom he had been talking—received an answer which I will not write down.

Though no man perhaps made such rough replies as Dr. Johnson, yet nobody had a more just aversion to general satire;[4] he always hated and censured Swift[5] for his unprovoked bitterness against the professors of medicine; and used to challenge his friends, when they lamented the exorbitancy of physicians fees, to produce him one instance of an estate raised by physic in England. When an acquaintance[6] too was one day exclaiming against the tediousness of the law and its partiality; 'Let us hear, Sir (said Johnson), no general abuse; the law[7] is the last result of human wisdom acting upon human experience for the benefit of the public.'

As the mind of Dr. Johnson was greatly expanded, so his first care was for general, not particular or petty morality; and those teachers had more of his blame than praise, I think, who seek to oppress life with unnecessary scruples: 'Scruples would (as he observed) certainly make men miserable, and seldom make them good. Let us ever (he said) studiously fly from those instructors against whom our Saviour denounces heavy judgments, for having bound up burdens grievous to be borne,[8] and laid them on the shoulders of mortal men.' No one had however higher notions of the hard task of true Christianity than Johnson, whose daily terror lest he had not done enough, originated in piety, but ended in little less than disease. Reasonable with regard to others, he had formed vain hopes of performing impossibilities himself; and finding his good works ever below his desires and intent, filled his imagination with fears that he should never obtain forgiveness for omissions of duty and criminal waste of time. These ideas kept him in constant anxiety concerning his salvation; and the vehement petitions he perpetually made for a longer continuance on earth, were doubtless the cause of his so prolonged existence; for when I carried Dr. Pepys[9] to him in the year

1782, it appeared wholly impossible for any skill of the physician or any strength of the patient to save him. He was saved that time however by Sir Lucas's prescriptions; and less skill on one side, or less strength on the other, I am morally certain, would not have been enough. He had however possessed an athletic constitution, as he said the man who dipped people in the sea at Brighthelmstone acknowledged; for seeing Mr. Johnson swim in the year 1766, Why Sir (says the dipper), you must have been a stout-hearted gentleman forty years ago.

Mr. Thrale and he used to laugh about that story very often: but Garrick told a better, for he said that in their young days, when some strolling players came to Litchfield, our friend had fixed his place upon the stage, and got himself a chair accordingly; which leaving for a few minutes, he found a man in it at his return, who refused to give it back at the first intreaty: Mr. Johnson however, who did not think it worth his while to make a second, took chair and man and all together, and threw them all at once into the pit. I asked the Doctor if this was a fact? 'Garrick has not *spoiled* it in the telling (said he), it is very *near* true to be sure.'

Mr. Beauclerc[1] too related one day, how on some occasion he ordered two large mastiffs into his parlour, to shew a friend who was conversant in canine beauty and excellence, how the dogs quarrelled, and fastening on each other, alarmed all the company except Johnson, who seizing one in one hand by the cuff of the neck, the other in the other hand, said gravely, 'Come, gentlemen! where's your difficulty? put one dog out at the door, and I will shew this fierce gentleman the way out of the window:' which, lifting up the mastiff and the sash, he contrived to do very expeditiously, and much to the satisfaction of the affrighted company. We inquired as to the truth of this curious recital. 'The dogs have been somewhat magnified, I believe Sir (was the reply): they were, as I remember, two stout young pointers; but the story has gained but little.'

One reason why Mr. Johnson's memory was so particularly exact, might be derived from his rigid attention to veracity;[2] being always resolved to relate every fact as it stood, he looked even on the smaller parts of life with minute attention, and remembered such passages as escape cursory and common observers. 'A story (says he) is a specimen of human manners, and derives its sole value from its truth. When Foote[3] has told me something, I dismiss it from my mind like a passing shadow: when Reynolds tells me something, I consider myself as possessed of an idea the more.'

Mr. Johnson liked a frolic or a jest well enough; though he had strange serious rules about it too: and very angry was he if any body offered to be merry when he was disposed to be grave. 'You have an ill-

founded notion (said he) that it is clever to turn matters off with a joke
(as the phrase is); whereas nothing produces enmity so certain, as one
person's shewing a disposition to be merry when another is inclined to
be either serious or displeased.'

One may gather from this how he felt, when his Irish friend Grierson,[1]
hearing him enumerate the qualities necessary to the formation of a poet,
began a comical parody upon his ornamented harangue in praise of a
cook, concluding with this observation, that he who dressed a good
dinner was a more excellent and a more useful member of society than
he who wrote a good poem. 'And in this opinion (said Mr. Johnson in
reply) all the dogs in the town will join you.'

Of this Mr. Grierson I have heard him relate many droll stories, much
to his advantage as a wit, together with some facts more difficult to be
accounted for; as avarice never was reckoned among the vices of the
laughing world. But Johnson's various life, and spirit of vigilance to
learn and treasure up every peculiarity of manner, sentiment, or general
conduct, made his company, when he chose to relate anecdotes of people
he had formerly known, exquisitely amusing and comical.[2] It is indeed
inconceivable what strange occurrences he had seen, and what surprising
things he could tell when in a communicative humour. It is by no means
my business to relate memoirs of his acquaintance; but it will serve to
shew the character of Johnson himself, when I inform those who never
knew him, that no man told a story with so good a grace, or knew so
well what would make an effect upon his auditors. When he raised
contributions for some distressed author, or wit in want, he often made
us all more than amends by diverting descriptions of the lives they were
then passing in corners unseen by any body but himself; and that odd
old surgeon,[3] whom he kept in his house to tend the out-pensioners, and
of whom he said most truly and sublimely, that

> In misery's darkest caverns known,
>   His useful care was ever nigh,
> Where hopeless anguish pours her groan,
>   And lonely want retires to die.

I have forgotten the year, but it could scarcely I think be later than
1765 or 1766,[4] that he was called abruptly from our house after dinner,
and returning in about three hours, said, he had been with an enraged
author, whose landlady pressed him for payment within doors, while the
bailiffs beset him without; that he was drinking himself drunk with
Madeira to drown care, and fretting over a novel which when finished
was to be his whole fortune; but he could not get it done for distraction,
nor could he step out of doors to offer it to sale. Mr. Johnson therefore

set away the bottle, and went to the bookseller, recommending the performance, and desiring some immediate relief; which when he brought back to the writer, he called the woman of the house directly to partake of punch, and pass their time in merriment.

It was not till ten years after, I dare say, that something in Dr. Goldsmith's behaviour struck me with an idea that he was the very man, and then Johnson confessed that he was so; the novel was the charming Vicar of Wakefield.

There was a Mr. Boyce[1] too, who wrote some very elegant verses printed in the Magazines of five-and-twenty years ago, of whose ingenuity and distress I have heard Dr. Johnson tell some curious anecdotes; particularly, that when he was almost perishing with hunger, and some money was produced to purchase him a dinner, he got a bit of roast beef, but could not eat it without ketchup, and laid out the last half guinea he possessed in truffles and mushrooms, eating them in bed too, for want of clothes, or even a shirt to sit up in.

Another man[2] for whom he often begged, made as wild use of his friend's beneficence as these, spending in punch the solitary guinea which had been brought him one morning; when resolving to add another claimant to a share of the bowl, besides a woman who always lived with him, and a footman who used to carry out petitions for charity, he borrowed a chairman's watch, and pawning it for half a crown, paid a clergyman to marry him to a fellow-lodger in the wretched house they all inhabited, and got so drunk over the guinea bowl of punch the evening of his wedding-day, that having many years lost the use of one leg, he now contrived to fall from the top of the stairs to the bottom, and break his arm, in which condition his companions left him to call Mr. Johnson, who relating the series of his tragi-comical distresses, obtained from the Literary Club[3] a seasonable relief.

Of that respectable society I have heard him speak in the highest terms, and with a magnificent panegyric on each member, when it consisted only of a dozen or fourteen friends; but as soon as the necessity of enlarging it brought in new faces,[4] and took off from his confidence in the company, he grew less fond of the meeting, and loudly proclaimed his carelessness *who* might be admitted, when it was become a mere dinner club. I *think* the original names, when I first heard him talk with fervor of every member's peculiar powers of instructing or delighting mankind, were Sir John Hawkins,[5] Mr. Burke, Mr. Langton,[6] Mr. Beauclerc,[7] Dr. Percy, Dr. Nugent,[8] Dr. Goldsmith, Sir Robert Chambers,[9] Mr. Dyer,[10] and Sir Joshua Reynolds, whom he called their Romulus,[11] or said somebody else of the company called him so, which was more likely: but this was, I believe, in the year 1775 or 1776. It was a supper meeting then, and I fancy Dr. Nugent ordered an omelet sometimes on a Friday or Saturday night; for I remember Mr. Johnson felt very painful sensations at the sight of that dish soon after his death, and cried, 'Ah, my poor dear friend! I shall never eat omelet with *thee* again!' quite in an agony. The truth is, nobody suffered more from pungent sorrow at a friend's death than Johnson, though he would suffer no one else to complain of their losses in the same way; 'for (says he) we must either outlive our friends you know, or our friends must outlive us; and I see no man that would hesitate about the choice.'

Mr. Johnson loved late hours extremely, or more properly hated early ones. Nothing was more terrifying to him than the idea of retiring to bed, which he never would call going to rest, or suffer another to call so. 'I lie down (said he) that my acquaintance may sleep; but I lie down to endure oppressive misery, and soon rise again to pass the night in anxiety and pain.' By this pathetic manner, which no one ever possessed in so eminent a degree, he used to shock me from quitting his company, till I hurt my own health not a little by sitting up with him when I was myself far from well: nor was it an easy matter to oblige him even by compliance, for he always maintained that no one forbore their own gratifications for the sake of pleasing another, and if one *did* sit up it was probably to amuse one's self. Some right however he certainly had to say so, as he made his company exceedingly entertaining when he had once forced one, by his vehement lamentations and piercing reproofs, not to quit the room, but to sit quietly and make tea for him, as I often did in London till four o'clock in the morning. At Streatham indeed I managed better, having always some friend[1] who was kind enough to engage him in talk, and favour my retreat.

The first time I ever saw this extraordinary man was in the year 1764,[2] when Mr. Murphy, who had been long the friend and confidential intimate of Mr. Thrale, persuaded him to wish for Johnson's conversation, extolling it in terms which that of no other person could have deserved, till we were only in doubt how to obtain his company, and find an excuse for the invitation. The celebrity of Mr. Woodhouse[3] a shoemaker, whose verses were at that time the subject of common discourse, soon afforded a pretence, and Mr. Murphy brought Johnson to meet him, giving me general cautions not to be surprised at his figure, dress, or behaviour. What I recollect best of the day's talk, was his earnestly recommending Addison's works to Mr. Woodhouse as a model for imitation. 'Give nights and days,[4] Sir (said he), to the study of Addison, if you mean either to be a good writer, or what is more worth, an honest man.' When I saw something like the same expression in his criticism on that author, lately published, I put him in mind of his past injunctions to the young poet, to which he replied, 'that he wished the shoemaker might have remembered them as well.' Mr. Johnson liked his new acquaintance so much however, that from that time he dined with us every Thursday through the winter, and in the autumn of the next year he followed us to Brighthelmstone, whence we were gone before his arrival; so he was disappointed and enraged, and wrote us a letter[1] expressive of anger, which we were very desirous to pacify, and to obtain his company again if possible. Mr. Murphy brought him back to us again very kindly, and from that time his visits grew more frequent, till in the year 1766 his health, which he had always complained of, grew so exceedingly bad, that he could not stir out of his room in the court[2] he inhabited for many *weeks* together, I think *months*.

Mr. Thrale's attentions and my own now became so acceptable to him, that he often lamented to us the horrible condition of his mind, which he said was nearly distracted; and though he charged *us* to make him odd solemn promises of secrecy on so strange a subject, yet when we waited on him one morning, and heard him, in the most pathetic terms, beg the prayers of Dr. Delap,[3] who had left him as we came in, I felt excessively affected with grief, and well remember my husband involuntarily lifted up one hand to shut his mouth, from provocation at hearing a man so wildly proclaim what he could at last persuade no one to believe; and what, if true, would have been so very unfit to reveal.

Mr. Thrale went away soon after, leaving me with him, and bidding me to prevail on him to quit his close habitation in the court, and come with us to Streatham, where I undertook the care of his health, and had the honour and happiness of contributing to its restoration. This task, though distressing enough sometimes, would have been less so had not my mother and he disliked one another extremely, and teized me often with perverse opposition, petty contentions, and mutual complaints. Her superfluous attention to such accounts of the foreign politics as are transmitted to us by the daily prints, and her willingness to talk on subjects he could not endure, began the aversion; and when, by the peculiarity of his style, she found out that he teized her by writing in the newspapers concerning battles and plots which had no existence, only to feed her with new accounts of the division of Poland perhaps, or the disputes between the states of Russia and Turkey, she was exceedingly angry to be sure, and scarcely I think forgave the offence till the domestic distresses[4] of the year 1772 reconciled them to and taught them the true value of each other; excellent as *they both* were, far beyond the excellence of any other man and woman I ever yet saw. As her conduct too extorted his truest esteem, her cruel illness excited all his tenderness; nor was the sight of beauty, scarce to be subdued by disease, and wit, flashing through the apprehension of evil, a scene which Dr. Johnson could see without sensibility. He acknowledged himself improved by her piety, and astonished at her fortitude, and hung over her bed with the affection of a parent, and the reverence of a son.[1] Nor did it give me less pleasure to see her sweet mind cleared of all its latent prejudices, and left at liberty to admire and applaud that force of thought and versatility of genius, that comprehensive soul and benevolent heart which attracted and commanded veneration from all, but inspired peculiar sensations of delight mixed with reverence in those who, like her, had the opportunity to observe these qualities, stimulated by gratitude, and actuated by friendship. When Mr. Thrale's perplexities disturbed his peace, dear Dr. Johnson left him scarce a moment, and tried every artifice to amuse as well as every argument to console him: nor is it more possible to describe than to forget his prudent, his pious attentions towards the man who had some years before certainly saved his valuable life, perhaps his reason, by half obliging him to change the foul air of Fleet-street for the wholesome breezes of the Sussex Downs.

The epitaph engraved on my mother's monument[2] shews how deserving she was of general applause. I asked Johnson why he named her person before her mind: he said it was, 'because every body could judge of the one, and but few of the other.'

> *Juxta sepulta est* HESTERA MARIA
> *Thomæ Cotton de Combermere baronetti Cestriensis filia,*
> *Johannis Salusbury armigeri Flintiensis uxor.*
> *Forma felix, felix ingenio;*
> *Omnibus jucunda, suorum amantissima.*
> *Linguis artibusque ita exculta*
> *Ut loquenti nunquam deessent*
> *Sermonis nitor, sententiarum flosculi,*
> *Sapientiæ gravitas, leporum gratia:*
> *Modum servandi adeo perita,*
> *Ut domestica inter negotia literis oblectaretur.*
> *Literarum inter delicias, rem familiarem sedulo curaret,*
> *Multis illi multos annos precantibus*
> *diri carcinomatis veneno contabuit,*
> *nexibusque vitæ paulatim resolutis,*
> *é terris—meliora sperans—emigravit.*
> *Nata 1707. Nupta 1739. Obiit 1773.*

Mr. Murphy, who admired her talents and delighted in her company, did me the favour to paraphrase this elegant inscription in verses which I fancy have never yet been published. His fame has long been out of my power to increase as a poet; as a man of sensibility perhaps these lines may set him higher than he now stands. I remember with gratitude

the friendly tears which prevented him from speaking as he put them
into my hand.

Near this place
Are deposited the remains of
HESTER MARIA,
The daughter of Sir Thomas Cotton of Combermere, in the county of Cheshire, Bart.
the wife of John Salusbury,
of the county of Flint, Esquire. She was born in the year
1707, married in 1739, and died in 1773.

A pleasing form, where every grace combin'd,
With genius blest, a pure enlighten'd mind;
Benevolence on all that smiles bestow'd,
A heart that for her friends with love o'erflow'd:
In language skill'd, by science form'd to please,
Her mirth was wit, her gravity was ease.
Graceful in all, the happy mien she knew,
Which even to virtue gives the limits due;
Whate'er employ'd her, that she seem'd to chuse,
Her house, her friends, her business, or the muse.
Admir'd and lov'd, the theme of general praise,
All to such virtue wish'd a length of days:
But sad reverse! with slow-consuming pains,
Th'envenom'd cancer revell'd in her veins;
Prey'd on her spirits—stole each power away;
Gradual she sunk, yet smiling in decay;
She smil'd in hope, by sore afflictions try'd,
And in that hope the pious Christian died.

The following epitaph on Mr. Thrale, who has now a monument close
by her's in Streatham church, I have seen printed and commended in
Maty's Review[1] for April 1784; and a friend[2] has favoured me with the
translation.

Hic conditur quod reliquum est
HENRICI THRALE,
Qui res seu civiles, seu domesticas, ita egit,
Ut vitam illi longiorem multi optarent;
Ita sacras,
Ut quam brevem esset habiturus præscire videretur;
Simplex, apertus, sibique semper similis,
Nihil ostentavit aut arte fictum aut cura
Elaboratum.
In senatu, regi patriœque
Fideliter studuit;
Vulgi obstrepentis contemptor animosus,
Domi inter mille mercaturœ negotia
Literarum elegantiam minimè neglexit.
Amicis quocunque modo laborantibus,
Conciliis, auctoritate, muneribus adfuit.

Inter familiares, comites, convivas, hospites,
Tam facili fuit morum suavitate
Ut omnium animos ad se alliceret;
Tam felici sermonis libertate
Ut nulli adulatus, omnibus placeret.
Natus 1724. Ob. 1781.
Confortes tumuli habet Rodolphum patrem, strenuum
fortemque virum, et Henricum filium unicum,
quem spei parentum mors inopina decennem
præripuit.
Ita
Domus felix et opulenta, quam erexit
Avus, auxitque pater, cum nepote decidit.
Abi viator![1]
Et vicibus rerum humanarum perspectis,
Æternitatem cogita![2]

Here are deposited the remains of
HENRY THRALE,
Who managed all his concerns in the present
world, public and private, in such a manner
as to leave many wishing he had continued
longer in it;
And all that related to a future world,
as if he had been sensible how short a time he
was to continue in this.
Simple, open, and uniform in his manners,
his conduct was without either art or affectation.
In the senate steadily attentive to the true interests
of his king and country,
He looked down with contempt on the clamours
of the multitude:
Though engaged in a very extensive business,
He found some time to apply to polite literature:
And was ever ready to assist his friends
labouring under any difficulties,
with his advice, his influence, and his purse.
To his friends, acquaintance, and guests,
he behaved with such sweetness of manners
as to attach them all to his person:
So happy in his conversation with them,
as to please all, though he flattered none.
He was born in the year 1724, and died in 1781.
In the same tomb lie interred his father
Ralph Thrale, a man of vigour and activity,
And his only son Henry, who died before his father,
Aged ten years.
Thus a happy and opulent family,
Raised by the grandfather, and augmented by the
father, became extinguished with the grandson.

Go, Reader!
And reflecting on the vicissitudes of
all human affairs,
Meditate on eternity.

I never recollect to have heard that Dr. Johnson wrote inscriptions for any sepulchral stones, except Dr. Goldsmith's in Westminster abbey, and these two in Streatham church.[1] He made four lines once on the death of poor Hogarth, which were equally true and pleasing: I know not why Garrick's[2] were preferred to them.

The hand of him here torpid lies,
That drew th'essential form of grace;
Here clos'd in death th' attentive eyes,
That saw the manners in the face.

Mr. Hogarth,[3] among the variety of kindnesses shewn to me when I was too young to have a proper sense of them, was used to be very earnest that I should obtain the acquaintance, and if possible the friendship of Dr. Johnson, whose conversation was to the talk of other men, like Titian's painting compared to Hudson's,[4] he said: but don't you tell people now, that I say so (continued he), for the connoisseurs and I are at war you know; and because I hate *them,* they think I hate *Titian*— and let them! Many were indeed the lectures I used to have in my very early days from dear Mr. Hogarth, whose regard for my father induced him perhaps to take notice of his little girl, and give her some odd particular directions about dress, dancing, and many other matters, interesting now only because they were his. As he made all his talents, however, subservient to the great purposes of morality, and the earnest desire he had to mend mankind, his discourse commonly ended in an ethical dissertation, and a serious charge to me, never to forget his picture of the *Lady's last Stake*.[5] Of Dr. Johnson, when my father and he were talking together about him one day: That man (says Hogarth) is not contented with believing the Bible, but he fairly resolves, I think, to believe nothing *but* the Bible. Johnson (added he), though so wise a fellow, is more like king David than king Solomon;[6] for he says in his haste that all men are liars.[7] This charge, as I afterwards came to know, was but too well founded: Mr. Johnson's incredulity amounted almost to disease, and I have seen it mortify his companions exceedingly. But the truth is, Mr. Thrale had a very powerful influence over the Doctor, and could make him suppress many rough answers: he could likewise prevail on him to change his shirt, his coat, or his plate, almost before it came[8] indispensably necessary to the comfortable feelings of his friends: But as I never had any ascendancy at all over Mr. Johnson, except just

The Thrales' house at Streatham

Johnson's introduction to a Highland hut

in the things that concerned his health, it grew extremely perplexing
and difficult to live in the house with him when the master of it was no
more;[1] the worse indeed, because his dislikes grew capricious; and he
could scarce bear to have any body come to the house whom it was
absolutely necessary for me to see. Two gentlemen, I perfectly well
remember, dining with us at Streatham in the summer 1782, when
Elliot's brave defence of Gibraltar[2] was a subject of common discourse,
one of these men naturally enough begun some talk about red-hot balls
thrown with surprising dexterity and effect: which Dr. Johnson having
listened some time to, 'I would advise you, Sir (said he with a cold sneer),
never to relate this story again: you really can scarce imagine how *very
poor* a figure you make in the telling of it.' Our guest being bred a
Quaker, and I believe a man of an extremely gentle disposition, needed
no more reproofs for the same folly; so if he ever did speak again, it was
in a low voice to the friend who came with him. The check was given
before dinner, and after coffee I left the room. When in the evening however our companions were returned to London, and Mr. Johnson and
myself were left alone, with only our usual family about us, 'I did not
quarrel with those Quaker fellows,' (said he, very seriously.) You did
perfectly right, replied I; for they gave you no cause of offence. 'No
offence! (returned he with an altered voice;) and is it nothing then to sit
whispering together when *I* am present, without ever directing their
discourse towards me, or offering me a share in the conversation?' That
was, because you frightened him who spoke first about those hot balls.
'Why, Madam, if a creature is neither capable of giving dignity to falsehood, nor willing to remain contented with the truth, he deserves no
better treatment.'

Mr. Johnson's fixed incredulity of every thing he heard, and his little
care to conceal that incredulity, was teizing enough to be sure: and I
saw Mr. Sharp[3] was pained exceedingly, when relating the history of a
hurricane that happened about that time in the West Indies, where, for
aught I know, he had himself lost some friends too, he observed Dr.
Johnson believed not a syllable of the account: 'For 'tis *so* easy (says he)
for a man to fill his mouth with a wonder, and run about telling the lie
before it can be detected, that I have no heart to believe hurricanes
easily raised by the first inventor, and blown forwards by thousands
more.' I asked him once if he believed the story of the destruction of
Lisbon[4] by an earthquake when it first happened: 'Oh! not for six
months (said he) at least: I *did* think that story too dreadful to be
credited, and can hardly yet persuade myself that it was true to the full
extent we all of us have heard.'

Among the numberless people however whom I heard him grossly and flatly contradict, I never yet saw any one who did not take it patiently excepting Dr. Burney, from whose habitual softness of manners I little expected such an exercise of spirit: the event was as little to be expected. Mr. Johnson asked his pardon generously and genteelly, and when he left the room rose up to shake hands with him, that they might part in peace. On another occasion, when he had violently provoked Mr. Pepys,[1] in a different but perhaps not a less offensive manner, till something much too like a quarrel was grown up between them, the moment he was gone, 'Now (says Dr. Johnson) is Pepys gone home[2] hating me, who love him better than I did before: he spoke in defence of his dead friend; but though I hope *I* spoke better who spoke against him, yet all my eloquence will gain me nothing but an honest man for my enemy!' He did not however cordially love Mr. Pepys, though he respected his abilities. 'I knew the dog was a scholar (said he, when they had been disputing about the classics for three hours together one morning at Streatham); but that he had so much taste and so much knowledge I did *not* believe: I might have taken Barnard's word though, for Barnard[3] would not lie.'

We had got a little French print among us at Brighthelmstone, in November 1782, of some people skaiting ,with these lines[4] written under:

> *Sur un mince chrystal l'hyver conduit leurs pas,*
> *Le precipice est sous la glace;*
> *Telle est de nos plaisirs la legere surface,*
> *Glissez mortels; n'appuyez pas.*

And I begged translations from every body: Dr. Johnson gave me this;

> O'er ice the rapid skaiter flies,
> · With sport above and death below;
> Where mischief lurks in gay disguise,
> Thus lightly touch and quickly go.

He was however most exceedingly enraged when he knew that in the course of the season I had asked half a dozen acquaintance[5] to do the same thing; and said, it was a piece of treachery, and done to make every body else look little when compared to my favourite friends the *Pepyses*, whose translations were unquestionably the best. I will insert them, because he *did* say so. This is the distich given me by Sir Lucas, to whom I owe more solid obligations, no less than the power of thanking him for the life he saved,[6] and whose least valuable praise is the correctness of his taste:

> O'er the ice as o'er pleasure you lightly should glide,
> Both have gulphs which their flattering surfaces hide.

This other more serious one was written by his brother:

> Swift o'er the level how the skaiters slide,
>   And skim the glitt'ring surface as they go:
> Thus o'er life's specious pleasures lightly glide,
>   But pause not, press not on the gulph below.

Dr. Johnson seeing this last, and thinking a moment, repeated,

> O'er crackling ice, o'er gulphs profound,
>   With nimble glide the skaiters play;
> O'er treacherous pleasure's flow'ry ground
>   Thus lightly skim, and haste away.

Though thus uncommonly ready both to give and take offence, Mr. Johnson had many rigid maxims concerning the necessity of continued softness and compliance of disposition: and when I once mentioned Shenstone's idea,[1] that some little quarrel among lovers, relations, and friends was useful, and contributed to their general happiness upon the whole, by making the soul feel her elastic force, and return to the beloved object with renewed delight:—'Why, what a pernicious maxim is this now (cries Johnson), *all* quarrels ought to be avoided studiously, particularly conjugal ones, as no one can possibly tell where they may end; besides that lasting dislike is often the consequence of occasional disgust, and that the cup of life is surely bitter enough, without squeezing in the hateful rind of resentment.' It was upon something like the same principle, and from his general hatred of refinement, that when I told him how Dr. Collier,[2] in order to keep the servants in humour with his favourite dog, by seeming rough with the animal himself on many occasions, and crying out, Why will nobody knock this cur's brains out? meant to conciliate their tenderness towards Pompey; he returned me for answer, 'that the maxim was evidently false, and founded on ignorance of human life: that the servants would kick the dog the sooner for having obtained such a sanction to their severity: and I once (added he) chid my wife for beating the cat before the maid, who will now (said I) treat puss with cruelty perhaps, and plead her mistress's example.'

I asked him upon this, if he ever disputed with his wife? (I had heard that he loved her passionately.) 'Perpetually (said he): my wife had a particular reverence for cleanliness, and desired the praise of neatness in her dress and furniture, as many ladies do, till they become troublesome to their best friends, slaves to their own besoms, and only sigh for the hour of sweeping their husbands out of the house as dirt and useless lumber: a clean floor is *so* comfortable, she would say sometimes, by way of twitting; till at last I told her, that I thought we had had talk enough about the *floor*, we would now have a touch at the *cieling*.'

On another occasion I have heard him blame her for a fault many people have, of setting the miseries of their neighbours half unintentionally half wantonly before their eyes, shewing them the bad side of their profession, situation, &c. He said, 'she would lament the dependence of pupillage[1] to a young heir, &c. and once told a waterman who rowed her along the Thames in a wherry, that he was no happier than a galley-slave, one being chained to the oar by authority, the other by want. I had however (said he, laughing), the wit to get her daughter[2] on my side always before we began the dispute. She read comedy better than any body he ever heard (he said); in tragedy she mouthed too much.'

Garrick told Mr. Thrale however, that she was a little painted puppet,[3] of no value at all, and quite disguised with affectation, full of odd airs of rural elegance; and he made out some comical scenes, by mimicking her in a dialogue he pretended to have overheard: I do not know whether he meant such stuff to be believed or no, it was so comical; nor did I indeed ever see him represent her ridiculously, though my husband did. The intelligence I gained of her from old Levett,[4] was only perpetual illness and perpetual opium. The picture I found of her at Litchfield was very pretty, and her daughter Mrs. Lucy Porter said it was like. Mr. Johnson has told me, that her hair was eminently beautiful, quite *blonde* like that of a baby; but that she fretted about the colour, and was always desirous to dye it black, which he very judiciously hindered her from doing. His account of their wedding we used to think ludicrous enough—'I was riding to church (says Johnson), and she following on another single horse: she hung back however, and I turned about to see whether she could get her steed along, or what was the matter. I had however soon occasion to see it was only coquetry, and *that I despised*, so quickening my pace a little, she mended hers; but I believe there was a tear or two——pretty dear creature!'

Johnson loved his dinner exceedingly, and has often said in my hearing, perhaps for my edification, 'that wherever the dinner is ill got there is poverty, or there is avarice, or there is stupidity; in short the family is somehow grossly wrong: for (continued he) a man seldom thinks with more earnestness of any thing than he does of his dinner; and if he cannot get that well dressed,[5] he should be suspected of inaccuracy in other things.' One day when he was speaking upon the subject, I asked him, if he ever huffed[6] his wife about his dinner? 'So often (replied he), that at last she called to me, and said, Nay, hold Mr. Johnson, and do not make a farce of thanking God for a dinner which in a few minutes you will protest not eatable.'

When any disputes arose between our married acquaintance however, Mr. Johnson always sided with the husband, 'whom (he said) the woman had probably provoked so often, she scarce knew when or how she had disobliged him first. Women (says Dr. Johnson) give great offence by a contemptuous spirit of non-compliance on petty occasions. The man calls his wife to walk with him in the shade, and she feels a strange desire just at that moment to sit in the sun: he offers to read her a play, or sing her a song, and she calls the children in to disturb them, or advises him to seize that opportunity of settling the family accounts. Twenty such tricks will the faithfullest wife in the world not refuse to play, and then look astonished when the fellow fetches in a mistress. Boarding-schools were established (continued he) for the conjugal quiet of the parents: the two partners cannot agree which child to fondle, nor how to fondle them, so they put the young ones to school, and remove the cause of contention. The little girl pokes her head,[1] the mother reproves her sharply: Do not mind your mamma, says the father, my dear, but do your own way. The mother complains to me of this: Madam (said I), your husband is right all the while; he is with you but two hours of the day perhaps, and then you teize him by making the child cry. Are not ten hours enough for tuition? And are the hours of pleasure so frequent in life, that when a man gets a couple of quiet ones to spend in familiar chat with his wife, they must be poisoned by petty mortifications? Put missey to school; she will learn to hold her head like her neighbours, and you will no longer torment your family for want of other talk.'

The vacuity[2] of life had at some early period of his life struck so forcibly on the mind of Mr. Johnson, that it became by repeated impression his favourite hypothesis, and the general tenor of his reasonings commonly ended there, wherever they might begin. Such things therefore as other philosophers often attribute to various and contradictory causes, appeared to him uniform enough; all was done to fill up the time, upon this principle. I used to tell him, that it was like the Clown's answer in *All's well that ends well*, of 'Oh Lord, Sir!'[3] for that it suited every occasion. One man, for example, was profligate and wild, as we call it, followed the girls, or sat still at the gaming-table. 'Why, life must be filled up (says Johnson), and the man who is not capable of intellectual pleasures must content himself with such as his senses can afford.' Another was a hoarder: 'Why, a fellow must do something; and what so easy to a narrow mind as hoarding halfpence till they turn into sixpences.'—Avarice was a vice against which, however, I never much heard Mr. Johnson declaim, till one represented it to him connected with cruelty, or some such disgraceful companion. 'Do not (said he) discourage your children from hoarding, if they have a taste to it: whoever lays up his penny rather than part with it for a cake, at least is not the slave of gross appetite; and shews besides a preference always to be esteemed, of the future to the present moment. Such a mind may be made a good one; but the natural spendthrift, who grasps his pleasures

111

greedily and coarsely, and cares for nothing but immediate indulgence, is very little to be valued above a negro.' We talked of Lady Tavistock,[1] who grieved herself to death for the loss of her husband—'She was rich and wanted employment (says Johnson), so she cried till she lost all power of restraining her tears: other women are forced to outlive their husbands, who were just as much beloved, depend on it; but they have no time for grief: and I doubt not, if we had put my Lady Tavistock into a small chandler's shop, and given her a nurse-child to tend, her life would have been saved. The poor and the busy have no leisure for sentimental sorrow.' We were speaking of a gentleman who loved his friend—'Make him prime minister (says Johnson) and see how long his friend will be remembered.' But he had a rougher answer for me, when I commended a sermon preached by an intimate acquaintance of our own at the trading end of the town. 'What was the subject, Madam (says Dr. Johnson)?' Friendship, Sir (replied I). 'Why now, is it not strange that a wise man, like our dear little Evans,[2] should take it in his head to preach on such a subject, in a place where no one can be thinking of it?' Why, what are they thinking upon, Sir (said I)? 'Why, the men are thinking on their money I suppose, and the women are thinking of their mops.'

Dr. Johnson's knowledge and esteem of what we call low or coarse life was indeed prodigious; and he did not like that the upper ranks should be dignified with the name of *the world.* Sir Joshua Reynolds said one day, that nobody *wore* laced coats now; and that once every body wore them. 'See now (says Johnson) how absurd that is; as if the bulk of mankind consisted of fine gentlemen that came to him to sit for their pictures. If every man who wears a laced coat (that he can pay for) was extirpated, who would miss them?' With all this haughty contempt of gentility, no praise was more welcome to Dr. Johnson than that which said he had the notions or manners of a gentleman:[3] which character I have heard him define with accuracy, and describe with elegance. 'Officers (he said) were falsely supposed to have the carriage of gentlemen; whereas no profession left a stronger brand behind it than that of a soldier; and it was the essence of a gentleman's character to bear the visible mark of no profession whatever.' He once named Mr. Berenger[4] as the standard of true elegance; but some one objecting that he too much resembled the gentleman in Congreve's comedies, Mr. Johnson said, 'We must fix them upon the famous Thomas Hervey,[5] whose manners were polished even to acuteness and brilliancy, though he lost but little in solid power of reasoning, and in genuine force of mind.' Mr. Johnson had however an avowed and scarcely limited partiality for all who bore the name or boasted the alliance of an Aston or a Hervey; and when Mr. Thrale once asked him which had been the happiest period of his past life? he replied, 'it was that year in which he spent one whole evening with M——y As——n.[1] That indeed (said he) was not happiness, it was rapture; but thoughts of it sweetened the whole year.' I must add, that the evening alluded to was not passed *tête-à-tête*, but in a select company, of which the present Lord Killmorey[2] was one. 'Molly (says Dr. Johnson) was a beauty and a scholar, and a wit and a whig; and she talked all in praise of liberty: and so I made this epigram upon her—She was the loveliest creature I ever saw!!!

> *Liber ut esse velim, suasisti pulchra Maria,*
> *Ut maneam liber—pulchra Maria, vale!'*

Will it do this way in English, Sir (said I)?

> Persuasions to freedom fall oddly from you:
> If freedom we seek—fair Maria, adieu!

'It will do well enough (replied he); but it is translated by a lady, and the ladies never loved M——y As——n.' I asked him what his wife thought of this attachment? 'She was jealous to be sure (said he), and teized me sometimes when I would let her; and one day, as a fortune-telling gipsey passed us when we were walking out in company with two or three friends in the country, she made the wench look at my hand, but soon repented her curiosity; for (says the gipsey) Your heart is divided, Sir, between a Betty and a Molly: Betty loves you best, but you take most delight in Molly's company: when I turned about to laugh, I saw my wife was crying. Pretty charmer! she had no reason!'

It was, I believe, long after the currents of life had driven him to a great distance from this lady, that he spent much of his time with Mrs. F—tzh—b—t, [3]of whom he always spoke with esteem and tenderness, and with a veneration very difficult to deserve. 'That woman (said he) loved her husband as we hope and desire to be loved by our guardian angel. F—tzh—b—t was a gay good-humoured fellow, generous of his money and of his meat, and desirous of nothing but cheerful society among people distinguished in *some* way, in *any way* I think; for Rousseau and St. Austin[4] would have been equally welcome to his table and to his kindness: the lady however was of another way of thinking; her first care was to preserve her husband's soul from corruption; her second to keep his estate entire for their children: and I owed my good reception in the family to the idea she had entertained, that I was fit company for F—tzh—b—t, whom I loved extremely. They dare not (said she) swear, and take other conversation-liberties before *you*.' I asked if her husband returned her regard? 'He felt her influence too power-fully (replied Mr. Johnson): no man will be fond of what forces him daily to feel himself inferior. She stood at the door of her Paradise in Derbyshire, like the angel with the flaming sword, to keep the devil at a distance. But she was not immortal, poor dear! she died, and her husband felt at once afflicted and released.' I enquired if she was handsome? 'She would have been handsome for a queen (replied the panegyrist); her beauty had more in it of majesty than of attraction, more of the dignity of virtue than the vivacity of wit.' The friend of this lady, Miss B—thby,[1] succeeded her in the management of Mr. F—tzh—b—t's family, and in the esteem of Dr. Johnson; though he told me she pushed her piety to bigotry, her devotion to enthusiasm; that she somewhat disqualified herself for the duties of *this* life, by her perpetual aspirations after the *next*: such was however the purity of her mind, he said, and such the graces of her manner, that Lord Lyttelton[2] and he used to strive for her preference with an emulation that occasioned hourly disgust, and ended in lasting animosity. 'You may see (said he to me, when the Poets Lives were printed) that dear B—thby is at my heart still. She *would* delight in that fellow Lyttelton's company though, all that I could do; and I cannot forgive even his memory the preference given by a mind like her's.' I have heard Baretti[3] say, that when this lady died, Dr. Johnson was almost distracted with his grief; and that the friends about him had much ado to calm the violence of his emotion. Dr. Taylor too related once to Mr. Thrale and me, that when he lost his wife, the negro Francis[4] ran away, though in the middle of the night, to Westminster, to fetch Dr. Taylor to his master, who was all but wild with excess of sorrow, and scarce knew him when he arrived: after some minutes however, the Doctor proposed their going to prayers, as the only rational method of calming the disorder this misfortune had occasioned in both their spirits. Time, and resignation to the will of God, cured every breach in his heart before I made acquaintance with him, though he always persisted in saying he never rightly recovered the loss of his wife. It is in allusion to her that he records the observation of a female critic, as he calls her, in Gay's Life;[5] and the lady of great beauty and elegance,[6] mentioned in the criticisms upon Pope's epitaphs, was Miss Molly Aston. The person spoken of in his strictures upon Young's poetry, is the writer of these Anecdotes,[7] to whom he likewise addressed the following verses[8] when he was in the Isle of Sky with Mr. Boswell. The letters written in his journey, I used to tell him, were better than the printed book; and he was not displeased at my having taken the pains to copy them all over. Here is the Latin ode:

> *Permeo terras, ubi nuda rupes*
> *Saxeas miscet nebulis ruinas,*
> *Torva ubi rident steriles coloni*
> > *Rura labores.*

Pervagor gentes, hominum ferorum
Vita ubi nullo decorata cultu,
Squallet informis, tugirique fumis
              Fœda latescit.

Inter erroris salebrosa longi,
Inter ignotæ strepitus loquelæ,
Quot modis mecum, quid agat requiro
              Thralia dulcis?

Seu viri curas pia nupta mulcet,
Seu fovet mater sobolem benigna,
Sive cum libris novitate pascit
              Sedula mentem:

Sit memor nostri, fideique merces,
Stet fides constans, meritoque blandum
Thraliæ discant resonare nomen
              Littora Skiæ.

On another occasion I can boast verses from Dr. Johnson.—As I went into his room the morning of my birth-day[1] once, and said to him, Nobody sends me any verses now, because I am five-and-thirty years old; and Stella was fed with them till forty-six,[2] I remember. My being just recovered from illness and confinement will account for the manner in which he burst out suddenly, for so he did without the least previous hesitation whatsoever, and without having entertained the smallest intention towards it half a minute before:

    Oft in danger, yet alive,
    We are come to thirty-five;
    Long may better years arrive,
    Better years than thirty-five.
    Could philosophers contrive
    Life to stop at thirty-five,
    Time his hours should never drive
    O'er the bounds of thirty-five.
    High to soar, and deep to dive,
    Nature gives at thirty-five.
    Ladies, stock and tend your hive,
    Trifle not at thirty-five:
    For howe'er we boast and strive,
    Life declines from thirty-five:
    He that ever hopes to thrive
    Must begin by thirty-five;
And all who wisely wish to wive,
Must look on Thrale at thirty-five.

'And now (said he, as I was writing them down), you may see what it is to come for poetry to a Dictionary-maker; you may observe that the rhymes run in alphabetical order exactly,'——And so they do.

Mr. Johnson did indeed possess an almost Tuscan power of improvisation:[1] when he called to my daughter, who was consulting with a friend about a new gown and dressed hat she thought of wearing to an assembly, thus suddenly, while she hoped he was not listening to their conversation,

> Wear the gown, and wear the hat,
> Snatch thy pleasures while they last;
> Hadst thou nine lives like a cat,
> Soon those nine lives would be past.

It is impossible to deny to such little sallies the power of the Florentines, who do not permit their verses to be ever written down though they often deserve it, because, as they express it, *cosi si perderebbe la poca gloria*.

As for translations, we used to make him sometimes run off with one or two in a good humour. He was praising this song of Metastasio,[2]

> *Deh, se piacermi vuoi,*
> *Lascia i sospetti tuoi,*
> *Non mi turbar con questo*
> *Molesto dubitar:*
> *Chi ciecamente crede,*
> *Impegna a serbar fede;*
> *Chi sempre inganno aspetto,*
> *Alletta ad ingannar.*

'Should you like it in English (said he) thus?'

> Would you hope to gain my heart,
> Bid your teizing doubts depart;
> He who blindly trusts, will find
> Faith from every generous mind:
> He who still expects deceit,
> Only teaches how to cheat.

Mr. Baretti coaxed him likewise one day at Streatham out of a translation of Emirena's speech to the false courtier Aquileius, and it is probably printed before now, as I think two or three people took copies; but perhaps it has slipt their memories.

> *Ah! tu in corte invecchiasti, e giurerei*
> *Che fra i pochi non sei tenace ancora*
> *Dell' antica onestà: quando bisogna,*
> *Saprai sereno in volto*
> *Vezzeggiare un nemico; acciò vi cada,*
> *Aprirgli innanzi un precipizio, e poi*
> *Piangerne la caduta. Offrirti a tutti*
> *E non esser che tuo; di false lodi*
> *Vestir le accuse, ed aggravar le colpe*
> *Nel farne la difesa, ognor dal trono*

I buoni allontanar; d'ogni castigo
Lasciar l'odio allo scettro, e d'ogni dono
Il merito usurpar: tener nascosto
Sotto un zelo apparente un empio fine,
Ne fabbricar che sulle altrui rovine.

Grown old in courts, thou art not surely one
Who keeps the rigid rules of ancient honour;
Well skill'd to sooth a foe with looks of kindness,
To sink the fatal precipice before him,
And then lament his fall with seeming friendship:
Open to all, true only to thyself,
Thou know'st those arts which blast with envious praise,
Which aggravate a fault with feign'd excuses,
And drive discountenanc'd virtue from the throne:
That leave the blame of rigour to the prince,
And of his every gift usurp the merit;
That hide in seeming zeal a wicked purpose,
And only build upon another's ruin.

These characters Dr. Johnson however did not delight in reading, or in hearing of: he always maintained that the world was not half as wicked as it was represented; and he might very well continue in that opinion, as he resolutely drove from him every story that could make him change it; and when Mr. Bickerstaff's flight[1] confirmed the report of his guilt, and my husband said in answer to Johnson's astonishment, that he had long been a suspected man: 'By those who look close to the ground, dirt will be seen, Sir (was the lofty reply): I hope I see things from a greater distance.'

His desire to go abroad, particularly to see Italy, was very great; and he had a longing wish too to leave some Latin verses[2] at the Grand Chartreux. He loved indeed the very act of travelling, and I cannot tell how far one might have taken him in a carriage before he would have wished for refreshment. He was therefore in some respects an admirable companion on the road, as he piqued himself upon feeling no inconvenience, and on despising no accommodations. On the other hand however, he expected no one else to feel any, and felt exceedingly inflamed with anger if any one complained of the rain, the sun, or the dust. 'How (said he) do other people bear them?' As for general uneasiness, or complaints of long confinement in a carriage, he considered all lamentations on their account as proofs of an empty head, and a tongue desirous to talk without materials of conversation. 'A mill that goes without grist (said he), is as good a companion as such creatures.'

I pitied a friend before him, who had a whining wife that found every thing painful to her, and nothing pleasing—'He does not know that she whimpers (says Johnson); when a door has creaked for a fortnight to-gether, you may observe—the master will scarcely give sixpence to get it oiled.'

Of another lady, more insipid than offensive, I once heard him say, 'She has some softness indeed, but so has a pillow.' And when one observed in reply, that her husband's fidelity and attachment were exemplary, notwithstanding this low account at which her perfections were rated—'Why Sir (cries the Doctor), being married to those sleepy-souled women, is just like playing at cards for nothing: no passion is excited, and the time is filled up. I do not however envy a fellow one of those honey-suckle wives for my part, as they are but *creepers* at best, and commonly destroy the tree they so tenderly cling about.'

For a lady of quality,[1] since dead, who received us at her husband's seat in Wales with less attention than he had long been accustomed to, he had a rougher denunciation: 'That woman (cries Johnson) is like sour small-beer, the beverage of her table, and produce of the wretched country she lives in: like that, she could never have been a good thing, and even that bad thing is spoiled.' This was in the same vein of asperity, and I believe with something like the same provocation, that he observed of a Scotch lady, 'that she resembled a dead nettle; were she alive (said he), she would sting.'

Mr. Johnson's hatred of the Scotch is so well known, and so many of his *bons mots* expressive of that hatred have been already repeated in so many books and pamphlets, that 'tis perhaps scarcely worth while to write down the conversation between him and a friend of that nation who always resides in London, and who at his return from the Hebrides asked him, with a firm tone of voice, What he thought of his country? 'That it is a very vile country to be sure, Sir;' (returned for answer Dr. Johnson.) Well, Sir! replies the other somewhat mortified, God made it. 'Certainly he did (answers Mr. Johnson again); but we must always remember that he made it for Scotchmen, and comparisons are odious, Mr. S——;[2] but God made hell.'

Dr. Johnson did not I think much delight in that kind of conversation which consists in telling stories:[3] 'every body (said he) tells stories of me, and I tell stories of nobody. I do not recollect (added he), that I have ever told *you*, that have been always favourites, above three stories; but I hope I do not play the Old Fool, and force people to hear uninteresting narratives, only because I once was diverted with them myself.' He was however no enemy to that sort of talk from the famous Mr. Foote,[4] 'whose happiness of manner in relating was such (he said) as subdued arrogance and roused stupidity: *His* stories were truly like those of

Biron in Love's Labour Lost,[1] so *very* attractive.

> That aged ears play'd truant with his tales,
> And younger hearings were quite ravish'd,
> So sweet and voluble was his discourse.

Of all conversers however (added he), the late Hawkins Browne[2] was the
most delightful with whom I ever was in company: his talk was at once
so elegant, so apparently artless, so pure, and so pleasing, it seemed a
perpetual stream of sentiment, enlivened by gaiety, and sparkling with
images.' When I asked Dr. Johnson, who was the *best* man he had ever
known? 'Psalmanazar,'[3] was the unexpected reply: he said, likewise,
'that though a native of France, as his friend imagined, he possessed
more of the English language, than any one of the other foreigners who
had separately fallen in his way.' Though there was much esteem however, there was I believe but little confidence between them; they conversed merely about general topics, religion and learning, of which both
were undoubtedly stupendous examples; and, with regard to true
Christian perfection, I have heard Johnson say, 'That George Psalmanazar's piety, penitence, and virtue exceeded almost what we read as
wonderful even in the lives of saints.'

I forget in what year it was that this extraordinary person lived and
died[4] at a house in Old-street, where Mr. Johnson was witness to his
talents and virtues, and to his final preference of the church of England,
after having studied, disgraced, and adorned so many modes of worship.[5]
The name he went by, was not supposed by his friend to be that of his
family, but all enquiries were vain; his reasons for concealing his original
were penitentiary;[6] he deserved no other name than that of the impostor,
he said. That portion of the Universal History[7] which was written by
him, does not seem to me to be composed with peculiar spirit, but all
traces of the wit and the wanderer were probably worn out before he
undertook the work.—His pious and patient endurance of a tedious
illness, ending in an exemplary death, confirmed the strong impression
his merit had made upon the mind of Mr. Johnson. 'It is so *very* difficult
(said he, always) for a sick man not to be a scoundrel. Oh! set the pillows
soft, here is Mr. Grumbler o'coming: Ah! let no air in for the world, Mr.
Grumbler will be here presently.'

This perpetual preference is so offensive, where the privileges of sickness are besides supported by wealth, and nourished by dependence,
that one cannot much wonder that a rough mind is revolted by them. It
was however at once comical and *touchant* (as the French call it), to observe Mr. Johnson so habitually watchful against this sort of behaviour,
that he was often ready to suspect himself of it; and when one asked him

gently, how he did?—'Ready to become a scoundrel, Madam (would commonly be the answer): with a little more spoiling you will, I think, make me a complete rascal.'

His desire of doing good was not however lessened by his aversion to a sick chamber: he would have made an ill man well by any expence or fatigue of his own, sooner than any of the canters.[1] Canter indeed was he none: he would forget to ask people after the health of their nearest relations, and say in excuse, 'That he knew they did not care: why should they (says he)? every one in this world has as much as they can do in caring for themselves, and few have leisure really to *think* of their neighbours distresses, however they may delight their tongues with *talking* of them.'

The natural depravity of mankind and remains of original sin were so fixed in Mr. Johnson's opinion, that he was indeed a most acute observer of their effects; and used to say sometimes, half in jest half in earnest, that they were the remains of his old tutor Mandeville's instructions. As a book however, he took care always loudly to condemn the Fable of the Bees,[2] but not without adding, 'that it was the work of a thinking man.'

I have in former days heard Dr. Collier[3] of the Commons loudly condemned for uttering sentiments, which twenty years after I have heard as loudly applauded from the lips of Dr. Johnson, concerning the well-known writer of that celebrated work: but if people will live long enough in this capricious world, such instances of partiality will shock them less and less, by frequent repetition. Mr. Johnson knew mankind, and wished to mend them: he therefore, to the piety and pure religion, the untainted integrity, and scrupulous morals of my earliest and most disinterested friend, judiciously contrived to join a cautious attention to the capacity of his hearers, and a prudent resolution not to lessen the influence of his learning and virtue, by casual freaks of humour, and irregular starts of ill-managed merriment. He did not wish to confound, but to inform his auditors; and though he did not appear to solicit benevolence, he always wished to retain authority, and leave his company impressed with the idea, that it was his to teach in this world, and theirs to learn. What wonder then that all should receive with docility from Johnson those doctrines, which propagated by Collier they drove away from them with shouts! Dr. Johnson was not grave however because he knew not how to be merry. No man loved laughing better, and his vein of humour[4] was rich, and apparently inexhaustible; though Dr. Goldsmith[5] said once to him, We should change companions oftener, we exhaust one another, and shall soon be both of us worn out. Poor Goldsmith was to him indeed like the earthen pot to the iron one in Fontaine's fables;[6] it had been better for *him* perhaps, that they had changed companions oftener;

yet no experience of his antagonist's strength hindered him from continuing the contest. He used to remind me always of that verse in Berni,[1]

> *Il pover uomo che non sen' èra accorto,*
> *Andava combattendo—ed era morto.*

Mr. Johnson made him a comical answer one day, when seeming to repine at the success of Beattie's Essay on Truth[2]—'Here's such a stir (said he) about a fellow that has written one book, and I have written many.' Ah, Doctor (says his friend), there go two-and-forty sixpences you know to one guinea.

They had spent an evening with Eaton Graham[3] too, I remember hearing it was at some tavern; his heart was open, and he began inviting away; told what he could do to make his college agreeable, and begged the visit might not be delayed. Goldsmith thanked him, and proposed setting out with Mr. Johnson for Buckinghamshire in a fortnight; 'Nay hold, Dr. *Minor* (says the other), I did not invite you.'

Many such mortifications arose in the course of their intimacy to be sure, but few more laughable than when the newspapers[4] had tacked them together as the pedant and his flatterer in Love's Labour lost. Dr. Goldsmith came to his friend, fretting and foaming, and vowing vengeance against the printer, &c. till Mr. Johnson, tired of the bustle, and desirous to think of something else, cried out at last, 'Why, what would'st thou have, dear Doctor! who the plague is hurt with all this nonsense? and how is a man the worse I wonder in his health, purse, or character, for being called *Holofernes?*' I do not know (replies the other) how you may relish being called Holofernes, but I do not like at least to play *Goodman Dull.*

Dr. Johnson was indeed famous for disregarding public abuse. When the people criticised and answered his pamphlets, papers, &c. 'Why now, these fellows are only advertising my book (he would say); it is surely better a man should be abused than forgotten.' When Churchill[5] nettled him however, it is certain he felt the sting, or that poet's works would hardly have been left out of the edition. Of that however I have no right to decide; the booksellers perhaps did not put Churchill on their list. I know Mr. Johnson was exceedingly zealous to declare how very little he had to do with the selection. Churchill's works too might possibly be rejected by him upon a higher principle; the highest indeed, if he was inspired by the same laudable motive which made him reject every authority for a word in his dictionary that could only be gleaned from writers dangerous to religion or morality—'I would not (said he) send people to look for words in a book,[6] that by such a casual seizure of the mind might chance to mislead it for ever.' In consequence of this delicacy, Mrs. Montague[1] once observed, That were an angel to give the *imprimatur*, Dr. Johnson's works were among those very few which would not be lessened by a line. That such praise from such a lady should delight him, is not strange; insensibility in a case like that, must have been the result alone of arrogance acting on stupidity. Mr. Johnson had indeed no dislike to the commendations which he knew he deserved: 'What signifies protesting so against flattery (would he cry)! when a person speaks well of one, it must be either true or false, you know; if true, let us rejoice in his good opinion; if he lies, it is a proof at least that he loves more to please me, than to sit silent when he need say nothing.'

That natural roughness of his manner, so often mentioned, would, notwithstanding the regularity of his notions, burst through them all from time to time; and he once bade a very celebrated lady,[2] who praised him with too much zeal perhaps, or perhaps too strong an emphasis (which always offended him), 'consider what her flattery was worth before she choaked *him* with it.' A few more winters passed in the talking world shewed him the value of that friend's commendations however; and he was very sorry for the disgusting speech he made her.

I used to think Mr. Johnson's determined preference of a cold monotonous talker over an emphatical and violent one, would make him quite a favourite among the men of *ton*, whose insensibility, or affectation of perpetual calmness, certainly did not give to him the offence it does to many. He loved 'conversation without effort (he said);' and the encomiums I have heard him so often pronounce on the manners of Topham Beauclerc[3] in society, constantly ended in that peculiar praise, that 'it was without *effort*.'

We were talking of Richardson who wrote Clarissa:[4] 'You think I love flattery (says Dr. Johnson), and so I do; but a little too much always disgusts me: that fellow Richardson, on the contrary, could not be contented to sail quietly down the stream of reputation, without longing to taste the froth from every stroke of the oar.'

With regard to slight insults from newspaper abuse, I have already declared his notions: 'They sting one (says he) but as a fly stings a horse;[5] and the eagle will not catch flies.'[6] He once told me however, that Cummyns[7] the famous Quaker, whose friendship he valued very highly, fell a sacrifice to their insults, having declared on his death-bed to Dr. Johnson, that the pain of an anonymous letter, written in some of the common prints of the day, fastened on his heart, and threw him into the slow fever of which he died.

Nor was Cummyns the only valuable member so lost to society: Hawkesworth,[8] the pious, the virtuous, and the wise, for want of that fortitude which casts a shield before the merits of his friend, fell a

David Garrick, 1771: drawing by George Dance

James Boswell in later life: drawing by Thomas Lawrence

lamented sacrifice to wanton malice and cruelty, I know not how provoked; but all in turn feel the lash of censure in a country where, as every baby is allowed to carry a whip, no person can escape except by chance. The unpublished crimes, unknown distresses, and even death itself, however, daily occurring in less liberal governments and less free nations, soon teach one to content one's self with such petty grievances, and make one acknowledge that the undistinguishing severity of newspaper abuse may in some measure diminish the diffusion of vice and folly in Great Britain, and while they fright delicate minds into forced refinements and affected insipidity, they are useful to the great causes of virtue in the soul, and liberty in the state; and though sensibility often sinks under the roughness of their prescriptions, it would be no good policy to take away their licence.

Knowing the state of Mr. Johnson's nerves, and how easily they were affected, I forbore reading in a new Magazine[1] one day, the death of a Samuel Johnson who expired that month; but my companion snatching up the book, saw it himself, and contrary to my expectation—'Oh (said he)! I hope Death will now be glutted with Sam. Johnsons, and let me alone for some time to come: I read of another namesake's departure[2] last week.'—Though Mr. Johnson was commonly affected even to agony at the thoughts of a friend's dying, he troubled himself very little with the complaints they might make to him about ill health. 'Dear Doctor[3] (said he one day to a common acquaintance, who lamented the tender state of his *inside*), do not be like the spider, man; and spin conversation thus incessantly out of thy own bowels.'—I told him of another friend who suffered grievously with the gout—'He will live a vast many years for all that (replied he), and then what signifies how much he suffers! but he will die at last, poor fellow, there's the misery; gout seldom takes the fort by a coup-de-main, but turning the siege into a blockade, obliges it to surrender at discretion.'

A lady he thought well of, was disordered in her health—'What help has she called in (enquired Johnson)?' Dr. James,[4] Sir; was the reply. 'What is her disease?' Oh, nothing positive, rather a gradual and gentle decline. 'She will die then, pretty dear (answered he)! When Death's pale horse[5] runs away with persons on full speed, an active physician may possibly give them a turn; but if he carries them on an even slow pace, down hill too! no care nor skill can save them!'

When Garrick was on his last sickbed,[6] no arguments, or recitals of such facts as I had heard, would persuade Mr. Johnson of his danger: he had prepossessed himself with a notion, that to say a man was sick, was very near wishing him so; and few things offended him more, than prognosticating even the death of an ordinary acquaintance. 'Ay, ay (said he), Swift[1] knew the world pretty well, when he said, that

> Some dire misfortune to portend,
> No enemy can match a friend.'

The danger then of Mr. Garrick, or of Mr. Thrale, whom he loved better, was an image which no one durst present before his view; he always persisted in the possibility and hope of their recovering from[2] disorders from which no human creatures by human means alone ever did recover. His distress for their loss was for that very reason poignant to excess; but his fears of his own salvation were excessive: his truly tolerant spirit, and Christian charity, which *hopeth all things*, and *believeth all things*,[3] made him rely securely on the safety of his friends, while his earnest aspiration after a blessed immortality made him cautious of his own steps, and timorous concerning their consequences. He knew how much had been given, and filled his mind with fancies of how much would be required, till his impressed imagination was often disturbed by them, and his health suffered from the sensibility of his too tender conscience: a real Christian is *so* apt to find his task above his power of performance!

Mr. Johnson did not however give into ridiculous refinements either of speculation or practice, or suffer himself to be deluded by specious appearances. 'I have had dust thrown in my eyes too often (would he say), to be blinded so. Let us never confound matters of belief with matters of opinion.'—Some one urged in his presence the preference of hope to possession; and as I remember, produced an Italian sonnet[4] on the subject. 'Let us not (cries Johnson) amuse ourselves with subtleties and sonnets, when speaking about hope, which is the follower of faith and the precursor of eternity; but if you only mean those air-built hopes which to-day excites and to-morrow will destroy, let us talk away, and remember that we only talk of the pleasures of hope; we feel those of possession, and no man in his senses would change the last for the first: such hope is a mere bubble, that by a gentle breath may be blown to what size you will almost, but a rough blast bursts it at once. Hope is an amusement rather than a good, and adapted to none but very tranquil minds.' The truth is, Mr. Johnson hated what we call unprofitable chat; and to a gentleman[5] who had disserted some time about the natural history of the mouse—' I wonder what such a one would have said (cried Johnson), if he had ever had the luck to see a *lion!*'

I well remember that at Brighthelmstone once, when he was not present, Mr. Beauclerc[6] asserted that he was afraid of spirits; and I, who was secretly offended at the charge, asked him, the first opportunity I could find, What ground he had ever given to the world for such a report?

'I can (replied he) recollect nothing nearer it, than my telling Dr. Lawrence[1] many years ago, that a long time after my poor mother's death, I heard her voice call *Sam!*' What answer did the Doctor make to your story, Sir, said I? 'None in the world,' (replied he;) and suddenly changed the conversation. Now as Mr. Johnson had a most unshaken faith, without any mixture of credulity, this story must either have been strictly true, or his persuasion of its truth the effect of disordered spirits. I relate the anecdote precisely as he told it me; but could not prevail on him to draw out the talk into length for further satisfaction of my curiosity.

As Johnson was the firmest of believers without being credulous, so he was the most charitable of mortals without being what we call an active friend. Admirable at giving counsel, no man saw his way so clearly; but he would not stir a finger for the assistance of those to whom he was willing enough to give advice: besides that, he had principles of laziness, and could be indolent by rule. To hinder your death, or procure you a dinner, I mean if really in want of one; his earnestness, his exertions could not be prevented, though health and purse and ease were all destroyed by their violence. If you wanted a slight favour, you must apply to people of other dispositions; for not a step would Johnson move to obtain a man a vote in a society, to repay a compliment which might be useful or pleasing, to write a letter of request, or to obtain a hundred pounds a year more for a friend, who perhaps had already two or three. No force could urge him to diligence, no importunity could conquer his resolution of standing still; 'What good are we doing with all this ado (would he say)? dearest Lady, let's hear no more of it!' I have however more than once in my life forced him on such services, but with extreme difficulty.

We parted at his door one evening when I had teized him for many weeks to write a recommendatory letter of a little boy to his schoolmaster; and after he had faithfully promised to do this prodigious feat before we met again—Do not forget dear Dick[2] Sir, said I, as he went out of the coach: he turned back, stood still two minutes on the carriage-step—'When I have written my letter for Dick, I may hang myself, mayn't I?'—and turned away in a very ill humour indeed.

Though apt enough to take sudden likings or aversions to people he occasionally met, he would never hastily pronounce upon their character; and when seeing him justly delighted with Solander's conversation,[3] I observed once that he was a man of great parts who talked from a full mind—'It may be so (said Mr. Johnson), but you cannot know it yet, nor I either: the pump works well, to be sure! but how, I wonder, are we to decide in so very short an acquaintance, whether it is supplied by a spring or a reservoir?'—He always made a great difference in his esteem between talents and erudition; and when he saw a person eminent for literature, though wholly unconversible, it fretted him. 'Teaching such tonies[1] (said he to me one day) is like setting a lady's diamonds in lead, which only obscures the lustre of the stone, and makes the possessor ashamed on't.' Useful and what we call every-day knowledge had the most of his just praise. 'Let your boy learn arithmetic dear Madam,' was his advice to the mother of a rich young heir:[2] 'he will not then be a prey to every rascal which this town swarms with: teach him the value of money, and how to reckon it; ignorance to a wealthy lad of one-and-twenty, is only so much fat to a sick sheep: it just serves to call the *rooks* about him.'

> And all that prey in vice or folly
>   Joy to see their quarry fly;
> Here the gamester light and jolly,
>   There the lender grave and sly.

These improviso lines, making part of a long copy of verses[3] which my regard for the youth on whose birth-day they were written obliges me to suppress lest they should give him pain, shew a mind of surprising activity and warmth; the more so as he was past seventy years of age when he composed them: but nothing more certainly offended Mr. Johnson, than the idea of a man's faculties (mental ones I mean) decaying by time; 'It is not true, Sir (would he say); what a man could once do, he would always do, unless indeed by dint of vicious indolence, and compliance with the nephews and nieces who crowd round an old fellow, and help to tuck him in, till he, contented with the exchange of fame for ease, e'en resolves to let them set the pillows at his back, and gives no further proof of his existence than just to suck the jelly that prolongs it.'

For such a life or such a death Dr. Johnson was indeed never intended by Providence: his mind was like a warm climate, which brings every thing to perfection suddenly and vigorously, not like the alembicated[4] productions of artificial fire, which always betray the difficulty of bringing them forth when their size is disproportionate to their flavour. *Je ferois un Roman tout comme un autre, mais la vie n'est point un Roman*, says a famous French writer;[5] and this was so certainly the opinion of the Author of the Rambler, that all his conversation precepts tended towards the dispersion of romantic ideas, and were chiefly intended to promote the cultivation of

> That which before thee lies in daily life.
>   MILTON.[6]

And when he talked of authors, his praise went spontaneously to such passages as are sure in his own phrase to leave something behind them useful on common occasions, or observant of common manners. For example, it was not the two *last*, but the two *first*, volumes of Clarissa[1] that he prized; 'For give me a sick bed, and a dying lady (said he), and I'll be pathetic myself: but Richardson had picked the kernel of life (he said), while Fielding was contented with the husk.'—It was not King Lear cursing his daughters, or deprecating the storm, that I remember his commendations of; but Iago's ingenious malice,[2] and subtle revenge or prince Hal's gay compliance with the vices of Falstaff, whom he all along despised. Those plays had indeed no rivals in Johnson's favour: 'No man but Shakespeare (he said) could have drawn Sir John.'[3]

His manner of criticising and commending Addison's prose, was the same in conversation as we read it in the printed strictures,[4] and many of the expressions used have been heard to fall from him on common occasions. It was notwithstanding observable enough (or I fancied so), that he did never like, though he always thought fit to praise it; and his praises resembled those of a man who extols the superior elegance of high painted porcelain, while he himself always chuses to eat off *plate*. I told him so one day, and he neither denied it nor appeared displeased.

Of the pathetick in poetry[5] he never liked to speak, and the only passage I ever heard him applaud as particularly tender in any common book, was Jane Shore's exclamation in the last act,[6]

Forgive me! *but* forgive me!

It was not however from the want of a susceptible heart that he hated to cite tender expressions, for he was more strongly and more violently affected by the force of words representing ideas capable of affecting him at all, than any other man in the world I believe; and when he would try to repeat the celebrated *Prosa Ecclesiastica pro Mortuis*, as it is called, beginning *Dies iræ, Dies illa*, he could never pass the stanza ending thus, *Tantus labor non sit cassus*, without bursting into a flood of tears; which sensibility I used to quote against him when he would inveigh against devotional poetry,[7] and protest that all religious verses were cold and feeble, and unworthy the subject, which ought to be treated with higher reverence, he said, than either poets or painters could presume to excite or bestow. Nor can any thing be a stronger proof of Dr. Johnson's piety than such an expression; for his idea of poetry was magnificent indeed, and very fully was he persuaded of its superiority over every other talent bestowed by heaven on man. His chapter upon that particular subject in his Rasselas,[8] is really written from the fullness of his heart, and quite in his best manner I think. I am not so sure that this is the proper place to mention his writing that surprising little volume in a week or ten days time, in order to obtain money for his journey to Litchfield[1] when his mother lay upon her last sickbed.

Promptitude of thought indeed, and quickness of expression, were among the peculiar felicities of Johnson: his notions rose up like the dragon's teeth sowed by Cadmus all ready clothed, and in bright armour too, fit for immediate battle. He was therefore (as somebody is said to have expressed it) a tremendous converser, and few people ventured to try their skill against an antagonist with whom contention was so hopeless. One gentleman[2] however, who dined at a nobleman's house[3] in his company and that of Mr. Thrale, to whom I was obliged for the anecdote, was willing to enter the lists in defence of King William's character,[4] and having opposed and contradicted Johnson two or three times petulantly enough; the master of the house began to feel uneasy, and expect disagreeable consequences: to avoid which he said, loud enough for the Doctor to hear, Our friend here has no meaning now in all this, except just to relate at club to-morrow how he teized Johnson at dinner to-day —this is all to do himself *honour*. No, upon my word, replied the other, I see no *honour* in it, whatever you may do. 'Well, Sir! (returned Mr. Johnson sternly) if you do not *see* the *honour*, I am sure I *feel* the *disgrace*.'

A young fellow,[5] less confident of his own abilities, lamenting one day that he had lost all his Greek—'I believe it happened at the same time, Sir (said Johnson), that I lost all my large estate in Yorkshire.'

But however roughly he might be suddenly provoked to treat a harmless exertion of vanity, he did not wish to inflict the pain he gave, and was sometimes very sorry when he perceived the people to smart more than they deserved. How harshly you treated that man to-day, said I once, who harangued us so about gardening—'I am sorry (said he) if I vexed the creature, for there certainly is no harm in a fellow's rattling a rattle-box, only don't let him think that he thunders.'—The Lincolnshire lady[6] who shewed him a grotto she had been making, came off no better as I remember: Would it not be a pretty cool habitation in summer? said she, Mr. Johnson! 'I think it would, Madam (replied he),—for a toad.'

All desire of distinction indeed had a sure enemy in Mr. Johnson. We met a friend driving six very small ponies, and stopt to admire them. 'Why does nobody (said our doctor) begin the fashion of driving six spavined horses, all spavined of the same leg? it would have a mighty pretty effect, and produce the distinction of doing something worse than the common way.'

When Mr. Johnson had a mind to compliment any one, he did it with more dignity to himself, and better effect upon the company, than any man. I can recollect but few instances indeed, though perhaps that may be more my fault than his. When Sir Joshua Reynolds left the room one day, he said, 'There goes a man not to be spoiled by prosperity.' And when Mrs. Montague[1] shewed him some China plates which had once belonged to Queen Elizabeth, he told her, 'that they had no reason to be ashamed of their present possessor, who was so little inferior to the first.' I likewise remember that he pronounced one day at my house a most lofty panegyric upon Jones the Orientalist,[2] who seemed little pleased with the praise, for what cause I know not. He was not at all offended, when comparing all our acquaintance to some animal or other, we pitched upon the elephant for his resemblance, adding that the proboscis of that creature was like his mind most exactly, strong to buffet even the tyger, and pliable to pick up even the pin. The truth is, Mr. Johnson was often good-humouredly willing to join in childish amusements, and hated to be left out of any innocent merriment that was going forward. Mr. Murphy always said, he was incomparable at buffoonery; and I verily think, if he had had good eyes, and a form less inflexible, he would have made an admirable mimic.

He certainly rode on Mr. Thrale's old hunter with a good firmness, and though he would follow the hounds fifty miles an end[3] sometimes, would never own himself either tired or amused. 'I have now learned (said he), by hunting, to perceive, that it is no diversion at all, nor ever takes a man out of himself for a moment: the dogs have less sagacity than I could have prevailed on myself to suppose; and the gentlemen often call to me not to ride over them. It is very strange, and very melancholy, that the paucity of human pleasures should persuade us ever to call hunting one of them.'—He was however proud to be amongst the sportsmen; and I think no praise ever went so close to his heart, as when Mr. Hamilton[4] called out one day upon Brighthelmstone Downs, Why Johnson rides as well, for aught I see, as the most illiterate fellow in England.

Though Dr. Johnson owed his very life to air and exercise, given him when his organs of respiration could scarcely play, in the year 1766,[5] yet he ever persisted in the notion, that neither of them had any thing to do with health. 'People live as long (said he) in Pepper-alley[6] as on Salisbury-plain; and they live so much happier, that an inhabitant of the first would, if he turned cottager, starve his understanding for want of conversation, and perish in a state of mental inferiority.'

Mr. Johnson indeed, as he was a very talking man himself, had an idea that nothing promoted happiness so much as conversation. A friend's erudition was commended one day as equally deep and strong—'He will not talk Sir (was the reply), so his learning does no good, and his wit, if he has it, gives us no pleasure: out of all his boasted stores I never heard him force but one word, and that word was *Richard*.'[1]— With a contempt not inferior he received the praises of a pretty lady's face and behaviour: 'She says nothing Sir (answers Johnson); a talking blackamoor were better than a white creature who adds nothing to life, and by sitting down before one thus desperately silent, takes away the confidence one should have in the company of her chair if she were once out of it.'—No one was however less willing to begin any discourse than himself: his friend Mr. Thomas Tyers[2] said, he was like the ghosts, who never speak till they are spoken to: and he liked the expression so well, that he often repeated it. He had indeed no necessity to lead the stream of chat to a favourite channel, that his fulness on the subject might be shewn more clearly, whatever was the topic; and he usually left the choice to others. His information best enlightened, his argument strengthened, and his wit made it ever remembered. Of him it might have been said, as he often delighted to say of Edmund Burke, 'that you could not stand five minutes with that man beneath a shed while it rained, but you must be convinced you had been standing with the greatest man[3] you had ever yet seen.'

As we had been saying one day that no subject failed of receiving dignity from the manner in which Mr. Johnson treated it, a lady at my house[4] said, she would make him talk about love; and took her measures accordingly, deriding the novels of the day because they treated about love. 'It is not (replied our philosopher) because they treat, as you call it about love, but because they treat of nothing, that they are despicable: we must not ridicule a passion which he who never felt never was happy, and he who laughs at never deserves to feel—a passion which has caused the change of empires, and the loss of worlds—a passion which has inspired heroism and subdued avarice.' He thought he had already said too much. 'A passion, in short (added he, with an altered tone), that consumes me always for my pretty Fanny[5] here, and she is very cruel (speaking of another lady in the room).' He told however in the course of the same chat, how his negro Francis[6] had been eminent for his success among the girls. Seeing us all laugh, 'I must have you know, ladies (said he), that Frank has carried the empire of Cupid further than most men. When I was in Lincolnshire[7] so many years ago, he attended me thither; and when we returned home together, I found that a female haymaker had followed him to London for love.' Francis was indeed no small favourite with his master, who retained however a prodigious influence over his most violent passions.

On the birth-day of our eldest daughter, and that of our friend Dr. Johnson, the 17th and 18th of September, we every year made up a little dance and supper, to divert our servants and their friends, putting the summer-house into their hands for the two evenings, to fill with acquaintance and merriment. Francis and his white wife[1] were invited of course. She was eminently pretty, and he was jealous, as my maids told me. On the first of these days amusements (I know not what year) Frank took offence at some attentions paid his Desdemona, and walked away next morning to London in wrath. His master and I driving the same road an hour after, overtook him. 'What is the matter, child (says Dr. Johnson), that you leave Streatham to-day? *Art sick?*' He is jealous (whispered I). 'Are you jealous of your wife, you stupid blockhead (cries out his master in another tone)?' The fellow hesitated; and, *To be sure Sir*, I *don't quite approve Sir*, was the stammering reply. 'Why, what do they *do* to her, man? do the footmen kiss her?' No Sir, no!—Kiss my *wife Sir!—I hope not Sir*. 'Why, what *do* they do to her, my lad?' Why nothing Sir, I'm sure Sir. 'Why then go back directly and dance you dog, do; and let's hear no more of such empty lamentations.' I believe however that Francis was scarcely as much the object of Mr. Johnson's personal kindness, as the representative of Dr. Bathurst,[2] for whose sake he would have loved any body, or any thing.

When he spoke of negroes, he always appeared to think them of a race naturally inferior, and made few exceptions in favour of his own; yet whenever disputes arose in his household among the many odd inhabitants of which it consisted, he always sided with Francis against the others, whom he suspected (not unjustly I believe) of greater malignity. It seems at once vexatious and comical to reflect, that the dissentions those people chose to live constantly in, distressed and mortified him exceedingly. He really was oftentimes afraid of going home, because he was so sure to be met at the door with numberless complaints; and he used to lament pathetically to me, and to Mr. Sastres the Italian master,[3] who was much his favourite, that they made his life miserable from the impossibility he found of making theirs happy, when every favour he bestowed on one was wormwood to the rest. If however I ventured to blame their ingratitude, and condemn their conduct, he would instantly set about softening the one and justifying the other; and finished commonly by telling me, that I knew not how to make allowances for situations I never experienced.

> To thee no reason who know'st only good,
> But evil hast not try'd.   MILTON.[4]

Dr. Johnson knew how to be merry with mean people too, as well as to be sad with them; he loved the lower ranks of humanity with a real affection: and though his talents and learning kept him always in the sphere of upper life, yet he never lost sight of the time when he and they shared pain and pleasure in common. A borough election[1] once shewed me his toleration of boisterous mirth, and his content in the company of people whom one would have thought at first sight little calculated for his society. A rough fellow one day on such an occasion, a hatter by trade, seeing Mr. Johnson's beaver in a state of decay, seized it suddenly with one hand, and clapping him on the back with the other; Ah, Master Johnson (says he), this is no time to be thinking about *hats*. 'No, no, Sir (replies our Doctor in a cheerful tone), hats are of no use now, as you say, except to throw up in the air and huzza with;' accompanying his words with the true election halloo.

But it was never against people of coarse life that his contempt was expressed, while poverty of sentiment in men who considered themselves to be company for *the parlour*, as he called it, was what he would not bear. A very ignorant young fellow,[2] who had plagued us all for nine or ten months, died at last consumptive: 'I think (said Mr. Johnson when he heard the news), I am afraid, I should have been more concerned for the death of the *dog*; but——(hesitating a while) I am not wrong now in all this, for the dog acted up to his character on every occasion that we know; but that dunce of a fellow helped forward the general disgrace of humanity.' Why dear Sir (said I), how odd you are! you have often said the lad was not capable of receiving further instruction. 'He was (replied the Doctor) like a corked bottle, with a drop of dirty water in it, to be sure; one might pump upon it for ever without the smallest effect; but when every method to open and clean it had been tried, you would not have me grieve that the bottle was broke at last.'

This was the same youth who told us he had been reading Lucius Florus; *Florus Delphini*[3] was the phrase; and my mother (said he) thought it had something to do with Delphos; but of that I know nothing. Who founded Rome then (enquired Mr. Thrale)? The lad replied, Romulus. And who succeeded Romulus (said I)? A long pause, and apparently distressful hesitation, followed the difficult question. 'Why will you ask him in terms that he does not comprehend (said Mr. Johnson enraged)? You might as well bid him tell you who phlebotomised Romulus. This fellow's dulness is elastic (continued he), and all we do is but like kicking at a wool-sack.'

The pains he took however to obtain the young man more patient instructors, were many, and oftentimes repeated. He was put under the care of a clergyman[4] in a distant province; and Mr. Johnson used both to write and talk to his friend concerning his education. It was on that occasion that I remember his saying, 'A boy should never be sent to Eton or Westminster school before he is twelve years old at least; for if in his years of babyhood he 'scapes that general and transcendent knowledge without which life is perpetually put to a stand, he will never get it at a public school, where if he does not learn Latin and Greek, he learns nothing.' Mr. Johnson often said, 'that there was too much stress laid upon literature as indispensably necessary: there is surely no need that every body should be a scholar, no call that every one should square the circle. Our manner of teaching (said he) cramps and warps many a mind, which if left more at liberty would have been respectable in some way, though perhaps not in that. We lop our trees, and prune them, and pinch them about (he would say), and nail them tight up to the wall, while a good standard is at last the only thing for bearing healthy fruit, though it commonly begins later. Let the people learn necessary knowledge; let them learn to count their fingers, and to count their money, before they are caring for the classics; for (says Mr. Johnson) though I do not quite agree with the proverb, that *Nullum numen abest si sit prudentia*, yet we may very well say, that *Nullum numen adest—ni sit prudentia.*'[1]

We had been visiting at a lady's house,[2] whom as we returned some of the company ridiculed for her ignorance: 'She is not ignorant (said he), I believe, of any thing she has been taught, or of any thing she is desirous to know; and I suppose if one wanted a little *run tea*,[3] she might be a proper person enough to apply to.'

When I relate these various instances of contemptuous behaviour shewn to a variety of people, I am aware that those who will now have heard little of Mr. Johnson will here cry out against his pride and his severity; yet I have been as careful as I could to tell them, that all he did was gentle, if all he said was rough. Had I given anecdotes of his actions instead of his words, we should I am sure have had nothing on record but acts of virtue differently modified, as different occasions called that virtue forth: and among all the nine biographical essays[4] or performances which I have heard will at last be written about dear Dr. Johnson, no mean or wretched, no wicked or even slightly culpable action will I trust be found, to produce and put in the scale against a life of seventy years, spent in the uniform practice of every moral excellence and every Christian perfection, save humility alone, says a critic,[5] but that I think *must* be excepted. He was not however wanting even in that to a degree seldom attained by man, when the duties of piety or charity called it forth.

Lowly towards God, and docile towards the church; implicit in his belief of the gospel, and ever respectful towards the people appointed to preach it; tender of the unhappy, and affectionate to the poor, let no one hastily condemn as proud, a character which may perhaps somewhat justly be censured as arrogant. It must however be remembered again, that even this arrogance was never shewn without some intention, immediate or remote, of mending some fault or conveying some instruction. Had I meant to make a panegyric on Mr. Johnson's well-known excellencies, I should have told his deeds only, not his words—sincerely protesting, that as I never saw him once do a wrong thing, so we accustomed ourselves to look upon him almost as an excepted being; and I should as much have expected injustice from Socrates or impiety from Paschal, as the slightest deviation from truth and goodness in any transaction one might be engaged in with Samuel Johnson. His attention to veracity was without equal or example: and when I mentioned Clarissa as a perfect character; 'On the contrary (said he), you may observe there is always something which she prefers to truth. Fielding's Amelia was the most pleasing heroine of all the romances (he said); but that vile broken nose[1] never cured, ruined the sale of perhaps the only book, which being printed off betimes one morning, a new edition was called for before night.'

Mr. Johnson's knowledge of literary history was extensive and surprising: he knew every adventure of every book you could name almost, and was exceedingly pleased with the opportunity which writing the Poets Lives gave him to display it. He loved to be set at work, and was sorry when he came to the end of the business he was about. I do not feel so myself with regard to these sheets: a fever which has preyed on me while I wrote them over for the press, will perhaps lessen my power of doing well the first, and probably the last work[2] I should ever have thought of presenting to the Public. I could doubtless wish so to conclude it, as at least to shew my zeal for my friend, whose life, as I once had the honour and happiness of being useful to, I should wish to record a few particular traits of, that those who read should emulate his goodness; but seeing the necessity of making even virtue and learning such as *his* agreeable, that all should be warned against such coarseness of manners, as drove even from *him* those who loved, honoured and esteemed him. His wife's daughter, Mrs. Lucy Porter of Litchfield, whose veneration for his person and character has ever been the greatest possible, being opposed one day in conversation by a clergyman who came often to her house, and feeling somewhat offended, cried out suddenly, Why, Mr. Pearson,[3] said she, you are just like Dr. Johnson, I think: I do not mean that you are a man of the greatest capacity in all the world like Dr. Johnson, but that you contradict one every word one speaks, just like him.

Mr. Johnson told me the story: he was present at the giving of the reproof. It was however observable that with all his odd severity, he could not keep even indifferent people from teizing him with unaccountable confessions of silly conduct which one would think they would scarcely have had inclination to reveal even to their tenderest and most intimate companions; and it was from these unaccountable volunteers in sincerity that he learned to warn the world against follies little known, and seldom thought on by other moralists.

Much of his eloquence, and much of his logic have I heard him use to prevent men from making vows on trivial occasions;[1] and when he saw a person oddly perplexed about a slight difficulty, 'Let the man alone (he would say), and torment him no more about it; there is a vow in the case I am convinced; but is it not very strange that people should be neither afraid nor ashamed of bringing in God Almighty thus at every turn between themselves and their dinner?' When I asked what ground he had for such imaginations, he informed me, 'That a young lady once told him in confidence, that she could never persuade herself to be dressed against the bell rung for dinner, till she had made a vow to heaven that she would never more be absent from the family meals.'

The strangest applications in the world were certainly made from time to time towards Mr. Johnson, who by that means had an inexhaustible fund of anecdote, and could, if he pleased, tell the most astonishing stories of human folly and human weakness that ever were confided to any man not a confessor by profession.

One day when he was in a humour to record some of them, he told us the following tale: 'A person (said he) had for these last five weeks often called at my door, but would not leave his name, or other message; but that he wished to speak with me. At last we met, and he told me that he was oppressed by scruples of conscience: I blamed him gently for not applying, as the rules of our church direct, to his parish priest or other discreet clergyman; when, after some compliments on his part, he told me, that he was clerk to a very eminent trader, at whose warehouses much business consisted in packing goods in order to go abroad: that he was often tempted to take paper and packthread enough for his own use, and that he had indeed done so so often, that he could recollect no time when he ever had bought any for himself.—But probably (said I), your master was wholly indifferent with regard to such trivial emoluments; you had better ask for it at once, and so take your trifles with consent.—Oh, Sir! replies the visitor, my master bid me have as much as I pleased, and was half angry when I talked to him about it.—Then pray Sir (said I), teize me no more about such airy nothings;[2] and was going on to be very angry, when I recollected that the fellow might be mad perhaps; so I asked him, When he left the counting-house of an evening?—At seven o'clock, Sir.—And when do you go to-bed, Sir?—At twelve o'clock.—Then (replied I) I have at least learned thus much by my new acquaintance;—that five hours of the four-and-twenty unemployed are enough for a man to go mad in; so I would advise you Sir, to study algebra,[1] if you are not an adept already in it: your head would get less *muddy*,[2] and you will leave off tormenting your neighbours about paper and pack-thread, while we all live together in a world that is bursting with sin and sorrow.—It is perhaps needless to add, that this visitor came no more.'

Mr. Johnson had indeed a real abhorrence of a person that had ever before him treated a little thing like a great one: and he quoted this scrupulous gentleman with his packthread very often, in ridicule of a friend who, looking out on Streatham Common from our windows one day, lamented the enormous wickedness of the times, because some bird-catchers were busy there one fine Sunday morning. 'While half the Christian world is permitted (said he) to dance and sing, and celebrate Sunday as a day of festivity, how comes your puritanical spirit so offended with frivolous and empty deviations from exactness. Whoever loads life with unnecessary scruples, Sir (continued he), provokes the attention of others on his conduct, and incurs the censure of singularity without reaping the reward of superior virtue.'

I must not, among the anecdotes of Dr. Johnson's life, omit to relate a thing that happened to him one day, which he told me of himself. As he was walking along the Strand a gentleman stepped out of some neighbouring tavern, with his napkin in his hand and no hat, and stopping him as civilly as he could—I beg your pardon, Sir; but you are Dr. Johnson, I believe. 'Yes, Sir.' We have a wager depending on your reply: Pray, Sir, is it irrèparable or irrepàirable that one should say? 'The *last* I think, Sir (answered Dr. Johnson), for the adjective ought to follow the verb; but you had better consult my Dictionary than me, for that was the result of more thought than you will now give me time for.' No, no, replied the gentleman gaily, the book I have no certainty at all of; but here is the *author*, to whom I referred: Is he not, Sir? to a friend with him: I have won my twenty guineas quite fairly, and am much obliged to you, Sir; so shaking Mr. Johnson kindly by the hand, he went back to finish his dinner or desert.

Another strange thing he told me once which there was no danger of forgetting: how a young gentleman[3] called on him one morning, and told him that his father having, just before his death, dropped suddenly into the enjoyment of an ample fortune, he, the son, was willing to qualify himself for genteel society by adding some literature to his other endowments, and wished to be put in an easy way of obtaining it. Johnson recommended the university; 'for you read Latin, Sir, with *facility*.' I read it a little to be sure, Sir. 'But do you read it *with facility*, I say?' Upon my word, Sir, I do not very well know, but I rather believe not.

Mr. Johnson now began to recommend other branches of science, when he found languages at such an immeasurable distance, and advising him to study natural history, there arose some talk about animals, and their divisions into oviparous and viviparous; And the cat here, Sir, said the youth who wished for instruction, pray in which class is she? Our Doctor's patience and desire of doing good began now to give way to the natural roughness of his temper. 'You would do well (said he) to look for some person to be always about you, Sir, who is capable of explaining such matters, and not come to us (there were some literary friends present as I recollect) to know whether the cat lays eggs or not: get a discreet man to keep you company, there are so many who would be glad of your table and fifty pounds a year.' The young gentleman retired, and in less than a week informed his friends that he had fixed on a preceptor to whom no objections could be made; but when he named as such one of the most distinguished characters in our age or nation, Mr. Johnson fairly gave himself up to an honest burst of laughter; and seeing this youth at such a surprising distance from common knowledge of the world, or of any thing in it, desired to see his visitor no more.

He had not much better luck with two boys that he used to tell of, to whom he had taught the classics, 'so that (he said) they were no incompetent or mean scholars:' it was necessary however that something more familiar should be known, and he bid them read the history of England. After a few months had elapsed he asked them, 'If they could recollect who first destroyed the monasteries in our island?' One modestly replied, that he did not know; the other said, *Jesus Christ.*

Of the truth of stories which ran currently about the town concerning Dr. Johnson, it was impossible to be certain, unless one asked him himself; and what he told, or suffered to be told before his face without contradicting, has every possible mark I think of real and genuine authenticity. I made one day very minute enquiries about the tale of his knocking down the famous Tom Osborne[1] with his own Dictionary in the man's own house. And how was that affair, in earnest? do tell me, Mr. Johnson? 'There is nothing to tell, dearest Lady, but that he was insolent and I beat him, and that he was a blockhead and told of it, which I should never have done; so the blows have been multiplying, and the wonder thickening for all these years, as Thomas was never a favourite with the Public. I have beat many a fellow, but the rest had the wit to hold their tongues.'

I have heard Mr. Murphy relate a very singular story,[2] while he was present, greatly to the credit of his uncommon skill and knowledge of life and manners: When first the Ramblers came out in separate numbers, as they were the objects of attention to multitudes of people, they happened, as it seems, particularly to attract the notice of a society who met every Saturday evening during the summer at Rumford in Essex, and were known by the name of The Bowling-green Club. These men seeing one day the character of Leviculus the fortune-hunter,[1] or Tetrica the old maid:[2] another day some account of a person who spent his life in hoping for a legacy,[3] or of him who is always prying[4] into other folks affairs, began sure enough to think they were betrayed; and that some of the coterie sate down to divert himself by giving to the Public the portrait of all the rest. Filled with wrath against the traitor of Rumford, one of them resolved to write to the printer and enquire the author's name; Samuel Johnson, was the reply. No more was necessary; Samuel Johnson[5] was the name of the curate, and soon did each begin to load him with reproaches for turning his friends into ridicule in a manner so cruel and unprovoked. In vain did the guiltless curate protest his innocence; one was sure that Aliger[6] meant Mr. Twigg, and that Cupidus[7] was but another name for neighbour Baggs: till the poor parson, unable to contend any longer, rode to London, and brought them full satisfaction concerning the writer, who from his own knowledge of general manners, quickened by a vigorous and warm imagination, had happily delineated, though unknown to himself, the members of the Bowling-green Club.

Mr. Murphy likewise used to tell before Dr. Johnson, of the first time *they* met, and the occasion of their meeting, which he related thus: That being in those days engaged in a periodical[8] paper, he found himself at a friend's house out of town; and not being disposed to lose pleasure for the sake of business, wished rather to content his bookseller by sending some unstudied essay to London by the servant, than deny himself the company of his acquaintance, and drive away to his chambers for the purpose of writing something more correct. He therefore took up a French *Journal Literaire* that lay about the room, and translating something he liked from it, sent it away without further examination. Time however discovered that he had translated from the French a Rambler[9] of Johnson's, which had been but a month before taken from the English; and thinking it right to make him his personal excuses, we went next day, and found our friend all covered with soot like a chimney-sweeper, in a little room, with an intolerable heat and strange smell, as if he had been acting Lungs in the Alchymist, making *æther*.[10] 'Come, come (says Dr. Johnson), dear Mur, the story is black enough now; and it was a very happy day for me that brought you first to my house, and a very happy mistake about the Ramblers.'

Dr. Johnson was always exceeding fond of chemistry;[11] and we made up a sort of laboratory at Streatham one summer, and diverted ourselves

Self-portrait by
Joshua Reynolds

Giuseppe Marc
Antonio Baretti

Johnson's letter to Mrs. Thrale, 17 January 1783

Mrs. Thrale to Johnson, 15 July 1784

with drawing essences and colouring liquors. But the danger Mr. Thrale found his friend in one day when I was driven to London, and he had got the children and servants round him to see some experiments performed, put an end to all our entertainment; so well was the master of the house persuaded, that his short sight would have been his destruction in a moment, by bringing him close to a fierce and violent flame. Indeed it was a perpetual miracle that he did not set himself on fire reading a-bed, as was his constant custom, when exceedingly unable even to keep clear of mischief with our best help; and accordingly the fore-tops of all his wigs were burned by the candle down to the very net-work. Mr. Thrale's valet-de-chambre, for that reason, kept one always in his own hands, with which he met him at the parlour-door when the bell had called him down to dinner, and as he went up stairs to sleep in the afternoon, the same man constantly followed him with another.

Future experiments in chemistry however were too dangerous, and Mr. Thrale insisted that we should do no more towards finding the philosophers stone.

Mr. Johnson's amusements were thus reduced to the pleasures of conversation merely: and what wonder that he should have an avidity for the sole delight he was able to enjoy? No man conversed so well as he on every subject; no man so acutely discerned the reason of every fact, the motive of every action, the end of every design. He was indeed often pained by the ignorance or causeless wonder of those who knew less than himself, though he seldom drove them away with apparent scorn, unless he thought they added presumption to stupidity: And it was impossible not to laugh at the patience he shewed, when a Welch parson of mean abilities, though a good heart, struck with reverence at the sight of Dr. Johnson, whom he had heard of as the greatest man living, could not find any words to answer his inquiries concerning a motto round some-body's arms which adorned a tomb-stone in Ruabon[1] church-yard. If I remember right the words were,

Heb Dw, Heb Dym,
Dw o' diggon.

And though of no very difficult construction, the gentleman seemed wholly confounded, and unable to explain them; till Mr. Johnson having picked out the meaning by little and little, said to the man, '*Heb* is a preposition, I believe Sir, is it not?' My countryman recovering some spirits upon the sudden question, cried out, So I humbly presume Sir, very comically.

Stories of humour do not tell well in books; and what made impression on the friends who heard a jest, will seldom much delight the distant acquaintance or sullen critic who reads it. The cork model of Paris is not more despicable as a resemblance of a great city, than this book, *levior cortice*,[1] as a specimen of Johnson's character. Yet every body naturally likes to gather little specimens of the rarities found in a great country; and could I carry home from Italy square pieces of all the curious marbles which are the just glory of this surprising part of the world, I could scarcely contrive perhaps to arrange them so meanly as not to gain some attention from the respect due to the places they once belonged to.——Such a piece of motley Mosaic work will these Anecdotes inevitably make: but let the reader remember that he was promised nothing better, and so be as contented as he can.

An Irish trader[2] at our house one day heard Dr. Johnson launch out into very great and greatly deserved praises of Mr. Edmund Burke: delighted to find his countryman stood so high in the opinion of a man he had been told so much of, Sir (said he), give *me* leave to tell something of Mr. Burke now. We were all silent, and the honest Hibernian began to relate how Mr. Burke went to see the collieries in a distant province; and he would go down into the bowels of the earth (in a bag),[3] and he would examine every thing: he went in a bag Sir, and ventured his health and his life for knowledge; but he took care of his clothes, that they should not be spoiled, for he went down in a bag. 'Well Sir (says Mr. Johnson good-humouredly), if our friend Mund should die in any of these hazardous exploits, you and I would write his life and panegyric together; and your chapter of it should be entitled thus: *Burke in a Bag.*'

He had always a very great personal regard and particular affection for Mr. Edmund Burke, as well as an esteem difficult for me to repeat, though for him only easy to express. And when at the end of the year 1774 the general election called us all different ways, and broke up the delightful society in which we had spent some time at Beconsfield,[4] Dr. Johnson shook the hospitable master of the house kindly by the hand, and said, 'Farewel my dear Sir, and remember that I wish you all the success which ought to be wished you, which can possibly be wished you indeed—*by an honest man.*'

I must here take leave to observe, that in giving little memoirs of Mr. Johnson's behaviour and conversation, such as I saw and heard it, my book lies under manifest disadvantages, compared with theirs, who having seen him in various situations, and observed his conduct in numberless cases, are able to throw stronger and more brilliant lights upon his character. Virtues are like shrubs, which yield their sweets in different manners according to the circumstances which surround them: and while generosity of soul scatters its fragrance like the honeysuckle, and delights the senses of many occasional passengers, who feel the pleasure, and half wonder how the breeze has blown it from so far, the more sullen but not less valuable myrtle waits like fortitude to discover its excellence, till the hand arrives that will *crush* it, and force out that perfume whose durability well compensates the difficulty of production.

I saw Mr. Johnson in none but a tranquil uniform state, passing the evening of his life among friends, who loved, honoured, and admired him: I saw none of the things he did, except such acts of charity as have been often mentioned in this book, and such writings as are universally known. What he said is all I can relate; and from what he said, those who think it worth while to read these Anecdotes, must be contented to gather his character. Mine is a mere *candle-light* picture of his latter days, where every thing falls in dark shadow except the face, the index of the mind; but even that is seen unfavourably, and with a paleness beyond what nature gave it.

When I have told how many follies Dr. Johnson knew of others, I must not omit to mention with how much fidelity he would always have kept them concealed, could they of whom he knew the absurdities have been contented, in the common phrase, to keep their own counsel. But returning home one day from dining at the chaplain's table,[1] he told me, that Dr. Goldsmith had given a very comical and unnecessarily exact recital there, of his own feelings when his play was hissed;[2] telling the company how he went indeed to the Literary Club at night, and chatted gaily among his friends, as if nothing had happened amiss; that to impress them still more forcibly with an idea of his magnanimity, he even sung his favourite song about an old woman tossed in a blanket seventeen times as high as the moon; but all this while I was suffering horrid tortures (said he), and verily believe that if I had put a bit into my mouth it would have strangled me on the spot, I was so excessively ill; but I made more noise than usual to cover all that, and so they never perceived my not eating, nor I believe at all imaged to themselves the anguish of my heart: but when all were gone except Johnson here, I burst out a-crying, and even swore by—— that I would never write again. 'All which, Doctor (says Mr. Johnson, amazed at his odd frankness), I thought had been a secret between you and me; and I am sure I would not have said any thing about it for the world. Now see (repeated he when he told the story) what a figure a man makes who thus unaccountably chuses to be the frigid narrator of his own disgrace. *Il volto sciolto, ed i pensieri stretti,*[3] was a proverb made on purpose for such mortals, to keep people, if possible, from being thus the heralds of their own shame: for what compassion can they gain by such silly narratives? No man should be expected to sympathise with the sorrows of vanity. If then you are mortified by any ill usage, whether real or supposed, keep at least the account of such mortifications to yourself, and forbear to proclaim how meanly you are thought on by others, unless you desire to be meanly thought of by all.'

The little history of another friend's superfluous ingenuity will contribute to introduce a similar remark. He had a daughter of about fourteen years old, as I remember, fat and clumsy: and though the father adored, and desired others to adore her, yet being aware that she was not what the French call *paitrie des graces*,[1] and thinking I suppose that the old maxim, of beginning to laugh at yourself first where you have any thing ridiculous about you, was a good one, he comically enough called his girl *Trundle*[2] when he spoke of her; and many who bore neither of them any ill-will felt disposed to laugh at the happiness of the appellation. 'See now (says Dr. Johnson) what haste people are in to be hooted. Nobody ever thought of this fellow nor of his daughter, could he but have been quiet himself, and forborne to call the eyes of the world on his dowdy and her deformity. But it teaches one to see at least, that if nobody else will nickname one's children, the parents will e'en do it themselves.'

All this held true in matters to Mr. Johnson of more serious consequence. When Sir Joshua Reynolds had painted his portrait looking into the slit of his pen, and holding it almost close to his eye, as was his general custom, he felt displeased, and told me 'he would not be known by posterity for his *defects* only, let Sir Joshua do his worst.' I said in reply, that Reynolds had no such difficulties about himself, and that he might observe the picture which hung up in the room where we were talking, represented Sir Joshua holding his ear in his hand to catch the sound. 'He may paint himself as deaf if he chuses (replied Johnson); but I will not be *blinking Sam*.'

It is chiefly for the sake of evincing the regularity and steadiness of Mr. Johnson's mind that I have given these trifling memoirs, to shew that his soul was not different from that of another person, but, as it was, greater; and to give those who did not know him a just idea of his acquiescence in what we call vulgar prejudices, and of his extreme distance from those notions which the world has agreed, I know not very well why, to call romantic. It is indeed observable in his preface to Shakespeare, that while other critics expatiate on the creative powers and vivid imagination of that matchless poet, Dr. Johnson commends him for giving so just a representation of human manners, 'that from his scenes a hermit might estimate the value of society,[3] and a confessor predict the progress of the passions.' I have not the book with me here, but am pretty sure that such is his expression.

The general and constant advice he gave too, when consulted about the choice of a wife, a profession, or whatever influences a man's particular and immediate happiness, was always to reject no positive good from fears of its contrary consequences. 'Do not (said he) forbear to marry a beautiful woman if you can find such, out of a fancy that she will be less constant than an ugly one; or condemn yourself to the society of coarseness and vulgarity for fear of the expences or other dangers of elegance and personal charms, which have been always acknowledged as a positive good, and for the want of which there should be always given some weighty compensation. I have however (continued Mr. Johnson) seen some prudent fellows who forbore to connect themselves with beauty lest coquetry should be near, and with wit or birth lest insolence should lurk behind them, till they have been forced by their discretion to linger life away in tasteless stupidity, and chuse to count the moments by remembrance of pain instead of enjoyment of pleasure.'[1]

When professions were talked of, 'Scorn (said Mr. Johnson) to put your behaviour under the dominion of canters;[2] never think it clever to call physic a mean study, or law a dry one; or ask a baby of seven years old which way *his genius* leads him, when we all know that a boy of seven years old has no *genius* for any thing except a peg-top and an apple-pye; but fix on some business where much money may be got and little virtue risqued: follow that business steadily, and do not live as Roger Ascham[3] says the wits do, *Men know not how; and at last die obscurely, men mark not where.*'

Dr. Johnson had indeed a veneration for the voice of mankind beyond what most people will own; and as he liberally confessed that all his own disappointments proceeded from himself, he hated to hear others complain of general injustice. I remember when lamentation was made of the neglect shewed to Jeremiah Markland,[4] a great philologist as some one ventured to call him—'He is a scholar undoubtedly Sir (replied Dr. Johnson), but remember that he would run from the world, and that it is not the world's business to run after him. I hate a fellow whom pride, or cowardice, or laziness drives into a corner, and does nothing[5] when he is there but sit and *growl*; let him come out as I do, and *bark*. The world (added he) is chiefly unjust and ungenerous in this, that all are ready to encourage a man who once talks of leaving it, and few things do really provoke me more, than to hear people prate of retirement, when they have neither skill to discern their own motives, or penetration to estimate the consequences: but while a fellow is active to gain either power or wealth (continued he), every body produces some hindrance to his advancement, some sage remark, or some unfavourable prediction; but let him once say slightly, I have had enough of this troublesome

143

bustling world, 'tis time to leave it now: Ah, dear Sir! cries the first old acquaintance he meets, I am glad to find you in this happy disposition: yes, dear friend! *do* retire and think of nothing but your own ease: there's Mr. William will find it a pleasure to settle all your accounts and relieve you from the fatigue; Miss Dolly makes the charmingest chicken broth in the world, and the cheesecakes we eat of her's once, how good they were: I will be coming every two or three days myself to chat with you in a quiet way; *so snug!* and tell you how matters go upon 'Change, or in the House, or according to the blockhead's first pursuits, whether lucrative or politic, which thus he leaves; and lays himself down a voluntary prey to his own sensuality and sloth, while the ambition and avarice of the nephews and nieces, with their rascally adherents and coadjutors, reap the advantage, while they fatten their fool.'

As the votaries of retirement had little of Mr. Johnson's applause, unless that he knew that the motives were merely devotional, and unless he was convinced that their rituals were accompanied by a mortified state of the body, the sole proof of their sincerity which he would admit, as a compensation for such fatigue as a worldly life of care and activity requires; so of the various states and conditions of humanity, he despised none more I think than the man who marries for a maintenance: and of a friend who made his alliance on no higher principles, he said once, 'Now has that fellow[1] (it was a nobleman of whom we were speaking) at length obtained a certainty of three meals a day, and for that certainty, like his brother dog in the fable, he will get his neck galled for life with a collar.'

That poverty was an evil to be avoided by all honest means however, no man was more ready to avow: concealed poverty particularly, which he said was the general corrosive that destroyed the peace of almost every family; to which no evening perhaps ever returned without some new project for hiding the sorrows and dangers of the next day. 'Want of money (says Dr. Johnson) is sometimes concealed under pretended avarice, and sly hints of aversion to part with it; sometimes under stormy anger, and affectation of boundless rage; but oftener still under a show of thoughtless extravagance and gay neglect—while to a penetrating eye, none of these wretched veils suffice to keep the cruel truth from being seen. Poverty is *hic et ubique* (says he), and if you do shut the jade out of the door, she will always contrive in some manner to poke her pale lean face in at the window.'

I have mentioned before, that old age had very little of Mr. Johnson's reverence: 'a man commonly grew wickeder as he grew older (he said), at least he but changed the vices of youth; headstrong passion and wild temerity, for treacherous caution, and desire to circumvent. I am always (said he) on the young people's side, when there is a dispute between them and the old ones: for you have at least a chance for virtue till age has withered its very root.' While we were talking, my mother's spaniel whom he never loved, stole our toast and butter; Fye Belle! said I, you used to be upon honour; 'Yes Madam (replies Johnson), *but Belle grows old.*' His reason for hating the dog was, 'because she was a professed favourite (he said), and because her Lady ordered her from time to time to be washed and combed: a foolish trick (said he) and an assumption of superiority that every one's nature revolts at; so because one must not wish ill to the Lady in such cases (continued he), one curses the cur.' The truth is, Belle was not well behaved, and being a large spaniel, was troublesome enough at dinner with frequent solicitations to be fed. 'This animal (said Dr. Johnson one day) would have been of extraordinary merit and value in the state of Lycurgus;[1] for she condemns one to the exertion of perpetual vigilance.'

He had indeed that strong aversion felt by all the lower ranks of people towards four-footed companions very completely, notwithstanding he had for many years a cat which he called Hodge, that kept always in his room at Fleet-street; but so exact was he not to offend the human species by superfluous attention to brutes, that when the creature was grown sick and old, and could eat nothing but oysters, Mr. Johnson always went out himself to buy Hodge's dinner, that Francis the Black's delicacy might not be hurt, at seeing himself employed for the convenience of a quadruped.

No one was indeed so attentive not to offend in all such sort of things as Dr. Johnson; nor so careful to maintain the ceremonies of life: and though he told Mr. Thrale once, that he had never sought to please till past thirty years old, considering the matter as hopeless, he had been always studious not to make enemies, by apparent preference of himself. It happened very comically, that the moment this curious conversation past, of which I was a silent auditress, was in the coach, in some distant province, either Shropshire or Derbyshire[2] I believe; and as soon as it was over, Mr. Johnson took out his pocket a little book and read, while a gentleman of no small distinction for his birth and elegance, suddenly rode up to the carriage, and paying us all his proper compliments, was desirous not to neglect Dr. Johnson; but observing that he did not see him, tapt him gently on the shoulder—'Tis Mr. Ch—lm—ley,[3] says my husband;—'Well, Sir! and what if it is Mr. Ch—lm—ley!' says the other sternly, just lifting his eyes a moment from his book, and returning to it again with renewed avidity.

He had sometimes fits of reading very violent; and when he was in earnest about getting through some particular pages, for I have heard him say he never read but one book, which he did not consider as obligatory, through in his whole life (and Lady Mary Wortley's Letters[1] was the book); he would be quite lost to company, and withdraw all his attention to what he was reading, without the smallest knowledge or care about the noise made round him. His deafness made such conduct less odd and less difficult to him than it would have been to another man; but his advising others to take the same method, and pull a little book out when they were not entertained with what was going forward in society, seemed more likely to advance the growth of science than of polished manners,[2] for which he always pretended extreme veneration.

Mr. Johnson indeed always measured other people's notions of every thing by his own, and nothing could persuade him to believe, that the books which he disliked were agreeable to thousands, or that air and exercise which he despised were beneficial to the health of other mortals. When poor Smart, so well known for his wit and misfortunes, was first obliged to be put in private lodgings, a common friend[3] of both lamented in tender terms the necessity which had torn so pleasing a companion from their acquaintance—'A madman must be confined, Sir,' (replies Dr. Johnson;) but, says the other, I am now apprehensive for his general health, he will lose the benefit of exercise. 'Exercise! (returns the Doctor) I never heard that he used any: he might, for aught I know, walk *to* the alehouse; but I believe he was always *carried* home again.'[4]

It was however unlucky for those who delighted to echo Johnson's sentiments, that he would not endure from them to-day, what perhaps he had yesterday, by his own manner of treating the subject, made them fond of repeating; and I fancy Mr. B——[5] has not forgotten, that though his friend one evening in a gay humour talked in praise of wine as one of the blessings permitted by heaven, when used with moderation, to lighten the load of life, and give men strength to endure it; yet, when in consequence of such talk *he* thought fit to make a Bacchanalian discourse in its favour, Mr. Johnson contradicted him somewhat roughly as I remember; and when to assure himself of conquest he added these words: You must allow me, Sir, at least that it produces truth; *in vino veritas*, you know, Sir.—'That (replied Mr. Johnson) would be useless to a man who knew he was not a liar when he was sober.'[6]

When one talks of giving and taking the lie familiarly, it is impossible to forbear recollecting the transactions between the editor of Ossian[7] and the author of the Journey to the Hebrides. It was most observable to me however, that Mr. Johnson never bore his antagonist the slightest degree of ill-will. He always kept those quarrels which belonged to him as a writer, separate from those which he had to do with as a man; but I never did hear him say in private one malicious word of a public enemy;

and of Mr. Macpherson I once heard him speak respectfully, though his reply to the friend[1] who asked him if *any man living* could have written such a book, is well known, and has been often repeated; 'Yes, Sir; many men, many women, and many children.'

I enquired of him myself if this story was authentic, and he said it was. I made the same enquiry concerning his account of the state of literature in Scotland, which was repeated up and down at one time by every body—'How knowledge was divided among the Scots, like bread in a besieged town, to every man a mouthful, to no man a bellyful.' This story he likewise acknowledged, and said besides, 'that some officious friend had carried it to Lord Bute, who only answered—Well, well! never mind what he says—he will have the pension[2] all one.'

Another famous reply to a Scotsman[3] who commended the beauty and dignity of Glasgow, till Mr. Johnson stopped him by observing, 'that he probably had never yet seen Brentford,' was one of the jokes he owned: and said himself, 'that when a gentleman of that country[4] once mentioned the lovely prospects common in his nation, he could not help telling him, that the view of the London road was the prospect in which every Scotsman most naturally and most rationally delighted.'

Mrs. Brooke[5] received an answer not unlike this, when expatiating on the accumulation of sublime and beautiful objects, which form the fine prospect UP the river St. Lawrence in North America; 'Come Madam (says Dr. Johnson), confess that nothing ever equalled your pleasure in seeing that sight reversed; and finding yourself looking at the happy prospect DOWN the river St. Lawrence.' The truth is, he hated to hear about prospects and views, and laying out ground and taste in gardening: 'That was the best garden (he said) which produced most roots and fruits; and that water was most to be prized which contained most fish.' He used to laugh at Shenstone[6] most unmercifully for not caring whether there was any thing good to *eat* in the streams he was so fond of, 'as if (says Johnson) one could fill one's belly with hearing soft murmurs, or looking at rough cascades!'

He loved the sight of fine forest trees however, and detested Brighthelmstone Downs, 'because it was a country so truly desolate (he said), that if one had a mind to hang one's self for desperation at being obliged to live there, it would be difficult to find a tree on which to fasten the rope.' Walking in a wood when it rained, was, I think, the only rural image he pleased his fancy with; 'for (says he) after one has gathered the apples in an orchard, one wishes them well baked, and removed to a London eating-house for enjoyment.'

With such notions, who can wonder he passed his time uncomfortably enough with us, whom he often complained of for living so much in the country; 'feeding the chickens (as he said I did) till I starved my own understanding. Get however (said he) a book about gardening, and study it hard, since you will pass your life with birds and flowers, and learn to raise the *largest* turnips, and to breed the *biggest* fowls.' It was vain to assure him that the goodness of such dishes did not depend upon their size; he laughed at the people who covered their canals[1] with foreign fowls, 'when (says he) our own geese and ganders are twice as large: if we fetched better animals from distant nations, there might be some sense in the preference; but to get cows from Alderney, or water-fowl from China, only to see nature degenerating round one, is a poor ambition indeed.'

Nor was Mr. Johnson more merciful with regard to the amusements people are contented to call such: 'You hunt in the morning (says he), and crowd to the public rooms at night, and call it *diversion*; when your heart knows it is perishing with poverty of pleasures, and your wits get blunted for want of some other mind to sharpen them upon. There is in this world no real delight (excepting those of sensuality), but exchange of ideas in conversation; and whoever has once experienced the full flow of London talk, when he retires to country friendships and rural sports, must either be contented to turn baby again and play with the rattle, or he will pine away like a great fish in a little pond, and die for want of his usual food.'—'Books without the knowledge of life are useless (I have heard him say); for what should books teach but the art of *living?* To study manners however only in coffee-houses, is more than equally imperfect; the minds of men who acquire no solid learning, and only exist on the daily forage that they pick up by running about, and snatching what drops from their neighbours as ignorant as themselves, will never ferment into any knowledge valuable or durable; but like the light wines we drink in hot countries, please for the moment though incapable of keeping. In the study of mankind much will be found to swim as froth, and much must sink as feculence, before the wine can have its effect, and become that noblest liquor which rejoices the heart, and gives vigour to the imagination.'

I am well aware that I do not, and cannot give each expression of Dr. Johnson with all its force or all its neatness; but I have done my best to record such of his maxims, and repeat such of his sentiments, as may give to those who knew him not, a just idea of his character and manner of thinking. To endeavour at adorning, or adding, or softening, or meliorating such anecdotes, by any tricks my inexperienced pen could play, would be weakness indeed; worse than the Frenchman[2] who presides over the porcelain manufactory at Seve, to whom when some Greek vases were given him as models, he lamented *la tristesse de telles formes*;

and endeavoured to assist them by clusters of flowers, while flying Cupids served for the handles of urns originally intended to contain the ashes of the dead. The misery is, that I can recollect so few anecdotes, and that I have recorded no more axioms of a man whose every word merited attention, and whose every sentiment did honour to human nature. Remote from affectation as from error or falsehood, the comfort a reader has in looking over these papers, is the certainty that those were *really* the opinions of Johnson, which are related as such.

Fear of what others may think, is the great cause of affectation; and he was not likely to disguise his notions out of cowardice. He hated disguise, and nobody penetrated it so readily. I shewed him a letter written to a common friend, who was at some loss for the explanation of it: 'Whoever wrote it (says our Doctor) could, if he chose it, make himself understood; but 'tis the letter of an *embarrassed man, Sir;*' and so the event proved it to be.

Mysteriousness in trifles offended him on every side: 'it commonly ended in guilt (he said); for those who begin by concealment of innocent things, will soon have something to hide which they dare not bring to light.' He therefore encouraged an openness of conduct, in women particularly, 'who (he observed) were often led away when children, by their delight and power of surprising.' He recommended, on something like the same principle, that when one person meant to serve another, he should not go about it slily, or as we say underhand, out of a false idea of delicacy, to surprise one's friend with an unexpected favour; 'which, ten to one (says he), fails to oblige your acquaintance, who had some reason against such a mode of obligation, which you might have known but for that superfluous cunning which you think an elegance. Oh! never be seduced by such silly pretences (continued he); if a wench wants a good gown, do not give her a fine smelling-bottle, because that is more delicate: as I once knew a lady[1] lend the key of her library to a poor scribbling dependant, as if she took the woman for an ostrich that could digest iron.' He said indeed, 'that women were very difficult to be taught the proper manner of conferring pecuniary favours; that they always gave too much money or too little; for that they had an idea of delicacy accompanying their gifts, so that they generally rendered them either useless or ridiculous.'

He did indeed say very contemptuous things of our sex; but was exceedingly angry when I told Miss Reynolds[2] that he said, 'It was well managed of some one to leave his affairs in the hands of his wife, because in matters of business (said he), no woman stops at integrity.' This was, I think, the only sentence I ever observed him solicitous to explain away after he had uttered it. He was not at all displeased at the recollection of a sarcasm thrown on a whole profession at once; when a gentleman leaving the company, somebody who sate next Dr. Johnson asked him, who he was? 'I cannot exactly tell you Sir (replied he), and I would be loth to speak ill of any person who I do not know deserves it, but I am afraid he is an *attorney*.'[1] He did not however encourage general satire,[2] and for the most part professed himself to feel directly contrary to Dr. Swift,[3] 'who (says he) hates the world, though he loves John and Robert, and certain individuals.'

Johnson said always, 'that the world was well constructed, but that the particular people disgraced the elegance and beauty of the general fabric.' In the same manner I was relating once to him, how Dr. Collier[4] observed, that the love one bore to children was from the anticipation one's mind made while one contemplated them: 'We hope (says he) that they will some time make wise men, or amiable women; and we suffer 'em to take up our affection beforehand. One cannot love *lumps of flesh*, and little infants are nothing more. On the contrary (says Johnson), one can scarcely help wishing, while one fondles a baby, that it may never live to become a man; for it is *so* probable that when he becomes a man, he should be sure to end in a scoundrel.' Girls were less displeasing to him; 'for as their temptations were fewer (he said), their virtue in this life, and happiness in the next, were less improbable; and he loved (he said) to see a knot of little misses dearly.'

Needle-work had a strenuous approver in Dr. Johnson, who said, 'that one of the great felicities of female life, was the general consent of the world, that they might amuse themselves with petty occupations, which contributed to the lengthening their lives, and preserving their minds in a state of sanity.' A man cannot hem a pocket-handkerchief (said a lady of quality to him one day), and so he runs mad, and torments his family and friends. The expression struck him exceedingly, and when one acquaintance grew troublesome, and another unhealthy, he used to quote Lady Frances's observation,[5] 'That a man cannot hem a pocket-handkerchief.'

The nice[6] people found no mercy from Mr. Johnson; such I mean as can dine only at four o'clock, who cannot bear to be waked at an unusual hour, or miss a stated meal without inconvenience. *He* had no such prejudices himself, and with difficulty forgave them in another. 'Delicacy does not surely consist (says he) in impossibility to be pleased, and that is false dignity indeed which is content to depend upon others.'

The saying of the old philosopher,[7] who observes, That he who wants least is most like the gods, who want nothing; was a favourite sentence with Dr. Johnson, who on his own part required less attendance, sick or well, than ever I saw any human creature. Conversation was all he required to make him happy; and when he would have tea made at two o'clock in the morning, it was only that there might be a certainty of detaining his companions round him. On that principle it was that he preferred winter to summer, when the heat of the weather gave people an excuse to stroll about, and walk for pleasure in the shade, while he wished to sit still on a chair, and chat day after day, till somebody proposed a drive in the coach; and that was the most delicious moment of his life. 'But the carriage must stop sometime (as he said), and the people would come home at last;' so his pleasure was of short duration.

I asked him why he doated on a coach so? and received for answer, 'That in the first place, the company was shut in with him *there*; and could not escape, as out of a room: in the next place, he heard all that was said in a carriage, where it was my turn to be deaf:' and very impatient was he at my occasional difficulty of hearing. On this account he wished to travel all over the world; for the very act of going forward was delightful to him, and he gave himself no concern about accidents, which he said never happened: nor did the running-away of the horses on the edge of a precipice between Vernon and St. Denys in France[1] convince him to the contrary; 'for nothing came of it (he said), except that Mr. Thrale leaped out of the carriage into a chalk-pit, and then came up again, looking *as white!*' When the truth was, all their lives[2] were saved by the greatest providence ever exerted in favour of three human creatures; and the part Mr. Thrale took from desperation was the likeliest thing in the world to produce broken limbs and death.

Fear was indeed a sensation to which Mr. Johnson was an utter stranger, excepting when some sudden apprehensions seized him that he was going to die; and even then he kept all his wits about him, to express the most humble and pathetic petitions to the Almighty: and when the first paralytic stroke took his speech from him, he instantly set about composing a prayer in Latin,[3] at once to deprecate God's mercy, to satisfy himself that his mental powers remained unimpaired, and to keep them in exercise, that they might not perish by permitted stagnation. This was after we parted; but he wrote me an account of it, and I intend to publish that letter,[4] with many more.

When one day he had at my house taken tincture of antimony instead of emetic wine, for a vomit, he was himself the person to direct us what to do for him, and managed with as much coolness and deliberation as if he had been prescribing for an indifferent person. Though on another occasion, when he had lamented in the most piercing terms his approaching dissolution, and conjured me solemnly to tell him what I thought, while Sir Richard Jebb[5] was perpetually on the road to Streatham, and Mr. Johnson seemed to think himself neglected if the physician left him for an hour only, I made him a steady, but as I thought a very gentle harangue, in which I confirmed all that the Doctor had been saying, how no present danger could be expected; but that his age and continued ill health must naturally accelerate the arrival of that hour which can be escaped by none. 'And this (says Johnson, rising in great anger) is the voice of female friendship I suppose, when the hand of the hangman would be softer.'

Another day, when he was ill, and exceedingly low-spirited, and persuaded that death was not far distant, I appeared before him in a dark-coloured gown, which his bad sight, and worse apprehensions, made him mistake for an iron-grey. 'Why do you delight (said he) thus to thicken the gloom of misery that surrounds me? is it not here sufficient accumulation of horror without anticipated mourning?' This is not mourning Sir (said I), drawing the curtain, that the light might fall upon the silk, and shew it was a purple mixed with green. 'Well, well (replied he, changing his voice), you little creatures should never wear those sort of clothes however; they are unsuitable in every way. What! have not all insects gay colours?' I relate these instances chiefly to shew that the fears of death itself could not suppress his wit, his sagacity, or his temptation to sudden resentment.

Mr. Johnson did not like that his friends should bring their manuscripts for him to read,[1] and he liked still less to read them when they were brought: sometimes however when he could not refuse he would take the play or poem, or whatever it was, and give the people his opinion from some one page that he had peeped into. A gentleman carried him his tragedy, which, because he loved the author,[2] Johnson took, and it lay about our rooms some time. What answer did you give your friend, Sir? said I, after the book had been called for. 'I told him (replied he), that there was too much *Tig* and *Tirry* in it.' Seeing me laugh most violently, 'Why what would'st have, Child? (said he.) I looked at nothing but the dramatis, and there was *Ti*granes and *Tiri*-dates, or Teribazus, or such stuff. A man can tell but what he knows, and I never got any further than the first page. Alas, Madam! (continued he) how few books are there of which one ever can possibly arrive at the *last* page! Was there ever yet any thing written by mere man that was wished longer by its readers, excepting Don Quixote, Robinson Crusoe, and the Pilgrim's Progress?' After Homer's Iliad, Mr. Johnson confessed that the work of Cervantes was the greatest in the world, speaking of it I mean as a book of entertainment; and when we consider that every other author's admirers are confined to his countrymen, and perhaps to the literary classes among *them*, while Don Quixote is a sort of common property, an universal classic, equally tasted by the court and the cottage, equally applauded in France and England as in Spain, quoted by every servant, the amusement of every age from infancy to decrepitude; the first book you see on every shelf, in every shop, where books are sold, through all the states of Italy; who can refuse his consent to an avowal of the superiority of Cervantes to all other modern writers? Shakespeare himself has, till lately, been worshipped only at home, though his plays are now the favourite amusements of Vienna; and when I was at Padua some months ago,[1] Romeo and Juliet was acted there under the name of *Tragedia Veronese*; while engravers and translators *live* by the Hero of La Mancha in every nation, and the sides of miserable inns all over England and France, and I have heard Germany too, are adorned with the exploits of Don Quixote. May his celebrity procure my pardon for a digression in praise of a writer who, through four volumes of the most exquisite pleasantry and genuine humour, has never been seduced to overstep the limits of propriety, has never called in the wretched auxiliaries of obscenity or profaneness; who trusts to nature and sentiment alone, and never misses of that applause which Voltaire and Sterne labour to produce, while honest merriment bestows her unfading crown upon Cervantes.

Dr. Johnson was a great reader of French literature, and delighted exceedingly in Boileau's works.[2] Moliere I think he had hardly sufficient taste of; and he used to condemn me for preferring La Bruyere to the Duc de Rochefoucault, 'who (he said) was the only *gentleman* writer who wrote like a professed author.' The asperity of his harsh sentences, each of them a sentence of condemnation, used to disgust me however; though it must be owned that, among the necessaries of human life, a *rasp* is reckoned one as well as a *razor*.

Mr. Johnson did not like any one who said they were happy, or who said any one else was so. 'It is all *cant* (he would cry), the dog knows he is miserable all the time.' A friend whom he loved exceedingly, told him on some occasion notwithstanding, that his wife's sister was *really* happy, and called upon the lady to confirm his assertion, which she did somewhat roundly as we say, and with an accent and manner capable of offending Mr. Johnson, if her position had not been sufficient, without any thing more, to put him in very ill humour. 'If your sister-in-law is really the contented being she professes herself Sir (said he), her life gives the lie to every research of humanity; for she is happy without health, without beauty, without money, and without understanding.' This story he told me himself; and when I expressed something of the horror I felt, 'The same stupidity (said he) which prompted her to extol felicity she never felt, hindered her from feeling what shocks you on repetition. I tell you, the woman is ugly, and sickly, and foolish, and poor; and would it not make a man hang himself to hear such a creature say, it was happy?

'The life of a sailor was also a continued scene of danger and exertion (he said); and the manner in which time was spent on shipboard would make all who saw a cabin envy a gaol.'[1] The roughness of the language used on board a man of war, where he passed a week on a visit to Capt. Knight,[2] disgusted him terribly. He asked an officer what some place was called, and received for answer, that it was where the loplolly man kept his loplolly:[3] a reply he considered, not unjustly, as disrespectful, gross, and ignorant; for though in the course of these Memoirs I have been led to mention Dr. Johnson's tenderness towards *poor* people, I do not wish to mislead my readers, and make them think he had any delight in *mean* manners or coarse expressions.[4] Even dress itself, when it resembled that of the vulgar, offended him exceedingly; and when he had condemned me many times for not adorning my children with more show than I thought useful or elegant, I presented a little girl to him who came o'visiting one evening covered with shining ornaments, to see if he would approve of the appearance she made. When they were gone home, Well Sir, said I, how did you like little miss? I hope she was *fine* enough. 'It was the finery of a beggar (said he), and you know it was; she looked like a native of Cow-lane dressed up to be carried to Bartholomew fair.'[5]

His reprimand to another lady for crossing her little child's handkerchief before, and by that operation dragging down its head oddly and unintentionally, was on the same principle. 'It is the beggar's fear of cold (said he) that prevails over such parents, and so they pull the poor thing's head down, and give it the look of a baby that plays about Westminster-Bridge, while the mother sits shivering in a *niche*.'

I commended a young lady for her beauty and pretty behaviour one day however, to whom I thought no objections could have been made. 'I saw her (says Dr. Johnson) take a pair of scissars in her left hand though; and for all her father is now become a nobleman, and as you say excessively rich, I should, were I a youth of quality ten years hence, hesitate between a girl so neglected, and a *negro*.'

It was indeed astonishing how he *could* remark such minutenesses with a sight so miserably imperfect; but no accidental position of a ribband escaped him, so nice was his observation, and so rigorous his demands of propriety. When I went with him to Litchfield and came down stairs to breakfast at the inn,[6] my dress did not please him, and he made me alter it entirely before he would stir a step with us about the town, saying most satirical things concerning the appearance I made in a riding-habit; and adding, ' 'Tis very strange that such eyes as yours cannot

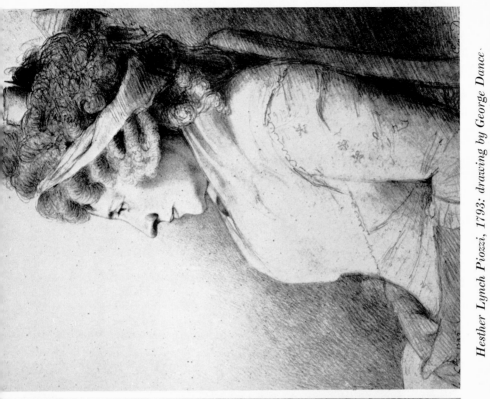

Gabriele Piozzi, 1793: drawing by George Dance

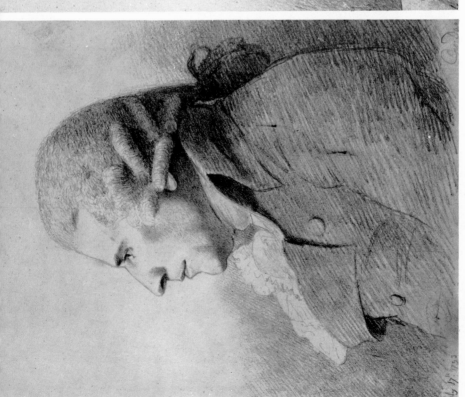

Hesther Lynch Piozzi, 1793: drawing by George Dance

Mrs. Piozzi, c. 1810

discern propriety of dress: if I had a sight only half as good, I think I should see to the centre.'

My compliances however were of little worth; what really surprised me was the victory he gained over a Lady little accustomed to contradiction, who had dressed herself for church at Streatham one Sunday morning, in a manner he did not approve, and to whom he said such sharp and pungent things concerning her hat, her gown, &c. that she hastened to change them, and returning quite another figure received his applause, and thanked him for his reproofs, much to the amazement of her husband, who could scarcely believe his own ears.

Another lady,[1] whose accomplishments he never denied, came to our house one day covered with diamonds, feathers, &c. and he did not seem inclined to chat with her as usual. I asked him why? when the company was gone. 'Why; her head looked so like that of a woman who shews puppets (said he), and her voice so confirmed the fancy, that I could not bear her to-day; when she wears a large cap, I can talk to her.'

When the ladies wore lace trimmings to their clothes, he expressed his contempt of the reigning fashion in these terms: 'A Brussels trimming is like bread sauce (said he), it takes away the glow of colour from the gown, and gives you nothing instead of it; but sauce was invented to heighten the flavour of our food, and trimming is an ornament to the manteau, or it is nothing. Learn (said he) that there is propriety or impropriety in every thing how slight soever, and get at the general principles of dress and of behaviour; if you then transgress them, you will at least know that they are not observed.'

All these exactnesses in a man who was nothing less than exact himself, made him extremely impracticable as an inmate, though most instructive as a companion, and useful as a friend. Mr. Thrale too could sometimes over-rule his rigidity, by saying coldly, There, there, now we have had enough for one lecture, Dr. Johnson; we will not be upon education any more till after dinner, if you please—or some such speech: but when there was nobody to restrain his dislikes, it was extremely difficult to find any body with whom he could converse, without living always on the verge of a quarrel, or of something too like a quarrel to be pleasing. I came into the room, for example, one evening, where he and a gentleman, whose abilities we all respect exceedingly, were sitting; a lady who walked in two minutes before me had blown 'em both into a flame, by whispering something to Mr. S——d,[2] which he endeavoured to explain away, so as not to affront the Doctor, whose suspicions were all alive. 'And have a care, Sir (said he), just as I came in; the Old Lion will not bear to be tickled.' The other was pale with rage, the Lady wept at the confusion she had caused, and I could only say with Lady Macbeth,[3]

Soh! you've displac'd the mirth, broke the good meeting
With most admir'd disorder.

Such accidents however occurred too often, and I was forced to take
advantage of my lost lawsuit,[1] and plead inability of purse to remain
longer in London or its vicinage. I had been crossed in my intentions of
going abroad,[2] and found it convenient, for every reason of health,
peace, and pecuniary circumstances, to retire to Bath, where I knew
Mr. Johnson would not follow me, and where I could for that reason
command some little portion of time for my own use; a thing impossible
while I remained at Streatham or at London, as my hours, carriage, and
servants had long been at his command, who would not rise in the
morning till twelve o'clock perhaps, and oblige me to make breakfast
for him till the bell rung for dinner, though much displeased if the toilet
was neglected, and though much of the time we passed together was
spent in blaming or deriding, very justly, my neglect of œconomy, and
waste of that money which might make many families happy. The
original reason of our connection, his *particularly disordered health and
spirits*,[3] had been long at an end, and he had not other ailments than old
age and general infirmity, which every professor of medicine was
ardently zealous and generally attentive to palliate, and to contribute all
in their power for the prolongation of a life so valuable. Veneration for
his virtue, reverence for his talents, delight in his conversation, and
habitual endurance of a yoke my husband first put upon me, and of
which he contentedly bore his share for sixteen or seventeen years, made
me go on so long with Mr. Johnson; but the perpetual confinement I will
own to have been terrifying in the first years of our friendship, and irksome in the last; nor could I pretend to support it without help, when
my coadjutor was no more. To the assistance we gave him, the shelter
our house afforded to his uneasy fancies, and to the pains we took to
sooth or repress them, the world perhaps is indebted for the three
political pamphlets,[4] the new edition and correction of his Dictionary,
and for the Poets Lives, which he would scarce have lived, I think, and
kept his faculties entire, to have written, had not incessant care been
exerted at the time of his first coming to be our constant guest in the
country; and several times after that, when he found himself particularly oppressed with diseases incident to the most vivid and fervent
imaginations.[5] I shall for ever consider it as the greatest honour which
could be conferred on any one, to have been the confidential friend of
Dr. Johnson's health; and to have in some measure, with Mr. Thrale's
assistance, saved from distress at least, if not from worse, a mind great
beyond the comprehension of common mortals, and good beyond all
hope of imitation from perishable beings.

Many of our friends were earnest that he should write the lives of our famous prose authors; but he never made any answer that I can recollect to the proposal, excepting when Sir Richard Musgrave[1] once was singularly warm about it, getting up and intreating him to set about the work immediately; he coldly replied, *'Sit down, Sir!'*

When Mr. Thrale built the new library at Streatham, and hung up over the books the portraits of his favourite friends,[2] that of Dr. Johnson was the last finished, and closed the number. It was almost impossible *not* to make verses on such an accidental combination of circumstances, so I made the following ones: but as a character written in verse will for the most part be found imperfect as a character, I have therefore written a prose one, with which I mean, not to complete, but to conclude these Anecdotes of the best and wisest man that ever came within the reach of my personal acquaintance, and I think I might venture to add, that of all or any of my readers:

> Gigantic in knowledge, in virtue, in strength,
> Our company closes with J O H N S O N at length;
> So the Greeks from the cavern of Polypheme past,
> When wisest, and greatest, Ulysses came last.
> To his comrades contemptuous, we see him look down,
> On their wit and their worth with a general frown.
> Since from Science' proud tree the rich fruit he receives,
> Who could shake the whole trunk while they turn'd a few leaves.
> His piety pure, his morality nice—
> Protector of virtue, and terror of vice;
> In these features Religion's firm champion display'd,
> Shall make infidels fear for a modern crusade.
> While th'inflammable temper, the positive tongue,
> Too conscious of right for endurance of wrong:
> We suffer from J O H N S O N, contented to find
> That some notice we gain from so noble a mind;
> And pardon our hurts, since so often we've found
> The balm of instruction pour'd into the wound.
> 'Tis thus for its virtues the chemists extol
> Pure rectified spirit, sublime alcohol;
> From noxious putrescence, preservative pure,
> A cordial in health, and in sickness a cure;
> But expos'd to the sun, taking fire at his rays,
> Burns bright to the bottom, and ends in a blaze.

It is usual, I know not why, when a character is given, to begin with a description of the person; that which contained the soul of Mr. Johnson deserves to be particularly described. His stature was remarkably high, and his limbs exceedingly large: his strength was more than common I believe, and his activity had been greater I have heard than such a form gave one reason to expect: his features were strongly marked, and his countenance particularly rugged; though the original complexion had certainly been fair, a circumstance somewhat unusual: his sight was near, and otherwise imperfect; yet his eyes, though of a light-grey colour, were so wild, so piercing, and at times so fierce, that fear was I believe the first emotion in the hearts of all his beholders. His mind was so comprehensive, that no language but that he used could have expressed its contents; and so ponderous was his language, that sentiments less lofty and less solid than his were, would have been encumbered, not adorned by it.

Mr. Johnson was not intentionally however a pompous converser; and though he was accused of using big words as they are called, it was only when little ones would not express his meaning as clearly, or when perhaps the elevation of the thought would have been disgraced by a dress less superb. He used to say, 'that the size of a man's understanding might always be justly measured by his mirth;' and his own was never contemptible. He would laugh at a stroke of genuine humour, or sudden sally of odd absurdity, as heartily and freely as I ever yet saw any man; and though the jest was often such as few felt besides himself, yet his laugh was irresistible, and was observed immediately to produce that of the company, not merely from the notion that it was proper to laugh when he did, but purely out of want of power to forbear it. He was no enemy to splendour of apparel or pomp of equipage—'Life (he would say) is barren enough surely with all her trappings; let us therefore be cautious how we strip her.' In matters of still higher moment he once observed, when speaking on the subject of sudden innovation,—'He who plants a forest may doubtless cut down a hedge; yet I could wish methinks that even he would wait till he sees his young plants grow.'

With regard to common occurrences, Mr. Johnson had, when I first knew him, looked on the still-shifting scenes of life till he was weary; for as a mind slow in its own nature, or unenlivened by information, will contentedly read in the same book for twenty times perhaps, the very act of reading it, being more than half the business, and every period being at every reading better understood; while a mind more active or more skilful to comprehend its meaning is made sincerely sick at the second perusal; so a soul like his, acute to discern the truth, vigorous to embrace, and powerful to retain it, soon sees enough of the world's dull prospect, which at first, like that of the sea, pleases by its extent, but soon, like that too, fatigues from its uniformity; a calm and a storm being the only variations that the nature of either will admit.

Of Mr. Johnson's erudition the world has been the judge; and we who produce each a score of his sayings, as proofs of that wit which in him was inexhaustible, resemble travellers who having visited Delhi or Golconda, bring home each a handful of Oriental pearl to evince the riches of the Great Mogul. May the Public condescend to accept my *ill-strung* selection with patience at least, remembering only that they are relics of him who was great on all occasions, and, like a cube in architecture, you beheld him on each side, and his size still appeared undiminished.

As his purse was ever open to almsgiving, so was his heart tender to those who wanted relief, and his soul susceptible of gratitude, and of every kind impression: yet though he had refined his sensibility, he had not endangered his quiet, by encouraging in himself a solicitude about trifles, which he treated with the contempt they deserve.

It was well enough known before these sheets were published, that Mr. Johnson had a roughness in his manner which subdued the saucy, and terrified the meek: this was, when I knew him, the prominent part of a character which few durst venture to approach so nearly; and which was for that reason in many respects grossly and frequently mistaken, and it was perhaps peculiar to him, that the lofty consciousness of his own superiority, which animated his looks, and raised his voice in conversation, cast likewise an impenetrable veil over him when he said nothing. His talk therefore had commonly the complexion of arrogance, his silence of superciliousness. He was however seldom inclined to be silent when any moral or literary question was started: and it was on such occasions, that, like the sage in Rasselas,[1] he spoke, and attention watched his lips; he reasoned, and conviction closed his periods: if poetry was talked of, his quotations were the readiest; and had he not been eminent for more solid and brilliant qualities, mankind would have united to extol his extraordinary memory. His manner of repeating deserves to be described, though at the same time it defeats all power of description; but whoever once heard him repeat an ode of Horace, would be long before they could endure to hear it repeated by another.

His equity in giving the character of living acquaintance[2] ought not undoubtedly to be omitted in his own, whence partiality and prejudice were totally excluded, and truth alone presided in his tongue: a steadiness of conduct the more to be commended, as no man had stronger likings or aversions. His veracity was indeed, from the most trivial to the most solemn occasions, strict, even to severity; he scorned to embellish a story with fictitious circumstances, which (he used to say) took off from its real value. 'A story (says Johnson) should be a specimen of life and manners; but if the surrounding circumstances are false, as it is no more a representation of reality, it is no longer worthy our attention.'

For the rest—That beneficence which during his life increased the comforts of so many, may after his death be perhaps ungratefully forgotten; but that piety which dictated the serious papers in the Rambler, will be for ever remembered; for ever, I think, revered. That ample repository of religious truth, moral wisdom, and accurate criticism, breathes indeed the genuine emanations of its great Author's mind, expressed too in a style so natural to him, and so much like his common mode of conversing, that I was myself but little astonished when he told me, that he had scarcely read over one of those inimitable essays before they went to the press.

I will add one or two peculiarities more, before I lay down my pen.——Though at an immeasurable distance from content in the contemplation of his own uncouth form and figure, he did not like another man much the less for being a coxcomb. I mentioned two friends[1] who were particularly fond of looking at themselves in a glass—'They do not surprise me at all by so doing (said Johnson): they see, reflected in that glass, men who have risen from almost the lowest situations in life; one to enormous riches, the other to every thing this world can give—rank, fame, and fortune. They see likewise, men who have merited their advancement by the exertion and improvement of those talents which God had given them; and I see not why they should avoid the mirror.'

The other singularity I promised to record, is this: That though a man of obscure birth himself, his partiality to people of family was visible on every occasion; his zeal for subordination warm even to bigotry; his hatred to innovation, and reverence for the old feudal times, apparent, whenever any possible manner of shewing them occurred. I have spoken of his piety, his charity, and his truth, the enlargement of his heart, and the delicacy of his sentiments; and when I search for shadow to my portrait, none can I find but what was formed by pride,[2] differently modified as different occasions shewed it; yet never was pride so purified as Johnson's, at once from meanness and from vanity. The mind of this man was indeed expanded beyond the common limits of human nature, and stored with such variety of knowledge, that I used to think it resembled a royal pleasure-ground, where every plant, of every name and nation, flourished in the full perfection of their powers, and where, though lofty woods and falling cataracts first caught the eye, and fixed the earliest attention of beholders, yet neither the trim parterre nor the pleasing shrubbery, nor even the antiquated ever-greens, were denied a place in some fit corner of the happy valley.[3]

Postscript

Naples, Feb. 10, 1786.
SINCE the foregoing went to the press, having seen a passage from Mr. Boswell's Tour to the Hebrides, in which it is said, that *I could not get through Mrs. Montagu's Essay on Shakespeare*, I do not delay a moment to declare, that, on the contrary, I have always commended it myself, and heard it commended by every one else; and few things would give me more concern than to be thought incapable of tasting, or unwilling to testify my opinion of its excellence.

Textual Notes

These are the main variants in Mrs. Piozzi's *Anecdotes* (references are to page and line, and to the first and fourth editions):

p. 8, 1. 21: for: but
p. 19, 1. 24: I: me
p. 27, 1. 4: bear: forbear
p. 48, 1. 7: Nichols: Nicholson
p. 61, 1. 5: Chiswick: Hammersmith
p. 67, 1. 5: *a quien: acquien*
p. 70, 1. 4: *où . . . où: ou . . . ou*
p. 78, 1. 9: forget: forgot
p. 78, 1. 24: notion: notions
p. 98, 1. 19: objections: observations
p. 103, 1. 22: cook-shops: cooks shops
p. 143, 1. 4: *n'appuyez: n'appayez*
p. 152, 1. 17: All's well that ends well:

As you like it
p. 156, 11. 1–2: said he had: he said had
p. 163, 1. 9: *tugurique: tigurique*
p. 173, 1. 1: no enemy: an enemy
p. 188, 1. 12: persons: a person
p. 207, 1. 2: aught: ought
p. 223, 11. 13–14: suddenly: sudden
p. 229, 1. 7: adjective: adverb
p. 234, 1. 21: Aliger: Aligu
p. 237, 1. 18: fore-tops: fore-top
p. 265, 1. 17: whom: who
p. 285, 11. 10–11: on shipboard: shipboard

Explanatory Notes

Anecdotes	Mrs. Piozzi, *Anecdotes of the Late Samuel Johnson, LL.D. During the Last Twenty Years of His Life,* 1786
Cooke	William Cooke, *The Life of Samuel Johnson, LL.D.* 1785; second edn, corrected, 1785
EM	*European Magazine*
Gleanings	A. L. Reade, *Johnsonian Gleanings,* 11 parts, 1909–52
GM	*Gentleman's Magazine*
Hayward	A. Hayward, *Autobiography, Letters and Literary Remains of Mrs. Piozzi (Thrale),* second edn, 2 vols., 1861
HLP	James L. Clifford, *Hester Lynch Piozzi (Mrs. Thrale),* second edn, 1952
JB	James Boswell
J Misc.	*Johnsonian Miscellanies,* ed. by G. B. Hill, 2 vols., 1897; references are to vol. i
Letters	*The Letters of Samuel Johnson,* ed. by R. W. Chapman, 3 vols, 1952
Life	James Boswell, *The Life of Samuel Johnson, LL.D.,* ed. by G. B. Hill, revised by L. F. Powell, 6 vols., 1934–50
Lives	Samuel Johnson, *Lives of the English Poets,* ed. by G. B. Hill, 3 vols., 1905
Mrs. P	Mrs. Piozzi
Poems	Samuel Johnson, *Poems,* ed. by E. L. McAdam, Jr. with George Milne, vol. vi of the Yale Edition of the Works of Samuel Johnson, 1964
Shaw	*Memoirs of the Life and Writings of the Late Dr. Samuel Johnson,* 1785
SJ	Samuel Johnson
Thraliana	*Thraliana: The Diary of Mrs. Hester Lynch Thrale (Later Mrs. Piozzi:) 1776–1809,* ed. by Katherine C. Balderston, 2 vols, second edn, 1951
Tyers	Thomas Tyers, *A Biographical Sketch of Dr. Samuel Johnson* in *GM* for Dec. 1784
UM	'Memoirs of the Life and Writings of Dr. Samuel Johnson,' in the *Universal Magazine of Knowledge and Pleasure* for August 1784

SHAW: *MEMOIRS*

Page 3.   (1) *Mrs. Du Maulin:* Mrs. Desmoulins, daughter of Dr. Swynfen. See *infra,* p. 7.

(2) *Mr. Thomas Davies:* actor, book-seller, biographer of David Garrick,

published *Miscellaneous and Fugitive Pieces* by SJ, 2 vols. 1773, with a third vol. in 1774.

(3) *Mr. Elphinston:* James Elphinston, who brought out an Edinburgh edition of the *Rambler*, had known SJ at least as early as April 1749. See *infra*, pp. 27–31.

Page 5.   (1) *sunk into the grave:* from the last paragraph of the Preface (1755). His most grievous loss was that of his wife.

Page 6.   (1) *September, 1709:* the day was the 18th, by new style dating.

(2) *Old Mr. Johnson:* Michael Johnson was both magistrate and sheriff of Lichfield during his residence there.

Page 7.   (1) *the times in which he lived:* see SJ's *Life* of Sprat, on Sprat's style of preaching: 'This I was told in my youth by my father, an old man, who had been no careless observer of the passages of those times' (*Lives* ii.37). Shaw follows *UM*, p. 91 in his wording. Elsewhere, however, the italicized remarks by SJ were presumably made with Shaw present.

(2) *Chearfulness:* SJ's father suffered from melancholy; see, for example, *Thraliana*, p. 159.

(3) *Mr. Swynfen:* Dr. Samuel Swinfen (or Swynfen); Shaw's is the fullest account of his relationship with the Johnsons.

(4) *Mr. Hunter:* according to SJ, 'abating his brutality,' the Rev. John Hunter was 'a very good master' (*Life*, ii. 146).

(5) *a Wollaston, a Newton, a Willis, a Garrick, and a Hawkesworth:* William Wollaston, writer of ecclesiastical and philosophical treaties; Thomas Newton, Bishop of Bristol; Sir John Willis, Chief Justice of the Common Pleas; David Garrick, the famous actor; and Dr. John Hawkesworth, miscellaneous writer and friend of SJ.

Page 8.   (1) *his pupils and his friends:* Garrick was at Lichfield grammar school two years after SJ; there is no evidence that Hawkesworth was ever in attendance there or at SJ's Edial school. Garrick and his brother George did, however, attend the Edial school.

(2) *the initials:* the initial stages; the beginnings.

(3) *Lives of the Poets:* published 1779–81 and revised in 1783. See *infra*, pp. 49–50.

(4) *at whose expense:* SJ's mother had fallen heir to a modest legacy, and one Andrew Corbet, then at Pembroke College, Cambridge, paid part of his expenses.

Page 9.   (1) *Pembroke college, Oxford, October 31, 1728:* Dr. Swinfen's college; the date had appeared in the *GM* obituary on SJ in December 1784, p. 957, in Tyers, p. 900, in Cooke, p. 3, and in *UM*, p. 91.

(2) *he studied several terms:* Tyers, p. 900 had written 'several terms'; SJ was at Oxford from 31 October 1728 to about 12 December 1729.

(3) *rudeness and contumely:* there is good evidence that this is true, despite Shaw's contrary opinion. See for example Tyres, p. 900.

(4) *Husband:* Rev. John Husbands, Fellow of Pembroke College, collected *A Miscellany of Poems* which was published at Oxford in 1731. Compare the wording with Tyers, p. 900, 'his elegant translation of Pope's *Messiah* into Latin verse found its way into a volume of poems published by one Husbands.'

(5) *Market Bosworth in Leicestershire:* SJ went there in 1732, probably in March, but remained only until July.

Page 10.   (1) *never in pay to booksellers:* Shaw reverts to this subject; see *infra*,
                pp. 31–2. Compare Tyers, p. 903, 'Robertson, Gibbon, and a few
                more, have raised the price of manuscript copies.'

              (2) *Blackwall:* Blackwall died on 8 April 1730, a date that appears in
                SJ's obituary in *GM*, December 1784, p. 957. See *Gleanings*, v. 75–80
                on the vexed problem of SJ and Blackwall. Tyers, p. 900, says SJ
                had been an usher to Blackwall for some time.

              (3) *marks of authenticity:* Shaw refers to 'An Account of the Writings of
                Dr. Samuel Johnson,' in the *EM* for December 1784, p. 412.

              (4) *at Litchfield:* Tom Davies (see Preface, p. 3, n. 2) wrote *Memoirs of the
                Life of David Garrick,* 2 vols. (1780); Shaw supposes there were two
                schools; there was only that at Edial, *near* Lichfield. Davies had
                given 1735 as the year of SJ's commencing instruction in the first
                edition of the *Memoirs,* but corrected it in the third edition, 1781,
                p. 7. *UM,* p. 91 and Cooke, p. 4, also speak of two schools. Shaw
                follows *UM,* p. 91, very closely.

Page 11.   (1) *Mrs Porter:* Elizabeth, widow of Harry Porter, and SJ were married
                on 9 July 1735 at Derby. She was forty-six years old and no beauty.
                See *infra*, pp. 33–5.

              (2) *romantic or impractical:* cf. Boswell's similar account of the Edial
                failure (*Life*, i. 97–9).

              (3) *the same subject:* the letter had appeared in Cooke and was cited by
                Tyers.

Page 12.   (1) *the Rev. Mr. COLSON:* John Colson, son of the Rev. Francis Colson,
                Vicar-Choral of Lichfield Cathedral, was Vicar of Chalk, Kent in
                1736.

              (2) *a Tragedy: Irene* was not acted until 6 February 1749 although
                Boswell states it was finished in 1737 (*Life*, i. 107). However, SJ was
                still revising his first draft as late as 1746 (*Poems*, p. 109).

              (3) *Gilb. Walmsley:* Gilbert Walmsley, Registrar of the Ecclesiastical
                Court of Lichfield, was one of SJ's earliest and dearest friends.

              (4) *treated with much respect:* Shaw is evidently wrong again; a second
                edition of *London* appeared a week after the first. See *Life,* i. 118–131,
                for further details of its reception. Tyers, p. 900, reports on the
                popularity of the poem. Shaw may be following Cooke, p. 10.

Page 13.   (1) *Bishop of Litchfield and Coventry:* Shaw is the only authority for this
                statement.

              (2) *the editors of newspapers:* Shaw, with his disregard of chronology, may
                refer to *The Birmingham Journal* for which SJ wrote some pieces
                now not extant. See *supra,* p. 10.

              (3) *Cave:* Edward Cave, founder of the *Gentleman's Magazine,* assumed
                the pseudonym Sylvanus Urban. SJ's poem appeared in the *GM* in
                March 1738 signed with his initials. See *infra,* p. 14, n. 4.

Page 14.   (1) *To URBAN:* the translator is not known (possibly Shaw himself?);
                an earlier English translation had appeared in the *GM* in May 1738.

              (2) *no documents before the public:* John Nichols reprinted letters from SJ
                to Cave, dated 23 November 1734 and 12 July 1737, in the January
                1785 *GM,* pp. 3–4.

              (3) *the Gentleman's Magazine:* the *GM* was founded in 1731; SJ is not
                known to have contributed until 1738.

              (4) *a few petit pieces:* of ten contributions to the *GM* in 1738 only *Ad*

Urbanum (above, pp. 13–14 and n. 1) and *The Life of Father Paul Sarpi* bore SJ's initials.

Page 15. (1) *several sessions: Debates in the Senate of Magna Lilliputia* began in 1738; the debates generally accepted as SJ's appeared in the *GM* from July 1741 through March 1744, although he was reporting debates that took place as early as November 1740. Compare Tyers, p. 900: 'his speeches . . . were begun in 1740, and continued for several sessions.' But see *PMLA*, 1959, pp. 76–8.

(2) *perceiving an imposture:* there are many anecdotes attesting to the truth of this statement.

(3) *Mr. Woodfall and Mr. Sheridan:* William Woodfall was a dramatic critic as well as a parliamentary reporter. I discover no Sheridan connected with the debates.

Page 16. (1) *his alphabet:* Shaw obviously means SJ's orthography.

(2) *Guthrie:* William Guthrie, miscellaneous writer, reported proceedings and debates for the *GM* from 1732 until SJ took over. Tyers, p. 901, calls Guthrie SJ's 'predecessor'.

(3) *Hawkesworth:* he succeeded SJ as parliamentary reporter in 1744; Tyers, p. 901, calls him SJ's 'successor'.

(4) *The Life of Savage:* Shaw errs again; SJ wrote to the *GM* in August 1743 that his biography of Richard Savage was soon to be published. It appeared in February 1744. SJ said he wrote forty-eight of the printed octavo pages of the *Life* in one sitting, 'but then I sat up all night' (*Life*, i, 166). Tyers, p. 901, says SJ took thirty-six hours to write the biography; he also reports that SJ was trying to prove himself to Cave.

(5) *this work was laid aside:* see *supra*, p. 14, n. 4. The work was abandoned because a rival, John Johnson, had already undertaken the same project. *Life*, i. 135. Shaw's language in this paragraph owes much to *UM*, p. 92.

(6) *the necessary information: Lives*, i. 335.

(7) *Fugitive Pieces: Miscellaneous and Fugitive Pieces*, see above, Preface, p. 3, n. 2. Cooke had listed the contents of the 3 vols. in an appendix.

Page 17. (1) *third Satire of Juvenal:* see *supra* p. 12, n. 4. The poem appeared in May 1738.

(2) *he had any genius:* compare Cooke, p. 11, quoting SJ: 'Dodsley was the only bookseller in London that found out I had any genius.'

(3) *Mr. Pope:* verbatim as in Cooke, p. 11. Tyers, p. 900, has Pope say 'he will soon be *déterré*.' *UM*, p. 93, may be Cooke's source.

(4) *his commentator:* William Warburton, Pope's editor: SJ's criticism of Pope's works is not marked by any exceptional 'rigidness'.

(5) *neither ancient nor modern: Lives*, iii. 246–47.

(6) *a warm admirer of Pope:* Shaw himself? See *Poems*, p. 91.

Page 18. (1) *Johnson's Imitation:* this is the opening couplet of SJ's *Vanity of Human Wishes:* Shaw is confused, what is more, as the second line should read 'Survey mankind, from China to Peru.'

(2) *ill employed: Lives*, iii, 271.

Page 19. (1) *a school in the neighbourhood of Litchfield:* Appleby School in Leicestershire. Pope recommended SJ to John Leveson-Gower, First Earl of Gower, who wrote the letter which follows.

Page 20.   (1) *Dean Swift:* the recipient of this letter was almost surely Deane Swift, Jonathan Swift's cousin.

(2) *1738:* Cooke gives 1737 (p. 17) but changes to 1738 in the second edition; Boswell has 1739 (*Life*, i. 134).

(3) *the life of this very extraordinary genius:* in *The Lives of the Poets* SJ is more than unkind to Swift.

(4) *in the year 1759:* Shaw, or the printer, is in error; the poem was published in 1749, SJ having composed it the previous year.

(5) *Cave became the publisher:* Cave published the *GM* from its beginnings in 1731; his name first appeared on the title-page in volume v.

Page 21.   (1) *Thomas Morris, Esq.:* Morris wrote a *Letter to a Friend* on the acting of tragedy and a travel *Journal*; both are in his *Miscellanies in Prose and Verse*, 1791. The *Juvenal* seems to have been abortive.

(2) *what goes by the name of Dryden:* Dryden translated the tenth Satire of Juvenal, among others.

(3) *the same gentleman:* see *supra*, p. 17 and n. 6. *Poems*, p. 91 n., attributes the strictures to Shaw.

(4) *Pope's epitaph:* *Lives*, iii. 271; the epitaph is for Edmund, Duke of Buckingham.

Page 22.   (1) *Pope's epitaph:* see *supra*, p. 21, n. 4.

Page 24.   (1) *this species of composition: An Account of the Life of Richard Savage*, published in February, 1744, came at the *end* of a series of lives, largely published in the *GM*. Cooke, pp. 26 and 29, errs similarly.

(2) *Osborne:* Thomas Osborne had hired SJ to catalogue the library of Edward Harley, 2nd Earl of Oxford. Tyers and Cooke had already printed the anecdote that follows.

Page 25.   (1) *the year 1748:* the *Plan* is dated 1747; the 4th Earl of Chesterfield died in 1773.

Page 26.   (1) *no tasting it without danger:* the intimate friend may have been Garrick, to whom SJ had unburdened himself about Chesterfield on at least one other occasion about this time.

(2) *Chambers's Dictionary:* Boswell reports that SJ told him 'he had formed his style upon that of Sir William Temple, and upon Chambers's Proposals for his Dictionary.' *Life*, i. 218–19. Ephraim Chambers's *Cyclopedia*, to which reference is made, was first published in 1728. Tyers, p. 902, has as SJ's model 'the Preface of Chambers to his *Cyclopedia*.'

Page 27.   (1) *written before he came to town:* most of the play was finished by the summer of 1737; there is evidence that SJ was still working on it as late as June 1746. It did not appear before 1749 because SJ could not find a producer.

(2) *the green-room:* but compare Boswell, under the year 1749: 'He for a considerable time used to frequent the *Green Room*' (*Life*, i. 201).

(3) *excelled in the profession:* among others Garrick and Spranger Barry and Mrs. Cibber and Mrs. Pritchard. Cooke had given most of the cast, pp. 32–3.

Page 28.   (1) *oraculous:* 'oracular'; obsolete and curiously joined with 'coarse' by Shaw.

(2) *unskilful writing:* Shaw is virtually alone in this opinion.

(3) *he might have excelled in the higher species of the drama:* Shaw follows Cooke, p. 35*.

(4) *the usage of Irene:* Shaw is also alone in advancing this suggestion. The periodical paper was SJ's *Rambler.*

(5) *Mr. Elphinston:* see the Preface, p. 3 *supra.* The Edinburgh *Ramblers* were published from 1 June 1750 to July 1752.

(6) *a collection of them:* Elphinston's translations of the mottoes were printed at the end of each volume of the Edinburgh edition. SJ's acknowledgement comes on the first page of the fourth edition, 1756.

Page 29. (1) *the celebrated Ruddiman:* Thomas Ruddiman, famous Scots philologist and editor.

(2) *the Magazine:* the *GM* for Sept. 1750 and Oct. 1752.

(3) *[Without any date]:* G. B. Hill sets the limits as Nov. 1751 and July 1752, explaining that SJ referred only to the Sept. 1750 *GM* in this letter (*Life,* ii. 210–11 and notes).

Page 30. (1) *Mrs. Strahan:* William Strahan, the printer, was Elphinston's brother-in-law.

(2) *fifty-second and fifty-fourth numbers:* 'The contemplation of the calamities of others, a remedy for grief' and 'A death-bed the true school of wisdom. The effects of death upon the survivors,' 15 and 22 September, 1750.

Page 31. (1) *five guineas a week:* SJ was paid two guineas for each paper; they appeared on Tuesdays and Saturdays.

(2) *David Hume:* Shaw refers to *Essays, Moral and Political,* 1751; an *Enquiry Concerning the Principles of Morals,* 1751; and *Political Discourses,* 1752.

(3) *a gentle-man author:* see *supra,* p. 9.

Page 32. (1) the *Rambler:* Hume's remark does not appear in his published work.

(2) *several petty pieces:* the small (petty) pieces SJ wrote between 1745 and 1753 or '54 are many and varied – and not all small. Shaw also refers to 'petit pieces' above, p. 14.

(3) *the day that was passing over me:* Cooke, p. 40* misquotes the same passage.

Page 33. (1) *cumberous:* 'unwieldy,' 'clumsy.'

(2) *three hundred pounds a year:* Shaw mistakes; SJ was in need again in 1755.

Page 34. (1) *so handsome:* see *supra,* p. 11, n. 1.

(2) *Bromley Church, Kent:* 'He deposited the remains of Mrs. Johnson in the church of Bromley in Kent, to which he was probably led by the residence of his friend Hawkesworth at that place' (*Life,* i. 241). The date on the stone is wrong as Mrs. Johnson died in 1752. The error is SJ's. Shaw echoes the *GM* for December 1784: 'an epitaph, inscribed on a black marble grave stone in Bromley church, Kent' (p. 884). I have corrected some errors in transcription.

Page 35. (1) *The North Briton:* by John Wilkes, who made capital of SJ's definition of 'pension': 'an allowance made to any one without an equivalent. In England it is generally understood to mean pay given to state hireling for treason to his country.'

(2) *c'est un falballa: EOD* has 'furbelow' as 'an alteration of "falbala".'

(3) *the word 'oats':* 'a grain, which in England is generally given to horses, but in Scotland supports the people.'

Page 36. (1) *'pension' or 'pensioners':* for 'pension,' see *supra*, p. 35, n. 1. A pensioner is 'One who is supported by an allowance paid at the will of another; a dependant.'

(2) *the excise:* 'A hateful tax levied upon commodities, and adjudged not by the common judges of property, but wretches hired by those to whom excise is paid.'

(3) *Moore, author of the World:* Edward Moore; *The World* ran from January 1753 to December 1756. There is no evidence that he acted for Chesterfield in the matter of the *Dictionary.*

(4) *two very elegant papers in the World:* those for Nov. 28 and Dec. 5, 1754. Shaw again relies heavily on *UM*, p. 95.

(5) *a Lord among wits:* Shaw is conflating two anecdotes. The 'cockboats' anecdote is a blown-up version of something SJ said to Garrick; the 'Lord among wits,' is a variant on SJ's statement to Joseph Fowke. See *Life*, i. 260, n. 1 and 266, n. 1. Tyers, p. 903, has the cock-boat anecdote. Cooke, p. 39*, has both anecdotes, although worded differently; both appear in *UM*, p. 95.

(6) *In the year following:* 1756; the two political essays appeared in the *Literary Magazine, or Universal Review.*

Page 37. (1) *the year forty-five:* his *Miscellaneous Observations on the Tragedy of Macbeth* was published in that year with proposals for an edition of all the plays.

(2) *respect and gratitude to him to the last:* Warburton praised SJ's *Miscellaneous Observations* in the Preface to his own edition of Shakespeare (1747). SJ was severe on many of Warburton's notes on Shakespeare in his edition (1765), but he paid tribute to him in his *Life* of Pope (1781). And see *supra*, p. 17, n. 4.

(3) *the text of Shakespear:* Shaw is saying that SJ, the *Dictionary* out of the way, now wrote his Shakespeare *Proposals.*

Page 38. (1) *the Idler:* the periodical ran from 15 April 1758 to 5 April 1760. Shaw's 'subsequent year' is 1757, as he had been discussing the 1756 Shakespeare *Proposals.*

(2) *on what terms is not known:* SJ was paid £84 for the first collected edition of the *Idler.*

(3) *our English soldiers: An Essay on the Bravery of the English Common Soldiers* first appeared in the *British Magazine,* January 1760.

(4) *second parts:* Cooke, p. 36, writes of the 'general faults of *second* parts.'

(5) *Voyage to Abyssinia:* Shaw goes back abruptly to 1735.

Page 39. (1) *Rasselas or Prince of Abyssinia:* there can be no knowing how early SJ conceived the work, which was published in 1759 and written only weeks prior to its publication.

(2) *Protogenes:* celebrated Greek painter known for the perfect execution of his work.

(3) *credit for twenty guineas:* there is no evidence for this story. *Rasselas* was sold to Strahan to whom SJ first offered it.

Page 40. (1) *his Idler:* 'On the Death of a Friend.' Cooke had reprinted the entire essay, pp. 37–44.

(2) *sold to another bookseller:* Shaw follows Cooke, p. 49, even to the very words.

(3) *Lord Bute:* Boswell writes: 'Lord Bute [John Stuart, 3rd Earl of Bute, then Prime Minister] told me, that Mr. Wedderburne, now Lord

Loughborough, was the person who first mentioned this subject to him' (*Life*, i. 373).

(4) *Mr. Murphy:* Murphy's account is in his *Essay on the Life and Genius of Samuel Johnson*, 1792, much too late to be that to which Shaw refers. Most of one paragraph in the *EM* for March 1785, p. 191, is devoted to SJ's pension.

(5) *Memoirs of G. Anne Bellamy: By a Gentleman of Covent Garden Theatre*, 1785. The reference is probably to Dr. Philip Francis who got 'a promotion' to private chaplain for Lady Caroline Fox on Miss Bellamy's interceding for him with Fox (p. 126). Francis was also recommended for a pension of £300 by George Grenville.

(6) *to draw a tree:* Shaw is sole authority for this and the following anecdote.

(7) *in the newspapers:* unidentified.

(8) *Mr. Steevens:* George Steevens collaborated with SJ in a revised edition of the Shakespeare, published in 1773.

Page 41. (1) *one of the Popes:* unidentified.

(2) *to the conclusion:* in his Preface to the edition.

Page 42. (1) *from the year 1760 to about 1775:* the dates of publication are, respectively, 1774, 1770, 1771, and 1775. Cooke had given 1769–1775 as the dates, p. 50. *UM*, p. 96, gives the correct dates.

(2) *Fordyce:* Alexander Fordyce, banker, 'failed' in 1772; there is no other account of SJ's intimacy with him.

(3) *the title and advertisement: Sermons to Young Women*, 1765. A. T. Hazen, *Samuel Johnson's Prefaces and Dedications* (New Haven, 1937), p. 34, attributes the preface to SJ. See, however, my article, 'Some Observations on Johnson's Prefaces and Dedications' in *English Writers of the Eighteenth Century* (New York, 1972).

(4) *His account of this journey: A Journey to the Western Islands of Scotland.*

(5) *Ossian's poems:* James Macpherson claimed to have translated, from manuscripts, poems by Ossian, an ancient Gaelic poet.

(6) *of guilt:* Cooke, p. 54, quotes the same passage to somewhat greater length.

Page 43. (1) *S. JOHNSON:* dated 20 January 1775; Macpherson's letter has yet to be found. See *Life*, ii. 511–14 for a full account of SJ's part in the controversy. And see *Life*, ii. 298 for Boswell's slightly different and more dramatic text of SJ's letter. Shaw's is the same text he had quoted in his *Enquiry*, 1782, pp. 11–12.

(2) *General Melville:* Robert Melville combined antiquarian interests with a military career. Shaw acknowledged his aid in the Preface to his *Galic and English Dictionary*, 1780.

(3) *the Rev. Mr. Shaw:* William Shaw, anonymous author of these memoirs. SJ's first reference to Shaw is in a letter to Boswell dated 11 March 1777, but he had received all or part of the manuscript of Shaw's 'Erse Grammar' in 1776.

(4) *Dr. Beattie:* James Beattie, poet and philosopher, friend of SJ; Shaw alone records this anecdote so flattering to himself. He, too, is sole authority for the following anecdote about himself.

(5) *the present Earl of Eglintoun:* Archibald Eglinton (or Eglintoune), 11th Earl of Eglinton, to whom Shaw dedicated his *Analysis of the Galic Language*, 1778.

(6) *Galic:* Gaelic; SJ writes of Shaw's 'Erse Grammar' (*Life*, iii. 106).

Page 44.
(1) *Mr. Strahan:* William Strahan, well-known printer. See *supra*, p. 30, n. 1.

(2) *a collection . . . and MSS:* his *Galic and English Dictionary*, 1780, to which SJ subscribed.

Page 45.
(1) *the following letter:* first published in these *Memoirs*.

(2) *Mrs. Williams:* blind Mrs. Anna Williams had been a member of SJ's household since the death of his wife, whose friend she was.

(3) *Macnicol:* the Rev. Donald M'Nicol wrote scurrilous *Remarks on Dr. Samuel Johnson's Journey to the Hebrides*, 1779.

(4) *Clark's answer:* John Clark's *An Answer to Mr. Shaw's Inquiry*, 1781.

Page 46.
(1) *parliament:* Macpherson became member for Camelford, Cornwall in 1780.

(2) *asses, apes, and dogs!:* Milton, Sonnet xii.

Page 47.
(1) *religious . . . apostacy:* SJ persuaded Shaw to renounce the Church of Scotland for the Church of England.

Page 48.
(1) *ANTI-OSSIAN:* unidentified.

(2) *a state of the controversy:* this is not in the long list of SJ's projected works (*Life*, iv, 301–2).

Page 49.
(1) Τὸν πρῶτον κινοῦντα ἀκίνητον: Aristotle, *Metaphysics*, iii. 8, 'the prime mover is itself unmoved.'

(2) *men without hope:* I Thessalonians, iv. 13.

(3) *the year 1778:* SJ was solicited to undertake the work on 29 March 1777.

(4) *two hundred pounds:* he asked for and received two hundred guineas to which the booksellers added another hundred guineas. A further hundred guineas was given him when the *Lives* were published separately. Tyers, p. 905, had said the booksellers gave SJ £300 and added £100 as 'a gratuity'. Cooke, p. 60, has the price as £200.

(5) *the Apollo press:* the press of John Bell, the enterprising bookseller and publisher who specialized in books in small sizes.

Page 50.
(1) *the declension of those abilities:* compare Cooke, p. 61: 'the Doctor's powers had been thought to be rather on the decline.'

(2) *deprived him for some time of the power of speech:* compare Cooke, p. 67: 'deprived him of the powers of speech.'

(3) *Dr. Heberden and Dr. Brocklesby:* SJ called William Heberden *ultimus Romanorum*; Richard Brocklesby was co-founder with SJ of the Essex-Head Club. Cooke, p. 69, had called the two men SJ's 'usual physicians.'

(4) *the Essex-Head:* on Essex Street in the Strand. The club rules had already been printed in the *GM* for February 1785, p. 99. Cooke was a member of the club.

(5) *a dropsy . . . some months:* very close in wording to Cooke, pp. 70–1.

(6) *the Lord Chancellor:* Edward Thurlow, 1st Baron Thurlow.

Page 51.
(1) *five hundred pounds:* Cooke, p. 72, also includes this fact. Shaw, four lines below, echoes Cooke's 'unexpected'.

(2) *not the least happy of his productions:* the letter had appeared in the *GM* for December, 1784, pp. 892–3 and in Cooke, pp. 72–4.

(4) *Mrs. Thrale:* Mrs. Thrale married Gabriel Piozzi on 23 July 1784.

Page 52.
(1) *his last will:* the will was published in the *GM* for December 1784, p. 946 and printed in Cooke's *Life*.

Page 53. (1) *Mrs. Williams:* see *supra*, p. 45, and n. 2.

(2) *Mr. Leveret:* Robert Levett, whom Boswell describes as 'an obscure practitioner in physick amongst the lower people' (*Life*, i. 243) is the subject of a letter in the *GM* for February 1785, pp. 101–2. SJ wrote a well-known poem upon his death.

(3) *about seven o'clock:* the hour of SJ's death appears in his obituary in the *GM* for December 1784, p. 957 and in Cooke, p. 79. Shaw's '1785' is, of course, an error.

(4) *what he has said of Dryden: Lives*, i. 417.

Page 55. (1) *a bookseller of eminence:* J. L. Clifford, *Young Samuel Johnson* (London, 1955), pp. 260–1, conjectures that this is Thomas Osborne. See *supra*, p. 24, n. 2.

(2) *Goldsmith:* there is no other authority for the following anecdotes about SJ and Goldsmith.

MRS. PIOZZI: *ANECDOTES*

Page 59. (1) *somewhere heard or read:* unidentified.

(2) *A Midsummer Night's Dream:* V. i, 'Never excuse; for when the players are all dead there need none to be blamed.'

(3) *the river Jenisca:* the Yenesei river is in the U.S.S.R.

Page 60. (1) *eleven nameless rivers:* Mrs. P. forgot or had not read the account of the Nile in Father Lobo's *Voyage to Abyssinia*, translated by SJ in 1735.

(2) *the Telamonian shield:* the reference is to Ajax, son of Telamon's, covering the retreat of the Greeks in the *Iliad*, xi. 544–74.

Page 61. (1) *little had ever been said about Butler:* 'the mode and place of his education are unknown; the events of his life are variously related; and all that can be told with certainty is, that he was poor' (*Lives*, i. 209).

(2) *the request of the deceased:* see *infra*, p. 70.

(3) *'acted' by the lords and ladies:* the children of the Earl of Bridgewater.

(4) *I have found friends:* see *HLP*, pp. 235–59, for an account of some of these friends.

Page 62. (1) *lock the door:* Michael Johnson was used to locking the door of his parchment factory, not his bookshop (*Gleanings*, iii. 95).

(2) *the prevalence of imagination:* Mrs. P. echoes the title of *Rasselas*, ch. 43, 'The Dangerous Prevalance of Imagination.' See *infra*, p. 86 for SJ and 'the diseases of the imagination.'

(3) *an uncle, Cornelius Ford:* he was SJ's cousin; see *infra*, p. 14 where Mrs. P refers to SJ as Ford's 'cousin.'

(4) *kept the ring:* defended it successfully against challengers.

(5) *a cabriolet stool:* probably an aid to entering the light two-wheeled carriage. The leap must have been over the length of the stool. Mrs. P describes its location as indoors, however (*Thraliana*, p. 190).

(6) *upwards of forty:* Michael was fifty; his wife, thirty-seven. They wed in 1706.

(7) *Nathaniel:* he was twenty-four when he died.

Page 63. (1) *in Rasselas:* ch. 26.

(2) *age of seventy-six:* Michael Johnson was seventy-five when he died.

(3) *the general friend:* 1. 297, part of a generalized portrait of virtuous old age (11. 291–8).

(4) *Mrs. Corbet:* 'On Mrs. Corbet, who Died of a Cancer in her Breast' (*Lives*, iii. 262–3).

(5) *Lucan:* SJ wrote of Lucan in his *Life* of Nicholas Rowe that he 'is distinguished by a kind of dictatorial or philosophic dignity, rather, as Quintilian observes, declamatory than poetical; full of ambitious morality and pointed sentences, comprised in vigorous and animated lines' (*Lives*, ii. 77).

(6) *the scrophulous evil:* known as the 'King's evil' for which the royal touch was considered sovereign. SJ was touched on 30 March 1712.

(7) *christening of his brother:* SJ was just three years old on 14 October 1712 when the ceremony was performed.

Page 64. (1) *epitaph upon the duck:* the duck was one of thirteen. SJ said his father wrote half the epitaph. See *Poems*, p. 354 for further details and variant readings.

(2) *late marriages:* compare *Life*, ii. 128: 'He did not approve of late marriages' and see *Rasseles*, ch. 28.

(3) *I have forgot who the father was:* Hill conjectures he was Bennet Langton (*JMisc.* i. 154 n. 1).

(4) *think higher of herself:* SJ's mother was proud of her descent from the Fords.

Page 65. (1) *of Fenton and of Broome:* Lives, ii. 261 and iii. 75. SJ refers to Ford's notoriety in the first of these passages.

(2) *your pretensions as a writer:* SJ had spent more than six months with Ford in 1725–26.

(3) *jamais mal de personne:* Mrs. P has this largely right. Boileau's father said of him that he was *un bon garçon qui ne dirait jamais mal de personne.*

(4) *her old maid Catherine:* Catherine Chambers, of the same age as SJ, joined the John household in 1724 when she was fifteen. Mrs. P is in error.

(5) *she was dead:* SJ wrote a prayer on her death. She died 17 October 1767, aged fifty-eight years. See *JMisc.* i. 45.

(6) *Newbery's books:* John Newbery, well-known bookseller, did a thriving trade in children's books.

(7) *Mrs. Barbauld:* Anna Letitia Barbauld, née Aikin, wrote some famous 'Hymns in Prose for Children.' SJ spoke harshly of her, according to Dr. Burney (*Life* ii. 408, and iv. 8 n. 3).

Page 66. (1) *eight years old:* he was almost seven and a half, but he had already attended school under Dame Oliver and then under Thomas Browne.

(2) *De Veritate Religionis:* probably Hugo Grotius's work of that name. SJ admired Grotius. See *Life* iiii. 125 and *Lives* i. 57.

(3) *Dr. Taylor:* the Rev. Dr. John Taylor of Ashbourne, schoolfellow and friend of SJ.

(4) *Bathurst is dead!!!:* Dr. Richard Bathurst, member of SJ's Ivy-Lane Club, died in 1762.

(5) *an ingenious and learned friend:* possibly William Parsons, Robert Merry, or Bertie Creatheed. *HLP*, p. 249. Mrs. P was very fond of Rousseau herself. (*HLP*, pp. 28, 327).

(6) *the Ghost scene:* Act IV, i; compare his note on *Macbeth*, II. i, the description of night before Duncan's murder: 'He that peruses

Shakespeare, looks around alarmed, and starts to find himself alone.'

Page 67. (1) *Hunter:* see *supra*, p. 7, and n. 4.

(2) *His next master:* the Rev. John Wentworth, headmaster of Stourbridge School.

(3) *coffee:* see the *British Apollo*, ii, No. 19 (1709) where 'Turkey [Turkish] Coffee' is listed as costing 6s. 4d. per pound, making it a luxury item.

(4) *I will not repeat them here:* they are lost.

Page 68. (1) *before the next vacation:* Dr. Robert Carey Sumner, Head Master of Harrow, died in 1771. See *JMisc.* ii. 4 for his version of SJ's dining with Mrs. Macaulay.

(2) *cant:* SJ often inveighed against 'cant', which he defined in his *Dictionary* as '2. A particular form of speaking peculiar to some certain class or body of men . . . 3. A whining pretension to goodness, in formal and affected terms . . . 4. Barbarous jargon.'

Page 69. (1) *Pere Rollin:* Charles Rollin, French historian and educator; Mrs. P probably read his *Method of Teaching and Studying the Belles Lettres*. See the 6th edition, 1769, ii. 405 for the passage cited.

(2) *sorrow suffered:* schoolmasters were much given to the rod.

(3) *a favourite workman:* 'Thomas Jackson, their man-servant' (*Life* i. 38).

(4) *quitted school:* SJ 'quitted school' in 1729; he was twenty years old.

(5) *Dr. Adams:* the Rev. Dr. William Adams, then Fellow and later Master of Pembroke College, Oxford. See *The Correspondence and Other Papers of James Boswell Relating to the Making of the 'Life of Johnson'*, ed. Marshall Waingrow (New York, 1970), *passim*, for Adams and SJ.

(6) *Dr. Taylor:* see *supra*. p. 66, and n. 3, and Waingrow, op. cit., pp. 98–107 and *passim*.

Page 70. (1) *Mr. Jordan:* the Rev. William Jordan, for whom SJ translated Pope's *Messiah* into Latin, but from whose instruction, despite his affection for Jordan, he 'did not profit much' (*Life* i. 59 and 61).

(2) *who will be my biographer:* SJ knew by this time that Boswell intended to be his biographer.

(3) *him and Adams:* see *supra*, p. 69 and n. 5.

(4) *Dr. James:* Dr. Robert James, physician and SJ's schoolmate in Lichfield; SJ helped him with his *Medicinal Dictionary*, 1743. SJ was thirteen when James left for Oxford.

(5) *Jack Hawkesworth:* Dr. John Hawkesworth, miscellaneous writer, was associated with SJ in the *GM* and in *The Adventurer* essays.

(6) *you took me up:* in 1765.

(7) *a diary:* he burned it shortly before his death.

(8) *1768:* in the *GM* for September, p. 439. See *Poems*, pp. 79–80 for variants.

Page 71. (1) *dear Mund:* Edmund Hector, SJ's very dear friend, who solicited the verses for a friend in Birmingham in 1731.

(2) *Shenstone:* William Shenstone's *A Pastoral Ballad in Four Parts*. Omit the second 'that' in the first line.

Page 72. (1) *died about that time:* the Rev. Dr. Edward Barnard died in December 1781.

(2) *my good breeding:* see *infra,* pp. 96, 112, 146, 154, and *Thraliana,* p. 182.

(3) *M——'s:* William Mason, poet, dramatist, friend and biographer of Gray; SJ refers to his plays *Caractacus* and *Elfrida.*

(4) *Mr. Jordan:* see *supra,* p. 70, n. 2. In 1754 Thomas Warton told Boswell, SJ 'seemed to retain the highest regard' for Jordan, then dead fifteen years (*Life* i. 272).

(5) *Sir William Browne the physician:* he was noted for his wit and gallantry to the ladies. He died in 1774, aged 82.

Page 73. (1) *Dr. Trapp:* Dr. Joseph Trapp, first Professor of Poetry at Oxford, was poet, essayist, pamphleteer, and wit.

(2) *Junius:* Junius's identity is still unknown. His letters were published between 1769 and 1771. SJ attacked but did not destroy him in *Thoughts on the Late Transactions Respecting Falkland's Islands,* published in the spring of 1771.

(3) *The False Alarm:* published in 1770; the last, *Taxation No Tyranny,* was published in 1775.

Page 74. (1) *Lord Bathurst:* in his speech 'On Conciliation With America,' 22 March 1775 Burke imagined Lord Bathurst's guardian angel predicting for him the future importance of America. Allen Bathurst, friend of Pope, was 1st Earl of Bathurst, some of whose speeches SJ reported in the *GM.*

(2) *to Wharton, or to Marlborough:* Thomas Wharton, 1st Marquis of Wharton and John Churchill, 1st Duke of Marlborough.

(3) *see:* 'fee' in *Thraliana,* p. 194.

(4) *the force of the expressions:* Boswell casts doubt on the accuracy of Mrs. P's reporting (*Life* iv. 317).

(5) *sitting steadily:* Hill conjectures 'stealthily'; Mrs. P. refers of course to Boswell.

(6) *a common-place book: Thraliana.*

Page 75. (1) *Anacreon's Dove:* Ode ix.

(2) *Frank Fawkes:* Francis Fawkes, probably best known for his translation of Theocritus, published *The Works of Anacreon, Sappho, Bion, Moscus and Musaeus* in 1760.

Page 76. (1) *Mr. Hector:* see *supra,* p. 71, n. 1 for Hector; the work was SJ's translation of Father Lobo's *Voyage to Abyssinia.* Mrs. P got this bit of information from Samuel Lysons to whom it had been told by JB himself (*Bulletin of John Rylands Library,* 1936, p. 277).

(2) *the Poets Lives: Lives* iii. 120–5.

(3) *Mr. Nichols:* John Nichols printed the *Lives.*

(4) *in Sir Joshua Reynolds's parlour: Rambler* 134, 29 June 1751, appeared while Reynolds was in Italy.

(5) *in the Idler:* No. 131; Sober loves conversation and fears solitude.

(6) *story of Gelaleddin: Idler* 75. Gelaleddin is a learned and witty Persian student.

(7) *his favourite: Rambler* 33.

(8) *life and manners: Rambler* 165.

(9) *Garrick: Rambler* 200; the rich Prospero condescends to an old friend.

(10) *Sophron: Idler* 57; the original of Sophron is not known.

(11) *Mr. Coulson:* of *Rambler* 24. Probably a Mr. Coulson who was at

Oxford with SJ and not the Reverend John Colson the mathematician. See *infra*, p. 85, n. 3 and *Thraliana*, p. 162, n. 3.

(12) *a proctor in the Commons:* Doctors' Commons in London, concerned with admiralty and ecclesiastical matters. A William Busby, proctor of Doctors' Commons died in September 1726 and an Edward Busby, Marshal of the Admiralty in Doctors' Commons died on 17 May 1751. Musgrave's *Obituaries.* The *GM* obituary notice, however, describes Busby as a 'procurator general of the arches court of Canterbury' (p. 236), to which the *London Magazine* (also p. 236) adds 'marshal of the high court of Admiralty, and late high sheriff for Staffordshire.' William Busby seems too early to fit the anecdote.

(13) *Dr. Salter:* Samuel Salter, master of the Charterhouse, was son to Samuel, archdeacon of Norfolk and a member of SJ's Ivy-Lane Club.

(14) *Richardson, an attorney:* otherwise unknown to fame. He and the two preceding wags appear in *Rambler* 188.

(15) *Miss Talbot:* Catherine Talbot wrote *Rambler* 30. For her comments on the periodical, see *Life* i. 208, nn. 2 and 3.

(16) *Mrs. Chapone:* Hester Chapone, née Mulso, wrote four letters for the tenth *Rambler.*

(17) *Carter:* Elizabeth Carter, upon whom SJ wrote a Greek epigram and English verses (*Poems*, pp. 45 and 62), contributed *Ramblers* 44 and 100 (the latter is the allegory).

(18) *his own satire: The Vanity of Human Wishes*, 11. 135–164.

Page 77.   (1) *George Lewis:* George Lewis Scott, mathematician, sub-preceptor to Prince George (later George III), was made Commissioner of Excise in 1758. He married Sarah Robinson, sister to Mrs. Elizabeth Montagu.

(2) *prefaces . . . and dedications:* the standard work on these is Allen T. Hazen's *Samuel Johnson's Prefaces and Dedications* (New Haven, 1937).

(3) *a dead stay-maker and a dying parson:* SJ wrote a prologue for a benefit performance for the recently deceased Hugh Kelly's *A Word to the Wise.* Kelly had been an apprentice staymaker. Dr. William Dodd, for whom SJ wrote *The Convict's Address to his Unhappy Brethren,* was soon thereafter hanged for forgery.

(4) *porter:* Henry Thrale was a brewer.

(5) *his health:* there is no record of illness during the *Dictionary* period.

Page 78.   (1) *1768:* she is not sure of the date in *Thraliana*, p. 165.

(2) *have it done carefully:* the revised *Dictionary* was published in 1773. See *Philological Quarterly* 1952 on the extent and kind of revision.

(3) *its coming out first:* Mrs. P means 'upon its first appearance.'

(4) *the Greek language:* SJ was overly modest; his knowledge of Greek was praised by many. See *Life* iv. 384–5.

(5) *at our country-house:* George Colman brought Peter Sturz to Streatham. Johnson was there, and Sturz has left an account of the meeting. See *HLP*, p. 76 and *TLS*, 10 February 1940, p. 80.

(6) *Fugitive Pieces:* see *supra* p. 3 and n. 2.

(7) *Tom Davies:* Davies had fallen on evil days; he went bankrupt in 1778 and SJ solicited help for him (*Life* iii. 223).

Page 79.   (1) *has done wonders:* elsewhere SJ is more guarded in his praise of Pope's efforts.

(2) *Dryden:* for SJ's comparison of Dryden and Pope see *Lives* iii. 220–3.

(3) *the Rehearsal:* Dryden was satirized as the dramatist Mr. Bayes in the 2nd Duke of Buckingham's play, 1671. In 1772 SJ told Boswell he questioned whether the satire 'was meant for Dryden' (*Life* ii. 168).

(4) *from putrefaction:* SJ had originally said, 'It has not wit enough to keep it sweet' (*Life* iv. 320).

(5) *twenty lines in a series:* in his *Life* of Dryden SJ reduces the number to ten (*Lives* i. 464).

(6) *Mourning Bride:* William Congreve's sole tragedy (1697), II. i. The same judgement appears in Boswell, *Life* ii. 85–6 and 96 and in the *Life* of Congreve (*Lives* ii. 229–30).

(7) *Dryden and Shakespeare:* SJ had made this comparison of the passages in Dryden's *Indian Emperor*, III. ii and *Macbeth*, II. i as early as the 1745 *Miscellaneous Observations on the Tragedy of Macbeth.*

(8) *its end:* Edward Young's *Night Thoughts*, i. 23.

(9) *a clipped hedge is to a forest:* compare SJ's Preface to Shakespeare: 'The work of a correct and regular writer is a garden accurately formed . . . ; the composition of Shakespeare is a forest . . .'

(10) *Steele's essays:* SJ had almost nothing else to say about Steele's essays.

Page 80.   (1) *Hermes: Hermes, or a Philosophical Inquiry Concerning Universal Grammar*, 1751. The dedication is thirty lines long; however, the first page contains exactly fourteen lines. Harris is careless with 'you', 'My Lord', and 'your Lordship'. Mrs. P had the correct number of lines in the anecdote in her marginal comment opposite the dedication in her copy of *Hermes* (*HLP*, p. 27, n. 2).

(2) *Ordinary of Newgate's account:* for a more detailed version of this anecdote see *Life*, ii. 65.

(3) *Mr. Rose of Chiswick:* Dr. William Rose, schoolmaster and translator.

(4) *Ferguson upon Civil Society:* Adam Fergusson, *Essay on the History of Civil Society*, 1766. In Boswell's version of this anecdote Rose names 'Lord Bute, when he signed the warrant for your pension' instead of Fergusson. See *Life* iv. 168, n. 1 and iv. 509 for Murphy's conflation of the anecdotes.

(5) *Buckinger:* Matthew Buckinger, born without hands or feet, according to one account, could 'write the Lord's Prayer in the compass of a silver penny.' Walpole, *Letters*, ed. Cunningham, iv. 159. How Buckinger wrote at all is still unexplained. See *Notes and Queries*, clxxiii (1937), 296, on this remarkable person.

(6) *a modern Martial:* the translation by SJ's friend James Elphinston, 1782 (see above, p. 28 and n. 6). The work was universally ridiculed. Elphinston is named in *Thraliana*, p. 208.

(7) *a writer of the first eminence:* the historian, Dr. William Robertson. *Life* iii. 336.

(8) *a first cousin:* probably Thomas Cotton, but I cannot discover how he died.

Page 81.   (1) *Sir Robert Cotton's:* Mrs. P's cousin (*Life* v. 435–6, n. 2).

    (2) *to a 'pig':* Mrs. P explains, in a marginal note, 'because they were too little boiled' (Hayward, ii. 295).

    (3) *the year 1777:* Thomas Warton's *Poems:* for Boswell's account of this see *Life* iii. 158. Warton is named in *Thraliana*, p. 208.

    (4) *another eminent writer:* Thomas Gray; see *JMisc.* i. 191, n. 1.

    (5) *History of Music:* Charles Burney's *General History of Music* (1782), ii. 340. See *Poems*, p. 304. The eminent writer was Robert Potter.

Page 82.   (1) *the child squeal'd on:* in *Thraliana*, on 1 August 1779, Mrs. P writes that the verses were meant to make fun of Thomas Percy's *The Hermit of Warkworth*.

    (2) *A famous ballad:* found in Pérez de Hita, *Guerras civiles de Granada*, xvii, and translated by Percy for his *Reliques of Ancient English Poetry*, 1765.

    (3) *naming him:* he named Thomas Warton, see *supra* p. 81, n. 3 and *Life* iii. 159.

    (4) *Lopez de Vega:* from Lope de Vega's *Arcadia*, iv. See *Poems*, p. 296 for variants.

Page 83.   (1) *the friend:* Thomas Sheridan; the line parodied ends the first act of Henry Brooke's *The Earl of Essex*, 1761.

    (2) *a certain pantomime:* Isaac de Benserade's *Balet de Cassandre*. Read 'Cassander' for 'Cassandra'.

    (3) *Easy Phraseology:* Giuseppe Baretti's work, printed in 1775, has a preface by SJ. 'Hetty' is Mrs. P's daughter 'Queeney' whose name was also Hester.

    (4) *1742 or 1743:* the *GM* for 1742 reports a comet seen in February and March; in May the Duke of Modena fled before being attacked by the Sardinians.

Page 84.   (1) *M. de Benserade:* see *supra*, p. 83, n. 2.

    (2) *Sir Joseph Banks's goat:* for a detailed and more accurate account of this caprine world-traveller see *Poems*, p. 270. SJ wrote the lines in 1772.

    (3) *Perpetui:* R. W. Chapman makes a case for 'perpetua' (Boswell's reading) in *Review of English Studies* I (1925), 373.

    (4) *Lord Anson's house:* George Anson, Baron Anson; the house was at Moor Park in Hertfordshire. See *Poems*, p. 256. The anecdote is undated in *Thraliana*, p. 213.

    (5) *Dryden's epigram:* Mrs. P did not have it to herself because SJ dictated it to Boswell who published it in his *Journal of a Tour to the Hebrides*, 1785.

Page 85.   (1) *Covent-Garden theatre:* the performance was almost surely Isaac Bickerstaffe's *Love in a Village* with music by Dr. Thomas Arne. See *Poems*, p. 266.

    (2) *tibi crispe pompae:* read 'tibi, Crispe, pompae?'

    (3) *Bates or Coulson:* probably two of SJ's schoolfellows at Oxford; for Colson, see *supra*, p. 76, n. 11 and *Thraliana*, p. 162, n. 3.

    (4) *Brent:* Charlotte Brent, singer and favourite pupil of Dr. Arne.

    (5) *Guadagni:* Gaetano Guadagni, one of the most famous contraltos of the century.

    (6) *the climacteric eye:* in 1771 SJ was 62; the climacteric year is the 63rd.

Page 86.   (1) *Dr. Lawrence:* SJ's friend, Dr. Thomas Lawrence. Mrs. P printed the verses in her *Letters to and from the Late Samuel Johnson*, 1788. See *Poems*, p. 275.

      (2) *Mr. Langton:* Bennet Langton, of whom SJ asked for the return of the translation in a letter of 5 July 1774. The poem is by William Oldys.

      (3) *1781 or 1782:* Boswell puts this under March 1782 (*Life* iv. 143–4).

      (4) *he lived but few months after:* Lawrence died in June 1783.

      (5) *diseases of the imagination:* see *supra*, p. 62 and n. 2.

      (6) *the patience of a woman:* Mrs. P refers to herself of course.

Page 87.   (1) *Paschal and Soame Jennings:* the reference to Pascal's *Pensées* is probably to no. 72 and nos. 121 and 282; that to Jenyns is to his *Free Inquiry into the Nature and Origin of Evil* in his *Miscellaneous Pieces*, 1761.

      (2) *Swift:* from his *Cadenus and Vanessa*.

      (3) *the Punic war:* SJ expresses the same sentiment in a letter of July 1775 to Mrs. P.

      (4) *'living wight':* Paradise Lost ii. 613.

Page 88.   (1) *the two succeeding ones:* SJ quotes Swift's *To Stella*, 1720; the 'succeeding' lines are 'In such a case would Cato bleed?/And how would Socrates proceed?'

      (2) *a gentleman:* Charles James Fox (Hayward i. 292).

      (3) *then present minister:* Hill conjectures that the Duke of Grafton was meant, *JMisc.* i. 203, n. 1.

      (4) *an invasion:* threats of an invasion occurred in 1778 and 1779.

      (5) *Dear Bathurst:* see *supra*, p. 66, n. 4.

      (6) *a gentleman:* possibly Alderman William Lee. See *Life* iii. 78–9.

      (7) *Life of Addison:* see *Lives* ii. 97–8, where SJ refers to and quotes from *Spectator* 232 in evidence, but that essay is probably by Henry Martyn.

Page 89.   (1) *Tillotson:* John Tillotson, Archbishop of Canterbury (1630–94); reference is to his sermons.

Page 90.   (1) *Mandeville:* Bernard Mandeville's *Fable of the Bees;* for an extended comment by SJ see *Life* iii. 291–3 and *infra*, p. 120.

      (2) *Rochefoucault's maxim*: François, Duc de la Rochefoucauld, *Réflexions Morales*, no. 105: 'Dans l'adversité de nos meilleurs amis nous trouvons toujours quelque chose qui ne nous déplaist pas' (1692 edn.). See *Letters*, nos. 560 and 1016 for SJ's other references to this maxim.

      (3) *Prior's verses: Alma, or The Progress of the Mind*, Canto iii, 11. 590–3.

      (4) *Miss Reynolds:* Frances Reynolds, Sir Joshua's sister, 'for whom Johnson had a particular affection' (*Life* i. 486, n. 1).

      (5) *an acquaintance:* possibly Mrs. P herself, for she had hoped to inherit Offley Place in Hertfordshire. Hayward i. 293 and *Letters* i. 389. And see *Thraliana*, pp. 37, 54, 74, and 85.

      (6) *Sir George Colebrook's family:* Sir George lost considerable sums in 1774, but his family had had a fortune settled on it the previous year.

Page 91.   (1) *I was spared it!:* Mrs. P was estranged from SJ and in Italy at his death.

Page 92.

Page 93.

Page 94.

Page 95.

(2) *he had left off wine:* I have always believed that he gave up wine because of his wife's fondness for it.

(3) *the rod of reproof:* possibly an echo of Proverbs xxix. 15: rod and reproof give wisdom.

(4) *something must be endured:* a faint echo of SJ in *Rasselas:* 'Human life is every where a state in which much is to be endured, and little to be enjoyed' (ch. 11).

(5) *the Prior and he:* this was in 1775; he wrote to Levet, 'I am very kindly used by the English Benedictine friars' (*Letters* ii. 47). The Prior was Father Cowley.

(6) *two of that college:* Father Joseph Wilks and Father James Compton. *Letters* ii. 136, and J. W. Croker, ed., Boswell's *Life* of SJ, ix (1846), 36, n. 1.

(7) *Dr. Nugent:* Dr. Christopher Nugent, Burke's father-in-law, was a member of SJ's Literary Club.

(8) *a letter:* to Frederick Augusta Barnard, dated 28 May 1768; SJ's warning concludes the letter.

(1) *lumieres:* an allusion to *les lumières de la foi.*

(2) *lately dead:* Hill conjectures that this was Lord Mayor Beckford, but William Beckford died in 1770, and Mrs. P does not record the anecdote until 'Oct. to Nov. 1780' in *Thraliana,* p. 460.

(3) *the Abbé Reynal:* Abbé Guillaume Thomas François Raynal, historian and philosopher; the incident occurred in 1777 and the 'common friend' was Mrs. Eizabeth Vesey (*Life* iv. 435).

(4) *Tadmor in the wilderness:* Tadmor is another name for Palmyra; it occurs in 1 Kings ix. 18 and 2 Chron. viii. 4.

(5) *Dawkins and Wood:* James Dawkins and Robert Wood; they visited Palmyra together and the latter wrote *Ruins of Palmyra,* 1753.

(6) *a young gentleman:* Sir John Lade, Mr. Thrale's nephew (*Thraliana,* p. 167, n. 7).

(1) *the subject of marriage:* Chapters xxviii and xxix of *Rasselas* are devoted to this subject.

(2) *foppish:* 'foolish, idle, vain,' SJ's *Dictionary.* See *infra,* p. 95, 'foppish lamentations'.

(3) *a blade of grass is always a blade of grass:* see *Idler* 97 for SJ's views on travel literature.

(4) *at Rouen together:* in September 1775. The account in Mrs. P's French journals differs from this in the *Anecdotes* about SJ and the Abbé Roffette. See her journal edited by Tyson and Guppy, 1932, pp. 47, 82, 85.

(1) *Harry the Fifth:* Samuel Foote's *Englishman At Paris,* unlike *Henry V,* shows the English at a disadvantage.

(2) *copillaire:* a syrup flavoured with orange-flower water.

(3) *Lord Sandys:* Edwin, Lord Sandys, friend of the Thrales in whose company SJ visited him in September 1774. He is the 'nobleman' who married 'for a maintenance'; see *infra,* p. 144.

(1) *foppish:* see *supra,* p. 93, n. 1.

(2) *drony:* 'sluggish' not in SJ's *Dictionary,* but used by Mrs. P in her *British Synonymy.*

(3) *luxurious:* 'voluptuous; enslaved to pleasure' (SJ's *Dictionary*) is a possible meaning.

(4) *possibly mad:* SJ often links solitude and madness.

Page 96. (1) *Rousseau:* Mrs. P is thinking of *La Nouvelle Héloise;* see *Thraliana,* pp. 197–8.

(2) *Variety:* William Whitehead's *Variety* is subtitled 'A Tale for Married People'. SJ thought little of him as a poet (*Life* i. 402).

(3) *Prior:* Matthew Prior's *An English Padlock.*

(4) *society:* see *supra* p. 72, n. 2; also *Thraliana,* p. 182.

(5) *Cards:* SJ late in life wished that he had learned to play cards (*Life* iii. 23). See *Philological Quarterly* 1952, p. 379 for one example of his detailed knowledge of ombre and quadrille.

Page 97. (1) *a green coat . . . a grey one:* since there were charity schools known as the Green-coat Hospital and the Grey-coat Hospital SJ may be expressing the difference as one between tweedle-dum and tweedle-dee.

(2) *Lord Bolingbroke:* nephew to the famous Henry St John, 1st Viscount Bolingbroke.

(3) *divorces:* Lord Bolingbroke had been divorced by his wife.

(4) *general satire:* see *infra,* p. 150.

(5) *Swift:* SJ says nothing of Swift's hatred of physicians elsewhere.

(6) *an acquaintance:* Mrs. P herself. *Thraliana,* p. 200.

(7) *the law:* SJ knew much law, sought to become an advocate, and would have been a good one, according to Boswell (*Life* i. 134).

(8) *burdens grievous to be borne:* see Matthew xxiii. 4 and Luke xi. 46.

(9) *Dr. Pepys:* Sir Lucas Pepys, physician and friend of the Thrales. In 1783 he told SJ, 'If you were *tractable,* Sir, I should prescribe for you' (*Life* iv. 169).

Page 98. (1) *Mr. Beauclerc:* Topham Beauclerk, one of SJ's younger friends, figures prominently in Boswell's *Life.* Both his and Garrick's anecdotes are in the *Life.*

(2) *his rigid attention to veracity:* this is attested to by various passages in the *Life* and in SJ's writings.

(3) *Foote:* who, said SJ, 'tells lies of everybody' (*Life* ii. 433–34). And see *infra,* p. 118.

Page 99. (1) *his Irish friend Grierson:* George Abraham Grierson, his Majesty's printer at Dublin, whose abilities SJ 'highly respected' (*Life* ii. 117). See *Thraliana,* p. 25 for another anecdote about him.

(2) *exquisitely amusing and comical:* Cooke, p. 35, wrote that '*humour* was not the Doctor's *strong hold*', echoed by Shaw, above, p. 187, 'he was equally without humour and superior to every species of buffoonery.'

(3) *that odd old surgeon:* Robert Levett; Mrs. P quotes SJ's *On the Death of Dr. Robert Levett.* Read 'pour'd his' and 'retir'd'.

(4) *1765 or 1766:* the story is highly inaccurate. The year was 1762. See *Life* i. 416 for Boswell's account in which the year is also inaccurately put as 1763.

Page 100. (1) *Mr. Boyce:* Samuel Boyce died in 1749; hence Mrs. P's 'five-and-twenty years ago' is wrong by 12 years. He was associated with SJ in the early years of the *GM.*

(2) *Another man:* Joseph Simpson, barrister. Hayward ii. 84. Mrs. P's anecdote does not reflect the true circumstances of Simpson's life. See *Gleanings,* iv. 156–7.

(3) *the Literary Club:* it went without a name until Garrick's funeral.

(4) *new faces:* see Waingrow, *Correspondence and Other Papers*, pp. 147–8 and n. 5 on SJ's attitude towards new members.

(5) *Sir John Hawkins:* SJ's official biographer and the 1st editor of his writings.

(6) *Mr. Langton:* see *supra*, p. 64, n. 3.

(7) *Mr. Beauclerc:* see *supra*, p. 98, n. 1.

(8) *Dr. Nugent:* see *supra*, p. 91, n. 7.

(9) *Sir Robert Chambers:* judge; SJ helped him write his law lectures.

(10) *Mr. Dyer:* Samuel Dyer, miscellaneous translator, held in high esteem by SJ. He and Percy and Chambers were not original members. Anthony Chamier, a former stock-broker, is omitted in Mrs. P's account. But see *Thraliana*, pp. 106–7 and 188.

(11) *their Romulus:* the original idea for the club was Reynolds's, or his and SJ's.

Page 101. (1) *some friend:* possibly Charles Burney (*Life*, ii. 406–7).

(2) *1764:* Mrs. P wrote in *Thraliana* that the meeting took place 'on the second Thursday of the Month of January 1765', p. 158.

(3) *Mr. Woodhouse:* James Woodhouse, shoemaker turned poetaster, owed much to the efforts of William Shenstone on his behalf.

(4) *nights and days:* as Mrs. P notes, SJ used the same phrase in his *Life* of Addison (*Lives* ii. 150).

Page 102. (1) *a letter:* not extant; marked no. 173 in *Letters*.

(2) *the court:* Johnson's Court, Fleet Street. For the vexed question of his illness, see *Life* i. 521–22.

(3) *Dr. Delap:* the Rev. Dr. John Delap, poet and dramatist.

(4) *domestic distresses:* Mrs. P's mother's cancer, her husband's acute financial difficulties, and the death of Penelope Thrale who only lived 10 hours.

Page 103. (1) *the reverence of a son:* see *Thraliana*, pp. 182–83.

(2) *my mother's monument:* in Streatham Church. Mrs. P had put 1706 as her mother's birth date in *Thraliana*, p. 7. See also *ibid.* p. 7, n. 2.

Page 104. (1) *Maty's Review:* Paul Henry Maty's *A New Review*.

(2) *a friend:* Michael Lort. *Thraliana*, p. 629, n. 2.

Page 105. (1) *Abi viator!:* changed from *Thraliana*'s 'Abi lector!', p. 543.

(2) *Aeternitatem cognita:* for remarks on the epitaph see *Thraliana*, p. 543.

Page 106. (1) *these two in Streatham church:* SJ wrote epitaphs for his father, mother, and wife. He also wrote an English epitaph for a Mrs. Bell (*Life* ii. 204, n. 1).

(2) *Garrick's:* for Garrick's lines and variants in SJ's quoted lines, see *Poems*, pp. 267–8.

(3) *Mr. Hogarth:* for the early relationship between Mrs. P and the portrait-painter see *HLP*, pp. 23–4.

(4) *Hudson's:* Thomas Hudson was for a time the principal English portrait-painter, *faute de mieux*.

(5) *Lady's last Stake:* based on Colley Cibber's play of the same name and a picture for which Mrs. P may have sat as a young girl.

(6) *King Solomon:* in *Thraliana* Mrs. P takes credit for the remark, p. 468.

(7) *all men are liars:* Ps. cvi. 11: 'I said in my haste, all men are liars.'

(8) *came:* S. C. Roberts suggests 'became'.

Page 107. (1) *was no more:* Henry Thrale died in 1781.

(2) *Elliot's brave defence of Gibraltar:* General George Augustus Eliott, Lord Heathfield.

(3) *Mr. Sharp:* 'Mr. Sharp the Surgeon' in the *Thraliana* account of the anecdote (p. 468), but since Sharp died in 1778 and the hurricane occurred in late 1780 something is amiss.

(4) *the destruction of Lisbon:* the earthquake of 1756; in *Thraliana*, p. 468 SJ is reputed as saying 'for I did not give Credit a long Time to the Earthquake at Lisbon.'

Page 108. (1) *Mr. Pepys:* William Weller Pepys, brother to Sir Lucas; see *supra*, p. 97, n. 9.

(2) *Now . . . is Pepys gone home:* possibly the incident recorded by Fanny Burney; see *HLP*, p. 212.

(3) *Barnard:* see *supra*, p. 72, n. 1.

(4) *these lines:* Pierre Roy's *Sur un mince chrystal.*

(5) *acquaintance:* among them 'Mr. Selwin' (*Thraliana*, p. 548), almost surely her friend Charles Selwyn.

(6) *the life he saved:* Mrs. P's way of saying that Sir Lucas recognized her illness in 1783–4 was caused by her love for Gabriel Piozzi.

Page 109. (1) *Shenstone's idea:* in William Shenstone's *Essays on Men and Manners*, No. lxxxvi, in *Works in Verse and Prose* (1777), ii. 213.

(2) *Dr. Collier:* Arthur Collier, lawyer, of Doctor's Commons, an intimate of the Thrales.

Page 110. (1) *pupillage:* the condition or period of being a minor.

(2) *her daughter:* Lucy Porter, for whom he had a 'parental tenderness' (*Life* i. 462).

(3) *a little painted puppet:* Garrick told JB that Tetty was 'very fat' (*Life* i. 99). Mrs. P has 'poppet' in *Thraliana*, p. 178.

(4) *old Levett:* see *supra.*, 99, n. 3.

(5) *well dressed:* compare SJ's remark on the mutton that was 'ill-fed, ill-killed, ill-kept, and ill-drest' (*Life* iv. 284).

(6) *huffed:* treated with arrogance and insolence; hectored. Tetty's answer is one of the very few remarks attributed to her.

Page 111. (1) *pokes her head:* thrusts it forward.

(2) *vacuity:* a word favoured by SJ; it occurs in *Rasselas*, the *Rambler*, the *Life*, and the *Letters.*

(3) *'Oh Lord, Sir':* II. i.

Page 112. (1) *Lady Tavistock:* her husband died in 1767, she in 1768.

(2) *Evans:* the Rev. Mr. Evans knew Mrs. P well enough to cast doubt on the fidelity of her *Anecdotes* (*HLP*, p. 268, n. 1).

(3) *manners of a gentleman:* see *supra*, p. 72, n. 2.

(4) *Mr. Berenger:* Richard Berenger, Gentleman of the Horse, was 'mighty delicate and polite' (*Life* iv. 489).

(5) *Thomas Hervey:* his brother Henry, of whom SJ was very fond, married Catherine Aston. The Herveys were among SJ's first acquaintances in London. R. W. Chapman suggests 'then' for 'them' in the preceding line (*Review of English Studies*, I (1925) 373).

Page 113. (1) *M - - - y As - - n:* Molly Aston; the evening was Friday, 8 May 1778. In *Thraliana*, p. 538 SJ is reported as saying that he spent the evening 'Teste a Teste' with her.

(2) *Lord Killmorey:* John Needham, tenth Viscount Kilmorey.

(3) *F--zh--b--t:* Mrs. William Fitzherbert died in 1753; SJ's Latin lines on Molly Aston were first printed in the April 1738 *GM*.

(4) *St. Austin:* St. Augustine.

Page 114. (1) *Miss B--thby:* Miss Hill Boothby's mother was a Fitzherbert. SJ wrote a prayer on Miss Boothby's death.

(2) *Lord Lyttelton:* George Lyttelton, first Baron Littelton. SJ rather unwillingly wrote his *Life* for his *Lives of the Poets*, but the rivalry for Miss Boothby's regard was almost surely not the reason for his reluctance.

(3) *Baretti:* he knew SJ as early as 1751; Miss Hill Boothby died in 1756.

(4) *the negro Francis:* Francis Barber, SJ's servant. Mrs. P is wrong; Francis did not join SJ's household until shortly after Tetty's death (*Life* i. 239). *Gleanings* ii, 'Francis Barber, The Doctor's Negro Servant,' is the definitive biography.

(5) *in Gay's Life:* the observation was that Gay was a poet 'of a lower order' (*Lives* ii. 282). And see above, Shaw, p. 34 on Tetty's critical abilities.

(6) *elegance:* SJ wrote 'great beauty and excellence' (*Lives* iii. 262).

(7) *these Anecdotes:* SJ wrote 'a lady, of whose praise he would have been justly proud' (*Lives* iii. 398).

(8) *the following verses:* written 6 September 1773 and enclosed in a letter to Mrs. P dated 23 October 1773.

Page 115. (1) *my birth-day:* 16 January 1740/1, old style; she celebrated on 27 January (*HLP*, p. 8). And see *Thraliana*, p. 3, n. 1 for Mrs. P's confession about her birth date.

(2) *forty-six:* Swift's last birthday-poem for Stella is dated 13 March 1726–7; she was not quite forty-six at her death.

Page 116. (1) *power of improvisation:* SJ set great store upon 'invention' in a poet. Tuscan improvisers, 'canteri', were paid by the commune. One of the most famous of these early 'canteri' was the Florentine Antonio di Guido.

(2) *Metastasio:* Pietro Metastasio, contemporary Italian poet; the first passage is from his *La Clemenza di Tito*, i. ii and the second from *Adriano in Syria*, ii. i. Mrs. P's Italian has a few inaccuracies.

Page 117. (1) *Mr. Bickerstaff's flight:* Isaac Bickerstaffe the dramatist fled the country in 1772 suspected of a capital crime.

(2) *Latin verses:* SJ's desire may have been prompted by Gray's having done this.

Page 118. (1) *a lady of quality:* Lady Catherine Wynne, *Thraliana*, p. 169. SJ found dinner at their home 'mean' and Lady Catherine 'nothing' (*Life* v. 449).

(2) *Mr. S------:* William Strahan, named in *Thraliana*, p. 166.

(3) *telling stories:* but see *supra*, p. 99.

(4) *Mr. Foote:* see *supra*, p. 98; SJ admired his ready wit.

Page 119. (1) *Love's Labour Lost:* II. i; read 'at' for 'with'.

(2) *the late Hawkins Browne:* Isaac Hawkins Browne, the younger, poet and wit (*Gleanings*, iii. 124).

(3) *Psalmanazar:* George Psalmanazar, literary impostor, venerated by SJ. For a full account of him, see *Life* iii. 443–9.

(4) *died:* Psalmanazar died 3 May 1763.

Page 120.

Page 121.

Page 122.

(5) *so many modes of worship:* only Church of Rome and Church of England.

(6) *penitentiary:* Mrs. P means penitential.

(7) *Universal History:* Psalmanazar wrote the history of the Jews, Gauls, and Spaniards, as well as the account of 'Xenophon's Retreat', in this huge compendium (*Letters* iii. 253).

(1) *canters:* for 'cant', see *supra*, p. 68. SJ defines canter in the *Dictionary* as 'A term of reproach for hypocrites, who talk formally of religion, without obeying it'.

(2) *Fable of the Bees:* see *supra*, p. 90, n. 1.

(3) *Dr. Collier:* see *supra*, p. 109, n. 2.

(4) *his vein of humour:* see *supra*, p. 99, n. 2.

(5) *Dr. Goldsmith:* the anecdote is fuller and more memorable in JB's version (*Life* iv. 183).

(6) *Fontaine's fables:* Jean de la Fontaine, the second Fable of the fifth Book.

(1) *Berni:* Francesco Berni; the lines are in his parody of Boiardo's *Orlando Innamorato*, canto 53, stanza 60.

(2) *Beattie's Essay on Truth:* James Beattie's *Essay* was published in 1770; four editions and three translations were printed by 1772. SJ more than once praised the work.

(3) *Eaton Graham:* the Rev. George Graham of Eton College and author of *Telemachus, a Masque* which SJ reviewed for the *Critical Review* in 1763.

(4) *the newspapers:* the article is said to have appeared in the *St. James's Chronicle* on 14 June 1770.

(5) *Churchill:* Charles Churchill had satirized SJ in *The Ghost* (1762) but there is no reason to believe that he therefore excluded him from the *Lives of the Poets.*

(6) *in a book:* he names Shaftesbury and Chubb in *Thraliana*, p. 34.

(1) *Mrs. Montague:* Mrs. Elizabeth Montagu, the celebrated Blue Stocking, author of an *Essay on Shakespeare*, for which see *infra*, the Postscript.

(2) *a very celebrated lady:* Hannah More, another Blue Stocking author. JB castigates Mrs. P for her inaccuracy in this story (*Life* iv. 341).

(3) *Topham Beauclerc:* see *supra*, p. 98, n. 1. JB writes of his 'elegance of manners' (*Life* i. 248.)

(4) *Clarissa:* Richardson's inordinate vanity is well known. See *Life*, iv. 28, n. 7 for an example quoted by JB.

(5) *a fly stings a horse:* SJ made much the same comment about a critic, both in the *Life* (i. 263, n. 3) and in the Preface to his edition of Shakespeare.

(6) *eagle will not capture flies:* in *Thraliana* SJ quotes the classical adage, 'Aquila non capet [cepit] Muscas', p. 203.

(7) *Cummyns:* Tom Cumming, American Quaker, died 29 May 1774; the contents of the anonymous letter are not known. See *Thraliana*, p. 224 for the possible explanation of the insults.

(8) *Hawkesworth:* see *supra*, p. 7, n. 5. He died on 17 November 1773, his death being directly or indirectly owing to newspaper attacks on the Preface to his edition of Cook's voyages in which he implies doubt in the efficacy of providence.

Page 123. (1) *in a new Magazine:* in *Thraliana* it was only 'in the Paper', p. 204.

(2) *another namesake's departure:* deaths of men named Samuel Johnson are recorded for 3 June 1766, 26 February 1772, and 31 July 1782 in the *GM*. None of these dates is right for Mrs. P's anecdote.

(3) *Dear Doctor:* Dr. Delap, see *supra*, p. 102, n. 3, identified in Hayward i. 294.

(4) *Dr. James:* see *supra*, p. 70, n. 4.

(5) *Death's pale horse:* Rev. vi. 8.

(6) *last sickbed:* Garrick died on 20 January 1779, aged sixty-two.

Page 124. (1) *Swift: Verses on the Death of Dr. Swift*, ll. 119–20; read 'great' for 'dire'.

(2) *from:* added by G. B. Hill.

(3) *'believeth all things':* 1 Cor. xiii. 7.

(4) *an Italian sonnet:* unidentifiable. There is no mention of this sonnet in the account in *Thraliana*, p. 202.

(5) *a gentleman:* Dr. Robert Vansittart, Regius Professor of Civil Law, Oxford (*Life* ii. 194, n. 2).

(6) *Beauclerc:* see *supra*, p. 98, n. 1. Mrs. P hated him but respected his veracity (Hayward ii. 112).

Page 125. (1) *Dr. Lawrence:* see *supra*, p. 86, n. 1, for Dr. Lawrence and *Life* iv. 94 and 490 for proof of the inaccuracy of this anecdote.

(2) *dear Dick:* probably Richard Burney, Dr. Burney's youngest son (*Life* iii. 367).

(3) *Solander's conversation:* Dr. Daniel Charles Solander, a Swede who went with Capt. Cook on his first voyage round the world.

Page 126. (1) *tonics:* not in SJ's *Dictionary*; OED gives 'a foolish person; a simpleton'.

(2) *a rich young heir:* Sir John Lade, see *supra*, p. 92, n. 6 and *Thraliana*, p. 171.

(3) *a long copy of verses:* it is one of seven stanzas. See *Poems*, pp. 307–8. The verses were prophetic, as Sir John came to a bad end. Read 'on' for 'in'.

(4) *alembicated:* evidently of Mrs. P's own coinage.

(5) *a famous French writer:* Rousseau; see *Thraliana*, p. 183, n. 4.

(6) *Milton: Paradise Lost* viii. 193.

Page 127. (1) *Clarissa:* see *supra*, p. 122. Except for *Amelia* SJ had little good to say of Fielding's novels.

(2) *Iago's ingenious malice:* in his 'general observation' on *Othello* SJ writes of 'the cool malignity of Iago, silent in his resentment, subtle in his designs, and studious at once of his interest and his vengeance.'

(3) *Sir John:* SJ terms Falstaff 'unimitated' and 'inimitable' in the 'general observation' on *2 Henry IV*.

(4) *printed strictures:* see *supra*, p. 101, n. 4.

(5) *the pathetick in poetry:* the emotional element.

(6) *the last act:* of Nicholas Rowe's *The Tragedy of Jane Shore:* SJ had high praise for it in his *Life* of Rowe.

(7) *devotional poetry:* SJ expresses this thought in various of his works, especially in the *Lives of the Poets*.

(8) *Rasselas:* ch. 10, 'Imlac's History Continued. A Dissertation Upon Poetry'.

Page 128. (1) *his journey to Lichfield:* his mother died before he could make the journey.

(2) *One gentleman:* Richard Pottinger, Clerk of the Privy Seal. *Thraliana,* p. 166 makes this and the identification in the next note. This will serve to supplement Waingrow, *Correspondence and Other Papers,* p. 141, n. 8, where Pottinger remains unidentified.

(3) *a nobleman's house:* that of the Hon. Thomas Fitzmaurice, son of first Earl of Shelburne.

(4) *King William's character:* SJ had a very low opinion of this monarch (*Life* ii. 342 and v. 255).

(5) *A young fellow:* he is described as 'a Coxcomb' in *Thraliana,* p. 167, but not identified.

(6) *the Lincolnshire lady:* Mrs. Diana Langton, mother of SJ's friend Bennet, named in *Thraliana,* p. 188.

Page 129. (1) *Mrs. Montague:* see *supra,* p. 122, n.1.

(2) *Jones the Orientalist:* Sir William Jones, member of the Literary Club, was noted for his modesty.

(3) *an end:* S. C. Roberts (ed. *Anecdotes,* 1925, p. 198) resists the emendation 'on end' because SJ 'describes "an end" as probably corrupted from "on end".'

(4) *Mr. Hamilton:* William Gerard Hamilton, parliamentarian, whom SJ may have assisted in his single speech.

(5) *1766:* see *supra,* p. 102.

(6) *Pepper-Alley:* there were three alleys of this name in London at this time.

Page 130. (1) *Richard:* Dr. John Taylor, editor of Demosthenes, once corrected a friend in a mistaken name by giving the correct one—'Richard' (*Life,* iii. 318).

(2) *Thomas Tyers:* see *Life,* iii. 307 and v. 73.

(3) *the greatest man:* the remark in the *Life* is more subdued; there Burke is only 'extraordinary' (iv. 275).

(4) *a lady at my house:* Mrs. P herself, if I understand her in *Thraliana,* p. 197.

(5) *pretty Fanny:* Fanny Browne. *Thraliana,* p. xxvii.

(6) *his negro Francis:* Francis Barber, see *supra,* p. 114, n. 4.

(7) *in Lincolnshire:* probably an error for Hertfordshire (*Thraliana,* p. 174, n. 4).

Page 131. (1) *his white wife:* Elizabeth (Betsy) Barber, for whom see *Gleanings* ii *passim.*

(2) *Dr. Bathurst:* Barber was brought to England from Jamaica by Bathurst's father; he entered SJ's service in 1752.

(3) *the Italian master:* Francesco Sastres, translator as well as teacher of Italian, was a member of the Essex-Head Club.

(4) *Milton: Paradise Lost* iv. 895.

Page 132. (1) *a borough election:* doubtless in Southwark which Henry Thrale represented for some fifteen years. SJ helped Thrale by writing election addresses for him.

(2) *young fellow:* Ralph Plumbe, Mr. Thrale's nephew (*Thraliana,* p. 170).

(3) *Delphini:* the edition of Florus 'In Usum Serenissimi Delphini.'

(4) *a clergyman:* the Rev. Henry Bright of Abingdon Grammar Schoo (*Thraliana,* p. 102).

Page 133. (1) *ni sit prudentia: Thraliana,* p. 477 has this attributed to Mrs. P herself, but see *Life* iv. 180 where SJ makes the same comment to JB. The line is from Juvenal, *Satires* x. 365.

(2) *a lady's house:* not Lady Catherine Wynne, for whom see *supra,* p. 118, n. 1 (as Hill conjectured, *Life* v. 449, n. 1).

(3) *run tea:* coagulated (?) as in 'run milk'.

(4) *nine biographical essays:* Hill lists nine (*JMisc.* i. 296, n. 1), but I doubt Mrs. P knew all those in that list.

(5) *a critic:* possibly Shaw, see *supra,* p. 54.

Page 134. (1) *broken nose:* Henry Fielding's heroine had suffered an accident to that member in a fall (*Amelia,* Bk. II, chap. i); the nose was repaired for subsequent editions.

(2) *the last work:* Mrs. P was too modest as a glance at her bibliography will show.

(3) *Mr. Pearson:* the Rev. John Batteridge Pearson, Perpetual Curate of St. Michael's, Lichfield.

Page 135. (1) *vows on trivial occasions:* as an example, see *Life* iii. 357, where SJ tells JB that 'a vow is a horrible thing, it is a snare for sin'.

(2) *airy nothings: A Midsummer Night's Dream,* V. i.

Page 136. (1) *study algebra:* see *supra,* p. 87 for SJ's love of mathematics.

(2) *'muddy':* 'cloudy in mind, dull' in SJ's *Dictionary* and exemplified by *The Winter's Tale,* I. ii.

(3) *a young gentleman:* a Mr. Greete, about whom nothing else is known. See *Thraliana,* p. 100 where the anecdote differs in some important respects.

Page 137. (1) *Tom Osborne:* see *supra,* p. 24, n. 2. In *Thraliana,* p. 195 there is no mention of SJ's *Dictionary* being the weapon.

(2) *a very singular story:* JB heard it also; see *Life,* i. 215–16.

Page 138. (1) *the fortune-hunter: Rambler* 74.

(2) *the old maid: Rambler* 103.

(3) *hoping for a legacy: Rambler* 182.

(4) *always prying: Rambler* 197.

(5) *Samuel Johnson:* Hill refers to *Life* i. 135 for a curate of this name, but JB was mistaken, for that Johnson's name was John. See *Notes and Queries* for October 1954.

(6) *Aliger:* in *Rambler* 201; not in the *Thraliana* account, p. 161.

(7) *Cupidus: Rambler* 73.

(8) *a periodical: Gray's-Inn Journal.*

(9) *a Rambler:* no. 190.

(10) *Lungs, making 'aether':* Ben Jonson's Lungs made 'elixir' in *The Alchemist.*

(11) *fond of chemistry:* a number of passages in the *Life* attest to this fondness.

Page 139. (1) *Ruabon:* in Denbighshire. The motto means 'Without God, without all. God is all-sufficient'. The unnamed person was Thomas Trevor, incumbent from 14 June 1770 to 21 April 1784. Foster's *Index of Incumbents Since the Reformation,* Cambridge University Library Add. MSS. 6744 (Welsh Incumbents).

Page 140. (1) *levior cortice:* Horace, Odes III. ix. 22.

(2) *An Irish trader:* he is only 'a gentleman' in *Thraliana,* p. 175.

(3) *a bag:* evidently some kind of overall covering.

(4) *Beconsfield:* Beaconsfield, Bucks., where Burke's home was. SJ

arrived there September 24 and parliament was dissolved on the 30th.

Page 141.　(1) *the chaplain's table:* Hill identifies the chaplain as Percy (*JMisc.* i. 311, n. 1), but since the incident referred to took place in 1768 and Percy did not become a chaplain to George III until 1769 it could not have been he. At all events, there were a number of King's chaplains who dined together and who invited guests.

　　(2) *his play was hissed:* Goldsmith's *The Good-Natured* Man was put on in 1768; certain scenes were hissed as 'low'.

　　(3) *pensieri stretti:* this proverb, among other details, is not in the *Thraliana* account, p. 83.

Page 142.　(1) *paitrie des graces:* pétrie des graces.

　　(2) *Trundle:* 'any round rolling thing' (SJ's *Dictionary*).

　　(3) *the value of society:* the passage should read 'by scenes from which a hermit may estimate the transactions of the world'.

Page 143.　(1) *enjoyment of pleasure:* see *supra,* p. 93, n. 1, for more of SJ's views on marriage.

　　(2) *canters:* see *supra,* p. 120, n. 1; SJ does not use the word in that sense here.

　　(3) *Ascham:* SJ edited Ascham's *English Works* in 1761 although the nominal editor was James Bennet. The quoted passage, from the first book of *The Scholemaster,* is in p. 208 of this edition. Mrs. P quotes from memory.

　　(4) *Jeremiah Markland:* he published notes on some of the plays of Euripides.

　　(5) *and does nothing:* G. B. Hill emends to 'and who does nothing'.

Page 144.　(1) *that fellow:* Lord Sandys, see *supra,* p. 94, n. 3; in 1769 he married Anna Maria King, widow of a banker.

Page 145.　(1) *Lycurgus:* the legendary legislator of Sparta of whom Plutarch wrote a life.

　　(2) *Shropshire or Derbyshire:* it was in Derbyshire. *Thraliana,* p. 189.

　　(3) *Mr. Ch- -lm- -ley:* George James Cholmondeley, grandson to the third Earl of Cholmondeley (*HLP,* p. 269, n. 1). See J. W. Croker, ed., Boswell's *Life* of SJ, ix (1846), 92, n. 1 for Cholmondeley's version of this story.

Page 146.　(1) *Lady Mary Wortley's Letters:* Lady Mary Wortley Montagu's *Letters* were published in 1763.

　　(2) *polished manners:* see *supra,* p. 72, n. 2.

　　(3) *a common friend:* Dr. Burney, *Thraliana,* p. 176.

　　(4) *carried home again:* Christopher Smart was probably in private lodgings in 1757.

　　(5) *Mr. B- - - - - -:* James Boswell, authority for the story.

　　(6) *when he was sober:* JB seizes on this as another example of Mrs. P's inaccuracy (*Life,* ii. 188).

　　(7) *Ossian:* see Shaw's account, *supra,* pp. 42–8.

Page 147.　(1) *the friend:* the Rev. Dr. Hugh Blair, identified in *Thraliana,* p. 166 and in the *Life,* i. 396.

　　(2) *he will have the pension:* hence the anecdote is before July 1762.

　　(3) *a Scotsman:* Adam Smith (*Life* iv. 186).

　　(4) *a gentleman of that country:* the Rev. Mr. John Ogilvie (*Life* i. 425).

　　(5) *Mrs. Brooke:* Mrs. Frances Brooke had come back from Quebec where her husband was chaplain to the English garrison.

(6) *Shenstone:* 'The pleasure of Shenstone was all in his eye; he valued what he valued merely for its looks: nothing raised his indignation more, than to ask if there were any fishes in his water' (*Lives* iii. 352).

Page 148.   (1) *canals:* 'a bason of water in a garden' (SJ's *Dictionary*).

(2) *the Frenchman:* SJ and the Thrales had visited Sèvres in 1775; 'we saw the china at Sêve' the former noted (*Life* ii. 397).

Page 149.   (1) *a lady:* Mrs. Montagu (Hayward i. 296).

(2) *Miss Reynolds:* see *supra,* p. 90, n. 4.

Page 150.   (1) *he is an 'attorney':* see *Life* ii. 126 on SJ and attornies.

(2) *general satire:* see *supra,* p. 97.

(3) *Dr. Swift:* Swift to Pope, 29 Sept. 1725: 'I hate and detest that animal called man, although I heartily love John, Peter, Thomas, and so forth'.

(4) *Dr. Collier:* see *supra,* p. 109, n. 2, and *Thraliana,* pp. 12–14 for more anecdotes about him.

(5) *Lady Frances's observation:* 'Lady Frances Burgoyne, daughter of the last Lord Halifax' (Croker's *Boswell,* 1831, iv. 374, n. 1). Fanny Burney described her as a stiff, formal old lady in her diary under date 30 July 1781.

(6) *nice:* 'fastidious; squeamish' (SJ's *Dictionary*).

(7) *the old philosopher:* Socrates, *Memorabilia,* I. vi. 10.

Page 151.   (1) *St. Denys in France:* on 27 September 1766. See *The French Journals of Mrs. Thrale and Dr. Johnson,* ed. Moses Tyson and Henry Guppy (1932), p. 88.

(2) *their lives:* with Henry Thrale were his daughter, Queeney, and Baretti. Tyson and Guppy, ed. Mrs. Thrale's *French Journals,* p. 88.

(3) *a prayer in Latin:* composed 'Nocte, inter 16 et 17 Junii, 1783' (*Life* iv. 230, n. 1).

(4) *I intend to publish that letter:* the letter is dated 19 June 1783; see *supra,* p. 134 where Mrs. P writes that she intends to publish no more books.

(5) *Sir Richard Jebb:* physician to the Thrales. From Feb. to June 1781 there are a number of references to him in SJ's letters to Mrs. P.

Page 152.   (1) *manuscripts for him to read:* John Hoole disagreed; see Waingrow, *Correspondence and Other Papers,* p. 326, n. 8.

(2) *the author:* Arthur Murphy; the play is his *Tragedy of Zenobia* in which two of the characters are Tigranes and Teribazus.

Page 153.   (1) *at Padua some months ago:* in mid-1785.

(2) *Boileau's works:* Tyers and Murphy also bear witness to this as well as various comments in SJ's *Lives of the Poets.*

Page 154.   (1) *envy a gaol:* compare *Life,* i. 348: 'No man will be a sailor who has contrivance enough to get himself into a jail'.

(2) *Capt. Knight:* Captain Joseph Knight. See *Life,* v. 514–15, for a full account of this episode.

(3) *loplolly:* a ship-doctor's medicines.

(4) *coarse expressions:* see *supra,* p. 72, n. 2.

(5) *Bartholomew fair:* held in Smithfield and a great occasion for a show of finery.

(6) *the inn:* The Swan (*Life* v. 428).

Page 155.   (1) *Another lady:* Hill conjectures that it was Mrs. Montagu (*JMisc.* i. 338, n. 1).

Page 156.

(2) *Mr. S- - - -d:* William Seward, like Mrs. P, a compiler of anecdotes. The lady was almost surely Sophia Streatfield, an intimate friend of Mrs. P (*JMisc.* i. 339, n. 3).

(3) *Lady Macbeth:* III. v; 'Soh!' is Mrs. P's.

(1) *my lost lawsuit:* the suit involved Lady Salisbury, Mrs. P's uncle's widow, and Mrs. P's Welsh estate.

(2) *going abroad:* SJ was one of those opposed to her going abroad at this time, i.e. December 1782 (Hayward, ii. 192–5).

(3) *disordered health and spirits:* see *supra*, p. 102, n. 2.

(4) *three political pamphlets:* see *supra*, p. 73, n. 3.

(5) *fervent imaginations:* see *supra*, p. 62, n. 2 and p. 86.

Page 157.

(1) *Sir Richard Musgrave:* Irish political writer and extreme admirer of SJ.

(2) *the portraits of his favourite friends:* these are listed by Hill, *JMisc.* i. 342, n. 3; they include Burke, Burney, Baretti, Garrick, Goldsmith, Murphy, Reynolds. See *Thraliana*, pp. 471–6, for the rest of Mrs. P's 'Characters'. The purchasers of the portraits are listed in E. Mangin, *Piozziana* (1833), p. 51.

Page 159.

(1) *the sage in Rasselas:* Rasselas so describes the sage to Imlac in ch. 18.

(2) *acquaintance:* a possible plural according to SJ's *Dictionary*.

Page 160.

(1) *two friends:* John Cator, one of Henry Thrale's executors, and Alexander Wedderburne, Lord Loughborough (Hayward, i. 296).

(2) *pride:* there is no need to document this aspect of SJ's character.

(3) *the happy valley:* Mrs. P is thinking of *Rasselas* again.

Postscript p. 161: the best account of this episode is in *HLP*, pp. 272–3. The postscript was supplied by Sir Lucas Pepys and others of Mrs. P's friends. See *supra*, p. xiii.

Index of Persons

Adams, Dr. William (1706–89), Master of Pembroke College, Oxford: 69, 70

Addison, Joseph (1672–1719), essayist and critic: 19, 101, 127

Allen, Charles (c. 1730–95), Vicar of St. Nicholas, Rochester: ix, 45

Anacreon (late 6th century B.C.), Greek poet: 75

Anne, Queen (1665–1714): 63

Anson, George Anson, Baron (1697–1762), admiral: 84

Aristotle (384–322 B.C.): 27

Ascham, Roger (1515–68), writer: 143

Aston, Mary ('Molly') (1706–?65), J.'s friend, 'a beauty and a scholar, a wit and a whig': 113, 114

Augustine, St. (354–430): 113

Banks, Sir Joseph (1743–1820), naturalist: 84

Barbauld, Laetitia (1743–1825), writer and teacher: 65

Barber, Elizabeth (Francis's wife) (1756?–1816): 131

Barber, Francis (1745?–1810), J.'s servant: 114, 130, 131, 145

Barnard, Dr. Edward (1717–81), Provost of Eton: 72, 108

Barnard, Sir Frederick Augusta (1743–1830), King's Librarian: 91

Baretti, Giuseppe Marc' Antonio (1719–89), Italian writer, friend of J.: 83, 114, 116

Bathurst, Allen Bathurst, 1st Earl of (1684–1775): 74

Bathurst, Dr. Richard (d. 1762), close friend of J.: 66, 88, 131

Beattie, Dr. James (1735–1803), poet and essayist: 43

Beauclerk, the Hon Tipham (1739–80), friend to J.: 98, 100, 122, 124

Bell, John (1745–1831), bookseller: 49

Bellamy, Mrs George Anne (1731?–88), actress: 40

Benserade, Isaac de (1612–91), French poet: 84, 180

Berenger, Richard (d. 1782), Gentleman of the Horse to George III: 112

Berni, Francesco (?1490–1536), Italian poet: 121

Bickerstaff, Isaac (1733–?1811), dramatist: 117

Blackwall, Revd. Anthony (1674–1730), headmaster of Market Bosworth grammar school: xi, 10

Blair, Dr. Hugh (1718–1800): 191

Boileau, or Boileau Despréaux, Nicolas (1636–1711), French critic and satirist: 65, 153

Bolingbroke, Frederick St. John, 2nd Viscount (1734–87): 97

Boothby, Miss Hill (1708–56), dear friend of J.: 114

Boswell, James (1740–95): ix, xiii, xiv, 42, 43, 114, 146 (Mr. B—), 161, 177

Boyse, Samuel (1708–49), poet: 100

Brent, Charlotte (d. 1802), opera singer: 85

Bright, Revd. Henry (1724–1803), schoolmaster: 189

Brocklesby, Dr. Richard (1722–97), J.'s physician: 50

Brooke, Mrs. Frances (1724–89), writer: 147

Broome, William (1689–1745), poetaster: 65

Browne, Fanny, wife of Thomas

Date Due

1991

March 14, 1991